Ways not to pay

The Manual on Debt Avoidance

Ways not to pay

The Manual on Debt Avoidance

Soki Tomb

LEGAL DISCLAIMER

This book does not incite or encourage any reader to engage in any specific behaviour with regard to payment or non-payment of debts. It does not seek to offer financial advice and specifically admonishes any reader to act at all times within the law. Conclusions drawn are the opinion of the author; they are not offered as statements of absolute and universal truth and should not be relied upon as the basis for any financial decision.

ISBN 9780956870209

Published by THAFA Press 2011

Dramatis Personae

In this book we will meet a number of characters again and again. They are the primary actors in the Darwinian struggle between Creditors and Debtors. If we introduce them now, it will make it easier for the reader to understand who they are and to recognise them when they appear:

Creditor	A person or organisation which is owed money
Debtor	A person who owes money to a Creditor
Always-Pay	A person who readily pays any demand for cash: cattle eager to be milked
Might-Pay	A person in no hurry to pay, but who can be influenced to do so: sheep easily penned in and fleeced
Won't-Pay	A person who refuses to pay; under pressure they may turn out to be a Might-pay by caving in: either a goat or a Jackal
Can't-Pay	Someone who at a particular point in time cannot pay
Hold-out	Someone who may or may not be able to pay but resists cunningly
Jackal	A metaphor for a Hold-out, stealthy, opportunistic, invisible
Hyena	A metaphor for a lawyer, scavenger with large appetite
Lion	A metaphor for the Justice system, the Lion of the Law
Goat	A Might-pay who, if he pays, turns out to be a sheep
Ostrich	A Will-pay who just doesn't know it yet

DCA	A Debt Collection Agency, populated by short-winded salivating curdogs
Bailiff	A collector with limited legal powers to enter properties to seize goods
Litigant	Someone pursuing someone else by suing, eg a Creditor suing a Debtor
Plaintiff	The litigant doing the suing
Defendant	Usually the Debtor being sued
Castle dweller	A Debtor living in a property with their name on the title deed
Hunter Gatherer	A nomadic Debtor who does not have their name on a title deed
Occupier	A hypothetical customer who may or may not exist, but is treated as being real by utilities until proven otherwise, akin to the mythological chimera
Goneaway	A Debtor who has moved without leaving a forwarding address
Dog	An internal collections agent; also known as a cur-dog
Vampire Bat	A for-profit Debt management or Claims Management company, highly parasitic and selfish in nature, sustained by misguided cattle and sheep for victim-customers
Lemming	A Debtor fleeing in uncontrolled despair before the pursuit of the dogs and hyenas of debt collection to their physical destruction by suicide. Sadly this does happen.
Student	Idle young person with capacity to be a jackal but may graduate to become a sheep, cow, goat, dog, hyena or very possibly a lion cub, hence an enigma.

Contents

"I don't want money. It is only people who pay their bills who want that, and I never pay mine."
From *"The Picture of Dorian Gray"* by Oscar Wilde

Introduction

WHAT'S IN THIS CHAPTER

Can it ever be justifiable not to pay a bill which we know is properly due? We gain an introduction into the abilities but also the limitations of Debt Collection Agencies and learn that it is not illegal to refuse to pay most debts, but that people who succeed in not paying are those who find ways of persuading their Creditors that they are not worth chasing. Lastly, we set out to be objective in discussing what is real and practical rather than indulging in partisan moralistic arguments.

Introduction

"The payment of debts is necessary for social order. The non-payment is quite equally necessary for social order. For centuries humanity has oscillated, serenely unaware, between these two contradictory necessities."
Simone Weil

What the French philosopher Simone Weil is saying in this introductory quotation is that, on the one hand society needs people to pay their debts because the legal contract to pay is an integral part of the social contract that human beings must cooperate and trust each other to part with money and goods: if they did not there would be no economic life, only subsistence and perhaps anarchy. On the other hand, sometimes people in debt must either renege on their debts or perish – or become criminals, outlaws or revolutionaries to survive. Because this too would threaten society and cause anarchy, the occasional non-payment of debts and the survival of the Debtor comprise the lesser evil for society. In summary, this politically subversive thinker with impeccable French intellectual and academic credentials is making the case for the logic of non-payment as an active, philosophically and morally legitimate choice for the hard-pressed Debtor.

This book has been inspired by the fact that consumer debt in the UK is at an all time high at over £3,000,000,000, and according to our newspapers we are a nation "drowning in debt". Payday loan companies are booming, charging annualised interest rates of over 1500% on loans of £100 which people without access to bank credit borrow to tide them over until their next pay cheque. Consumer debts are sold on by retailers and credit card companies to be collected by Debt Purchase companies, increasingly backed by private capital and hedge funds who see debt collection as an easy way to make money.

Progressively debt collectors have gained access to extremely powerful credit bureau information - one debt collection agency boasted recently that it had access to information on over 15 million people in the UK – which can confirm who we are as individuals based on our address history and date of birth, and list what debts we owe to various Creditors, showing how we have kept up payments month by month. This information is used in sophisticated computer programmes to score and rank individual Debtors in terms of their ability and likelihood to pay.

Huge investments have been made in technology to enable easy telephone connection to Debtors, and to be able to trace them when they disappear; collectors are highly trained in techniques for customer negotiation and manipulation, and paid bonuses on results to collect via the telephone. Debt collectors speak of themselves as an "industry": there are hundreds of thousands of them in the UK, aided by thousands more based offshore in India or South Africa or Cyprus. Pity the poor consumer who finds themselves in debt; and indeed to protect the consumer there is ever increasing regulation by the *Office of Fair Trade, the Information Commission, the Consumer Protection and Markets Authority.*

What help does the Debtor have against the might of the "collection industry"? Well he or she can approach the *Consumer Credit Counselling Service* (*CCCS*) or the *Citizens Advice Bureau* (*CAB*) – both manned by part-time volunteers, who will explain how to prioritise debts, how to deal with court procedures and how to find compromises with debt collectors. This is the Establishment ensuring that the economically disenfranchised play the game by the rules of the Establishment. The alternative is not to play by these rules, but by the rules of cunning and strategy laid down by such masters as the Chinese warrior sage Sun Tzu in his seminal *Art of War* or Machiavelli following the pragmatic principles as laid down in *The Prince.* Their approach focuses less on what is moral or legal, and more on what is possible and practical, and it has interesting implications for the management of personal debt.

Is it not a crime to evade debt?

But is there anyone who will demonstrate dispassionately, not just how to collaborate and compromise with debt collectors, but how they can be beaten at their own game? That is just what this book is about: exposing the practices of retailers and debt collectors, including their many weaknesses from the perspective of a Debtor. It is not a crime not to pay consumer debts such as credit cards, utilities, hire purchase agreements, even if one can afford to pay and does not. Although the credit industry would like to make it so and may often try to trick Debtors into feeling criminalised, Debtors are at liberty to choose within the law not to collaborate with the attempts of the debt collection "industry" to enrich itself by extracting money from him or her which the Debtor may not be willing to afford. The exception to this is Government. Government takes itself very seriously as a debt collector and is wont to criminalise the non-payer of its non-discretionary services, such as council tax, income tax, road tax and sundry others.

In reality, debt collectors do not have things all their own way. At a time of recession and government cuts government agencies which try to collect money from citizens are faced with making significant reductions in customer-facing staff. Even the dreaded Taxman – Her Majesty' Revenue and Collection (HMRC) – is reputed to have had to recently write of £1.5bn of taxes more than two years old because they no longer have resources to collect it and therefore deem it more efficient to write the money off. Debt purchase companies have found that the portfolios of debts they have bought at a discount to face value – perhaps buying £1 of nominal debt for 10p – can only be collected at 2p or less per £1, so that they face massive losses on their investments and now back away from buying more. Retailers , utilities and credit card companies are also under pressure to reduce costs, relying ever more on automated processes including interactive voice robotics, and less on people to collect debt. The strategy everywhere is to pick "winners", Debtors who are likely to pay, concentrating resources fully on them, and leaving "dross" to one side, and to rely on empty threats which cannot be afforded to be carried out. This is known as *"churn and burn"*, in other words contact as many customers as possible and forget those who will not pay easily on demand.

By appearing less like a winner and more like dross - the Can't Pay - a Debtor can significantly improve their ability to escape payment altogether. Some of what Debtors do to avoid payment may not be strictly legal, and some is clearly fraudulent or indeed criminal and could lead to a custodial sentence. This book makes no recommendations on what Debtors should or should not do, and it certainly does not give legal advice. It simply describes what Debtors *actually do* to avoid payment. Knowledge of this derives from the author's extensive national and international personal experience as a consultant to credit granting and debt collecting organisations in both the private and public sectors as well as from encounters with anonymous clients as a consumer debt counsellor.

"By appearing less like a winner and more like dross – the Can't Pay – a Debtor can significantly improve their ability to escape payment altogether"

It is an unpartisan exposure of the fact that commercial systems and society at large, for reasons which are alluded to by Simone Weil above, allow or are at least unable to prevent a significant range of goods and services from being obtained without payment and financial obligations avoided by a minority of consumers. It shows how this is done and how commercial and government apparatuses fail either through incompetence or a calculation based on diminishing returns to prevent non-payers from succeeding in getting things for free.

To the outraged debt collector, fraud manager, legal practitioner or legislator, let this be an admonition to work harder and smarter, and meanwhile to be grateful that practices as are described here keep you in employment. To the interested consumer or Debtor, it is an opportunity to know how debt management works and what your choices are in either cooperating with it or evading it. Let us end this introduction by making homage to Machiavelli, taken from *The Prince*, his classical tome on the use of strategy and tactics to achieve survival, victory and endurance in Renaissance Italy:

"It remains now to discuss what methods and measures a prince should employ...
Many have written about this and I fear I might be considered presumptuous,
particularly as I intend to depart from the principles laid down by others. As my
intention is to write something useful for discerning minds, I find it more fitting
to seek the truth of the matter rather than imaginary conceptions"

What a precept, and what an act to try to follow!

1.0

The Decision To pay or not

WHAT'S IN THIS CHAPTER

We look in more depth at the moral and philosophical arguments which tell us we must always pay and learn that we are programmed from birth to think like this. But in fact throughout history people have taken from each other and justified it later; the problem for each generation now is that the rules are already made and the wealth distributed to select groups who make sure they hang on to it.

The Decision to Pay or Not

"Debt, grinding debt, whose iron face the widow, the orphan, and the sons of genius fear and hate; debt, which consumes so much time, which so cripples and disheartens a great spirit with cares that seem so base, is a preceptor whose lessons cannot be foregone, and is needed most by those who suffer from it most."
Ralph Waldo Emerson

How do people justify to themselves a refusal to pay for goods and services from which they know they have benefited? Is this not dishonest? What if we all did this? The answers are: "easy"; "of course" and often "criminal"; and "there is no chance of this".

Seen from the view of the debt collector, there are three types of people in the world: people who always pay for everything being the vast majority. Then there are those who sometimes pay if they are asked hard enough and they can't avoid it. Finally there is a small group of people who never pay – and get away with it. This book concerns itself primarily with the latter group and the simple but effective methods they use to get thousands of pounds worth of goods and services for free every year. But this group of Don't-pays further divides into two, forever hard to distinguish for the Creditor, and forever thus providing cover and excuse for one of the two. This is the "Won't Pay" (although he could if he chose) who will disguise himself as his cohort companion: "Can't Pay", and thus escape the full weight of collection enforcement.

It reveals how simple it can be to get things for nothing – and how retail, Government and benefits systems as well as the legal system are simply unable to afford the time and effort to stop the determined free-rider – under certain conditions.

Nothing described in here is recommended, we do not suggest that you as a consumer decide not to pay. But in a free society, why should not everyone know how some people manage to get things for nothing? If a parent leaves chocolates on a kitchen table, why would they be surprised to find that their children have taken them when they arrive home? If a bank or gas company is too negligent to guard its assets, because it does not think it worth investing in controls to prevent loss, how shall we be aghast that it does not collect all it should?

Banks, Utilities and Government – the "good guys"?

If you owe money to a bank or a gas company or indeed to the Taxman, you can be sure they will work very hard to track you down and try to squeeze it out of you. But what if they owe you money? How many people know that utilities are sitting on hundreds of millions of pounds owing to customers who have moved home while in credit on payment plans, leaving their account closed and in credit? Utilities including gas, electricity and water companies make ZERO effort to find people who have moved away while being owed money. Let it be said again, they are sitting on hundreds of millions of pounds of money belonging to their customers in anticipation that they can simply keep it as a source of capital.

Do you know that if you receive a payment in error to your account from the bank and do not tell them, you can be prosecuted for fraud? Do you also know that if you leave your bank account dormant, ie you do not make withdrawals or further payments into it, the bank will quietly absorb your cash into its reserves after a few years? Will they try to find you and pay it out to you? No chance! Is it right? We don't think so.

And how much effort does the Taxman make to send you back overpaid tax? You have to find out that you have paid too much and make a claim to get your own money back. How reasonable is that given the grief they give you if you owe *them* money! The taxman charges punitive interest for any tax that may be overdue – but if you are due a tax refund, unsurprisingly, you will not receive any interest to recompense you for the time (and loss of other investment opportunity to you) that the Government has been hanging on to your money. Is this fair and reasonable and ethical, or is it the leonine bargain of an overbearing and avaricious predator?

"Utilities are sitting on hundreds of millions of pounds owing to customers who have moved home while in credit"

Does this mean it is acceptable to hold back money from them or indeed to cheat or deceive them? Clearly, cheating, deceiving, scamming and stealing are all morally wrong and illegal. But lines of right and wrong can get blurred in the eye of the beholder when the other side displays ethics that are less than even. It makes it easier for non-payers to rationalise their behaviour when they realise that their Creditors (the people trying to get money out of them) aren't exactly lily white.

Look at the amounts of money these people pay themselves and for doing what...? Who says that it is right that a director of *Thames Water* should award himself a salary of £1,247,711 for simply doing his job? These people typically end up with pension plans which give them inflation-proofed pensions of more than £250,000 a year for life! Can their customers write themselves contracts awarding themselves fat salaries and pensions?

It's not like *Thames Water* actually makes the stuff – it rains on us all for free, yet the water companies manage to lose one fifth of the water they are supposed to control to leakage. And who owns nearly all of our water, electricity and gas companies these days: the French and the Germans with maybe a few sovereign Arab funds thrown in! Does that mean that it is actually patriotic to not pay for utilities because it reduces the profits and therefore the competitiveness of foreign economies competing with the UK?

Then look at the banks: they borrow our money from us, lend it back to us, gouge us with bank charges, fees for overdrafts, and fees for the privilege of them writing us a letter. They earn billions from us, they pay themselves even more than the utilities do, and ironically they will lend us all the money we like when we don't want it or need it - and lend us zero when we really do want it and need it. Companies who have banked loyally with one bank for years find their credit withdrawn overnight when bank policies change in a downturn. Businesses get wiped out, people thrown unemployed on the street.

Should we weep for bankers, should we give a damn when white collar wild-west gambling and chicanery leads to a Lehman bankruptcy, and cocaine-sniffing city dealers have to pack their laptops and *iphones* and coffee grinders into cardboard boxes and have a taste of the way the rest of the population lives? To quote the economist J K Galbraith: *"By all but the pathologically romantic, it is now recognised that this is not the age of the small man"*.

Tax Ethics of the Wealthy

When American billionairess Leona Helmsley was convicted of tax evasion in 1992 she famously declared: "Paying taxes is for the little people." Thus it is no surprise that Topshop fashion boss Philip Green was reported to have paid his wife in Monaco a dividend of £1.3 billion in 2010 in order to legally avoid (not illegally evade) income tax in UK.

Nor indeed is corporate Britain to be accused of being a slouch in the sport of paying minimum tax: writer Nicholas Shaxson describes how one third of the largest 700 UK businesses paid no tax in 2006. Does the average wage earner have such discretionary choice as to whether to pay or not to pay tax? It has been reported in the press that Vodafone can allegedly threaten the prime minister that they will relocate offshore if the government presses them too hard on tax. The small man will go to jail if he refuses to pay.

In short, there is an argument that those living gilded existences in a society described by the Nobel prize-winning economist JK Galbraith as being divided into *"private wealth and public squalor "* arrange the disposition and the price of the necessities which the rest of us must have. They ensure that their own

> "How can banks, utilities and government set themselves up as arbiters of what is good and right when they chase us whenever we owe them money, and leave it to us to find out if they owe us money?"

needs are more than well taken care of materially, and determine codes of behaviour which they can easily afford to adhere to. If the rest of the population also goes along with the codes they force upon us, it assures that the have's of this world will continue to have in plenty, served by the idiots who play their game by their rules, and who will struggle in large part to maintain themselves.

For many people, life is like a game of monopoly which is already in progress when they join it. Unfortunately, all the stations and utilities have already been taken, as has Park Lane which is full of hotels and costs unaffordable amounts to land on. Who made up the rules of the game? Generations of nobles, bastards to nobles, bourgeois *nouveaux riches*, lackeys who bent over for the foregoing , time-servers, and licensed crooks and gangsters.

People are rich today because their ancestor was a compliant but determined whore who slept with Charles II. From William the Conqueror onwards, kings gave land and hunting rights to nobles to keep them "on-side", governments gave grants and licences and monopolies to corporations run by "people like us". Peculation – where civil servants like the diarist and Secretary to the nascent British Navy Samuel Pepys, and Lord Clive of India used their offices to enrich themselves personally – was a way of life for early servants of commerce and government for centuries. Whether right or wrong, fair or unfair, this is the way it is: the way of the world.

Who then, the argument might run, is the thief? Is it the unemployed father who allows his children to watch television without a licence? Or is it the chairman of an oil company whose oil wells were stolen as recently as the mid 20th Century (or does "expropriated" sound less unpleasant) from the democratically elected ruler of Iran via a coup executed at the will of the British Government?

Life isn't fair: life indeed, according to the Buddha, is suffering. It is noticeable

"People are rich today because their ancestor was a compliant but determined whore who slept with Charles II"

that those who make the rules, run the corporations, and benefit from parliamentary allowances suffer a good deal less than those whom they expect to follow those rules. Is that fair? Is it right that Ernest Saunders, and Gerald Ronson, convicted in the famous Guinness share trading fraud case of 1990 , each was able to go free early, in Saunders's case due to "mental illness", only for him to promptly recover and start up in business again? They were freed by the same *"Good and Great"* who make the rules up for the little man – who gets no early release for mental illness; indeed the jails are full of people who are deranged or medically addicted but unhappily do not have connections.

So, as Jesus said, who shall cast the first stone? Well the answer is very easy: the Establishment. If the rules of the game as we know it were abandoned there would be chaos. Civilisation would collapse, rape and murder in the streets would be widespread in the short interval before social Armageddon. Luckily for all of us, but especially those who make the rules, there is no danger of this: If you don't pay, you can be pursued through the Law, and payment can be enforced on you, although the reality of debt collection is entirely different as we shall see later. If you steal (and if you are caught and convicted) you will be imprisoned – maybe. Civilisation is saved on these principles, and the Establishment therefore triumphs.

The Establishment determines what goods and services we are allowed to buy, at what prices and to what quality – blame the Government for Robert Maxwell's theft of the pensions of his employees – from whom and at what interest rate if we borrow and at what penalty if we default. Sherlock Holmes could consume cocaine and morphine to give himself rest and inspiration, but you today may not. In the First World War the pub opening hours were limited so that the great unwashed would return to the munitions factories sober after lunch to allow the war to continue to be prosecuted. Under New Labour limits on pub opening hours were abandoned almost entirely by a populist Tony Blair, hoping to mould a café culture on that same populous, now deemed to be overwhelmingly middle-class. The

Establishment giveth and the Establishment taketh away, ever to suit their own convenience.

So, to summarise: if property is theft, who to date has stolen the most? Is it the 5% of society who have managed to acquire 85% of all wealth, or is it the 5% of society who have acquired 0.1% of all wealth and who incidentally provide 90% of the prison population?

Original sin as the keystone of the Creditor:Debtor paradigm

"The big propagandistic lie that is promoted by the so-called Collection Industry is that it is morally right to pay. "

The big propagandistic lie that is promoted by the so-called Collection Industry is that it is morally right to pay. Hence it can at various times in history be morally obligatory to pay a tax on having windows in one's house, or on tea, or on the right to vote (Margaret Thatcher's ill-fated Poll Tax). Where does this come from? Elsewhere in this book we playfully categorise the players in the drama of credit and debt management as animals, describing those who feel an instinctive need to pay as **cattle** and **sheep** who willingly present themselves for farming.

The Judaeo-Christian ethic

The entire Judaeo-Christian ethic is based on the myth, legend or lie of Original Sin. According to this myth an all-knowing "loving God" placed a man and a woman in a beautiful garden and instructed them not to eat an apple. Being prescient he was of course aware that they would eat it anyway; he then acted surprised and angry that they had done so and cursed them with an "original sin" that they would carry through the generations such that everyone would be born with a burden of guilt or sin, a debt to the very fact of their existence. This debt must be expiated by worship, work and sacrifice of money to "God" or one of the hundreds of thousands of competing churches who claim his exclusive franchise and want 10% of everything you earn. So we are all programmed to pay up.

> **The Lie**
>
> *"If you tell a big enough lie and keep repeating it, people will eventually come to believe it. The lie can be maintained only so long as the State can withhold from the people the political, economic (and military) consequences of the lie. It thus becomes vitally important for the State to use all its powers to suppress dissent for the truth is the mortal enemy of the lie, and thus by extension the truth is the mortal enemy of the State" Josef Goebbels*

Thus our western culture brings us up with a sense of guilt at being alive and a feeling that we owe something to someone and need to pay to feel better. It can accordingly be argued that we are born and educated to be *cattle* and *sheep.* Capitalism in the form of consumerism and advertising then lies to us that we will feel better in the interval between now and dying if we give ourselves over to consumption of things that we not only don't need, but including stuff that can be actively injurious to our health, and then encourages us to take on lots of credit to be able do so. We can always pay later, can't we?

In fact it is always a matter of choice for a Debtor owing a non-government unsecured debt as to whether they decide to pay or not, just as it now is as to whether one worships a particular deity or none at all. The collection industry works almost entirely on the childhood nostrum that it is "right" to pay one's debts and plays on a sense of shame and guilt on the part of the Debtor. In a secular age of widespread unbelief in any deity and absence of hope for any kind of spiritual salvation they successfully position themselves as a commercial quasi-priesthood who can shrive the erring Debtor of the sin of owing money. Thus can the Debtor obtain "relief" and "rehabilitation", as if he were some kind of criminal or sufferer from a disease.

> "In fact it is always a matter of choice for a Debtor owing a non-Government unsecured debt as to whether they decide to pay or not"

None of the foregoing is intended to justify any action which anyone takes to either avoid payment or to cheat, defraud or steal from any government, corporation or institution. It simply points out the moral difficulty of the "Establishment" in arrogating right to itself in determining mechanisms for the acquisition and transfer of goods, services and benefits in our society. It shows how individuals within society might well rationalise to themselves any actions they might take in avoiding payment as being a moral choice no less valid to them than the moral imperative of payment set down by law, and commercial practice, both underpinned by an Establishment which forces its questionable ethics on a population locked into a system which keeps the high-ups firmly and permanently on top of the low-downs.

Nor is any of this intended to "prove" the argument in favour of the have-nots. It simply sets out how someone might not feel morally compromised in playing against the system, deliberately going against its codes, mores and indeed laws in order to re-gain some of the advantage which misfortune and miscasting of history, birth, lineage, genes, ethnicity, social class and educational opportunity may have withheld from them.

William the conquered would have been executed as a pirate, thief and traitor: William the Conqueror got lucky in that reigning King Harold and his army were exhausted from a 300 mile forced march after the Battle of Stamford Bridge just three days earlier. William was thus able to win his battle to end up owning all of England, making the laws and becoming the progenitor of an enduring sequence of God's representatives on English soil.

The question for many of those who decide to find ways around paying also boils down to that of the character *Dirty Harry* from the film *Magnum Force*: "Do you feel lucky?" They are helped in their luck, as we will see in the next section, by the calculation of the system that they will be the exceptions.

Corporations versus Sole Traders

Most Hold-out Debtors will have no compunction about avoiding payment to large corporations and government institutions. These are both seen as over-powerful, and can easily seem deserving of being out-smarted. If they are

"No one feels sorry for a large corporation or a tax office and their very facelessness make them seem inhuman"

wasteful in their own use of their resources, to compound their incompetence by depriving them of payment could be argued to be simply underpinning the case for their reform, abolition or bankruptcy. No one feels sorry for a large corporation or a tax office, and their very facelessness, rigidity and bureaucracy make them inhuman.

It is different with the corner-shop owner or the widow who runs a small bed-and-breakfast. To outsmart and take advantage of individual people who may themselves be struggling to make a living might be a different matter. If there is a difference between the Hold-out Debtor and the out-and-out conman (or the *jackal* and the *wolf* as we shall describe them more fully later), perhaps it is that the former would not seek to take from the weak, who might well be their kith and brethren.

2.0

Legalities

> **WHAT'S IN THIS CHAPTER**
>
> First we discover that the law is not at all clear in terms of what you can and cannot do. Then we examine the concepts of fraud and theft, seeking to define the line between these criminal acts and "sins of omission" which may or may not be illegal. We note that it is of key importance to be able to distinguish when one is at risk of crossing a legal boundary, although most of us have a sixth sense to help guide us.

Legalities

"One should always play fairly when one has the winning cards"
Oscar Wilde

When asked about Truth, a wise man once replied: "Which truth do you mean? There is your truth, my truth, his and her truths and maybe also *The Truth*". In other words, there are many perspectives on what is real and true, all depending on the point of view of the observer as to what he sees. So it arguably is also with regard to the Law. There are statutes aplenty to be sure, but apparently not enough to assure complete adherence to the path of rectitude, because every year our lawgiving parliamentarians create more of them. Was England so chaotically ungovernable in 1900 that for a full century thereafter parliamentarians needed to labour (and labour yet) to make ever more laws each year?

"Where the law should be in black and white there are frequently shades of grey"

If the Law were clear, there would be no need for courts of appeal and yet higher courts. Yet the Law Lords are always busy, deciding how the Law should be interpreted in a particular case. For in England, in addition to the statutory laws passed by Parliament there is the Common Law of precedence, expressing what a particular judge considered to be an appropriate interpretation of existing Law, or indeed a novel thrust into his own consideration as to what the Law should be to address a particular case.

Where the Law ideally should be in black and white, there are frequently shades of grey in practice. Something may be so, but in law it needs to be proven to be so. It is always a mistake to confuse our sense of natural justice (your natural justice, or my natural justice?) with the Law. So for the purposes of this book, something may be seen to be illegal, but it is only certainly so when it is so proven in court.

Fraud

A reasonable definition of fraud could be "obtaining goods or services by deception". This is certainly illegal. To borrow a million pounds in the clear knowledge that one never intended to pay it back would fall within the definition of obtaining goods by deception. The lender would never part with the money in the first place if they were aware of an intention not to repay. But how to prove such a thing in the absence of an unlikely full confession?

If the borrower were to provide information material to the conditions of the loan, however, which turned out to be knowingly false, that would be a different matter. A false name, age, address, statement of assets or income, stated expectation of future work or reward might all influence the lender to make a loan which he or she would refuse if the true information were provided. The provision of such false information with a view to obtaining pecuniary advantage is undoubtedly fraudulent and illegal. Anyone committing fraud and convicted of it will gain a criminal record and very likely a prison sentence.

But first of all they have to be caught, prosecuted and convicted. Big frauds are very visible eventually at least, though obviously not at the time they are being committed, otherwise they would be prevented and frustrated through preventive detection. All providers of credit today routinely have a fraud department which will seek to prevent fraud where possible by detecting untruths in the identity, date of birth, address history, employment record, asset detail, lease or mortgage documentation of the credit applicant. But just as burglars tend not to wear striped black and white pullovers and carry bags marked "swag" around with them as they ply their trade, fraudsters are by definition very adept at mimicking the behaviour of honest folk. *Goats* wander among the *sheep.*

A great deal of debt which retailers write off as unpaid is in fact fraud, in that the debt was never collectable, because the Debtor never intended to pay and successfully practiced a deception undetected by the retailer. The greatest crimes are those which remain undiscovered, and perhaps the most modest (because unreported) fraud success stories of all time are those intelligent criminals and fraudsters who did not boast about their achievements.

Theft

Theft is generally also associated with deceit in that the intelligent perpetrator disguises their identity as a precondition of not being caught and convicted. To take property or services without identifying oneself and without permission and without intent to pay for it is theft, and to commit the act of theft is to steal. Theft is forbidden in all cultures and religions, but it is endemic to human behaviour. Who among us as a child has not stolen a cake, or a sweet or an apple from a tree? We are all thieves in one way or another, although most westerners, schooled indirectly every day by the commercialised Judaeo-Christian morality of small town Hollywood, may have some remorse about that and a sincere intention not to repeat the offence.

An example of self-delusion

There is an old story that when a guest at a party asked a lady in jest: "Would you commit adultery for a million pounds?" she had no hesitation in replying immediately "Of course! Wouldn't anyone?" To which the guest responded: "Well, how about ten pounds then?" The lady then snorted: "What do you think I am?" The guest meekly replied: "We both know what you are madam, we are merely negotiating on price."

We delude ourselves in our interpretation of our own case as to right and wrong, morality is elastic. To steal may well be morally wrong in all cultures, but practiced thieves are able to quickly digest this fact and let it pass out of their ambient consciousness.

Sins of Omission

In fact it can be quite difficult to prove intent not to pay. If one moves into a property and begins to use the gas, water and electricity supply, at what point can it be said to be clear that the user has no intention to pay? There is a presumption of innocence, of good intent and it is only by non-performance or non-payment that this good intent can be called into question. Even where a borrower has had to provide voluminous information about their ability and intent to pay and signed clear contracts committing to specific payments on given dates, the sheer fact of non-payment is never of itself convincing evidence of intent not to pay or of a pre-meditated fraud.

> "In fact it can be quite difficult to prove intent not to pay"

Successful fraud requires intelligence and the ability to detect and outwit defences where theft merely demands speed and occasionally brute force of the perpetrator. Fraudsters are notoriously adept at distancing themselves from the proof of their misdemeanours, disguising their true identities and airbrushing their trails for would be detectors. They are helped in this regard by the fact that many debt collectors, particularly at the early stages of debt collection, have not been selected by qualification, career ambition or demonstrated high intelligence to carry out this role, and actually find the work distasteful and embarrassing, being at least unconsciously willing to give up.

This fact of presumed good intent is the gateway through which hold-out Debtors walk with impunity out of harm's way to the freedom of being able to enjoy treatment as a late payer or a Can't-pay. No one yet has been able to tell apart a Can't-pay from a Won't pay apart from hanging them by their heels from a high building and threatening to let go.

Warning!

The successful Hold-out Debtor may easily be tempted to cross the line of legality in terms of both fraud and theft, specifically in cases where they seek or obtain the benefit of a good or service with prior intent not to pay. In some cases this will be fairly self-evident, for example in making a credit application which contains material falsehoods, while in others it may be difficult to prove prior intent. Not to offer to pay for goods or services obtained on credit and not to cooperate with the collection attempts of the seller or agents acting on his behalf, not to provide information requested, or to be present and available to discuss a debt – these are not crimes. But most people do have a sense of what is lawful and unlawful and most of us know instinctively when we are taking what is not ours to take.

3.0

How Credit is obtained

WHAT'S IN THIS CHAPTER

Now it is time to look at the building blocks of credit management which are used to determine how much credit any individual may have and under what terms, including concepts such as credit limit, risk category, scoring and profiling. Very importantly we also examine the behavioural characteristics which credit grantors and debt collectors associate with non-payment or debt being recognised as uncollectable. An understanding of these characteristics is critical to the success or failure of payment refusal or debt evasion.

How Credit is Obtained

Thus hath the candle singed the moth. O, these deliberate fools!
The Merchant of Venice, William Shakespeare

Just as one man's meat is the other man's poison, the credit advanced by a Creditor is immediately a debt owed by a Debtor. Both parties take a risk at the outset: the Debtor that he will be able to sustain the conditions of the debt and later to repay it, and the Creditor that the Debtor will be willing and able to perform his obligation of repayment. The credit granting process is designed to give comfort to the Creditor in taking this risk. Of course, the point about risk is that betimes it falls against the risk-taker. That only makes him a fool if he calculated the risk incorrectly or ignored the analysis that his assessment delivered. Then he is the moth singed by the flame of the brightly beaconing candle of illusory potential profit.

But deliberate, voluntary and considered advancement or "granting" of credit is only one way in which credit is obtained or a debt entered into. In the case of government, an external agency can decide that a tax is due or that child support needs to be paid. By moving into a property supplied by a utility credit is generally given involuntarily in

Credit Checking

For nearly all commercially obtained credit it is necessary to undergo a credit check. This will determine:

- *Whether credit may be given and under what conditions*

- *To what value may credit be extended, ie what the credit limit will be*

- *To what risk category the new account will be assigned, ie high, medium or low risk*

that gas, electricity and water are all quite literally on tap. In these cases the Debtor "acquires" credit without any initial risk assessment or credit approval, and equally the Creditor takes on an unquantified risk, some of which must inevitably go against him.

Credit terms

The conditions under which credit is granted are almost universally non-negotiable for consumer credit, ie for loans, higher purchase agreements, mobile phone agreements, credit cards. If a consumer does not accept any of the individual terms, their application for credit will be refused.

However, it is often possible to negotiate individual conditions, with landlords for example, on the amount of deposit which they will require, on the length of lease or indeed the price. In the case of utilities, home movers who move into a property nominated as "owned" by an individual utility are generally subjected to deemed contract conditions. In other words, they will be sent the terms and conditions of the use of the utility offering by mail and, based on the assumption that they do not promptly reject the terms published by the utility, these terms will take effect.

"Under contract law if there is no agreement between the parties on payment terms, the party which last communicates its terms in writing to other party is recognised as obliging its terms upon the other"

Under contract law if there is no agreement between the parties on payment terms, the party which last communicates its terms in writing to the other party is recognised as obliging its terms and conditions upon the other. This opens up the possibility for a home-mover in possession of a property and the utility services on tap to write to the utility refuting its terms and inserting their own. Specifically in regard to refusing consent to have their data shared with other credit providers (which will give the utility access to previous address history, previous payment behaviour and subsequent addresses after they have moved out of the current property for tracing purposes) the new householder has a sustained right to disallow such sharing of their data provided that they give prompt notice in writing to the suppler after contact has been made.

Most credit providers have set terms of payment, that is to say, the means of payment and the length of time for which credit will be provided. In the case of credit card companies, provided one makes a minimum payment, the card company will be only too happy for the customer to take extended credit within their credit limit based on a high interest rate of between 20% and 30% per annum.

Energy utilities offer payment by cheque after the end of each quarter, or by standing order or direct debit monthly and their prices or tariffs for each offering will reflect the perceived risk and cost to the utility in supplying a customer on the specific term. A very high risk customer may only be offered a prepayment meter on a high tariff, while for the majority of assessed low or normal risk customers direct debit monthly payment will be promoted as the most economic tariff to the customer – but actually because it gives most control of revenue generation to the utility, on the assumption that the customer will honour the direct debt. Most do.

Credit Limit

The credit limit set by a supplier is the maximum amount which the supplier will permit the customer to be in debt to him before having to make a payment. In the case of credit and store cards and also mobile phone accounts, accumulated credit is now calculated in real time, so that electronic systems will automatically stop further use of the credit line when the credit limit is reached. The customer is informed of their credit limit in order that they realise they need to make payment when the limit is reached and do not attempt to overstep it. Banks are now beginning to offer this feature with regard to warning messages to mobile phones that customers are about to go into overdraft.

Often with store and credit cards, customers who use their credit facility close to the limit without hitting it and who pay regularly on time will find that they are given additional credit from time to time without having to request it. It is of course, the supreme irony of the credit economy that when one has no need of credit (and is therefore very creditworthy) one is inundated with offers of credit, but if one actually needs to borrow it can be very hard to obtain. Hence, writing to a credit or store card company under one's own initiative to ask for higher credit, may have the reverse effect of causing the limit to be reduced.

Risk Category

Every customer receiving credit from a supplier will also be assessed in terms of the risk they are believed to carry of not paying on time, or not paying at all. It is in the interest of the customer to have their risk assessed as lowly as possible, not least because the lowest risk customers will generally be offered the most attractive prices and service offerings.

"Anyone perceived as high risk will be placed on a shorter more aggressive path for enforcement"

Anyone categorised as high risk will be placed on a shorter, more aggressive debt path for enforcement, while low risk customers who miss payments will initially be assumed to be too busy and their excuses for lateness, or objections on the basis of alleged supplier contract failure given more credibility. Customers with varying perceived degrees of risk may be offered different pricing – to compensate for risk or indeed to deter an applicant from becoming a customer based on high and unattractive pricing. They may also be required to make a security deposit to offset the risk of non-payment, but again as a deterrent to the impecunious against becoming a customer and a probable bad Debtor.

Scoring

Consumers can be "scored" at numerous points in their life cycle as customers, and for different reasons. Application scoring or credit scoring is the most well-known use of scoring algorithms, and it is used to determine the factors just discussed: whether to offer a line of credit to a named individual, how much to offer, on what terms or payment tariff.

Profiling by Postcode

A large UK credit bureau famously states: "You are where you live". What this means is that the credit score for any individual is significantly influenced by their postcode. Scoring groups thousands of people together and attempts to categorise them into groups of similar types who will all behave in a similar way. Socio-demographic archetypes are defined, such as "retired older couples living in mortgage free properties" or "struggling singles in bed-sits". These categorisations are used for marketing purposes to determine what products to mail-shot to whom, and there can be approximately 70 different marketing categories which try to capture all of the possible groupings in age, sex, social class, wealth, ethnicity, cultural aspirations – and likely creditworthiness. Frequently post-coding is used to pre-screen offers not just in terms of likelihood of finding a customer, but targeting one who will pay.

An industry jargon uses the expression "red-lining" which is an approach defined by marketers to determine which postcodes they simply do not want to sell to and which they definitely do not want to give credit to. It is supposed to be illegal to refuse someone credit simply based on where they live, but the fact remains that certain postcodes will influence credit score, and the ability to secure credit and thereby become a Debtor, very highly.

Other factors used in scoring in addition to postcode include age, sex, marital status and names. Ethnic names may attract more negativity that native-sounding names. Currently unfashionable names – like Cyril, Edward, Mabel and Olive – may be linked to postcode to imply an elderly person. In a given postcode, a man aged 35 will be assumed to be either single and unemployed, or married with children, and if they are married with children it may be inferred that they are likely to be employed and have a steady income and a higher credit status.

"You are where you live" Much effort goes into modelling socio-demographic types to infer both propensity to buy and propensity to pay. The basic data used for developing these scoring models includes shopping surveys which are often found in magazines. The Scoring defines people into groups of populations which are "normed" into standard distribution curves shaped like a bell. The average performer is represented in the middle, high part of the bell, with small extremes on either side. The so-called "law of large numbers" means that most populations will have a large number of people at average value and small extremes, both high and low. From a marketing perspective this can be applied to likely spend, for example the average spend on a credit card might be £800 per month with very small number of people spending between £20 and £30 per month, or at the other extreme spending £8000 to £8500 per month.

It also extends to likelihood of non-payment. The credit bureaux retain vast amounts of historical data on payment behaviour and use sophisticated software applications with names like "neural network scoring" to determine which combinations of age, sex, marital status, payment history at both personal and postcode level either pre-dispose a given individual at a given address to either pay nor not pay.

What relevance is this to the credit applicant who may either intend to pay or not? It is massively relevant because scoring works on odds, just like betting on a horse. A low credit score may correlate with high odds of non-payment and a high one with low odds of non-payment. People scoring both high and low will fail to pay and become bad debts, but the one who scores high for propensity to pay will be granted credit. Just like a punter before a race meeting looking at horses to assess which characteristics might indicate it could be a winner, the informed credit applicant may want to know how to present themselves so that they maximise their credit score. In doing so they stand to be granted the greatest amount of initial credit.

Application scoring frequently asks questions of the credit applicant which cannot be answered from data shared with credit bureaux. This can include

> "The informed credit applicant may want to know how to present themselves so that they maximise their credit score"

nature of employment, marital status, number of children, owned or mortgaged or rented accommodation, length of time at current and at previous address. A married civil servant with two teenaged children, who lives in an owned house for the last 25 years and therefore owns it outright and has no mortgage will score highly. So will a policeman who does not have a credit record because he generally chooses to pay for things by saving cash for when he can afford them. A single self-employed contractor living in rented accommodation at four different addresses in the last three years might not score quite so highly...

Behavioural Scoring

The same borrower, now become a Debtor in arrears, who was keen to appear in the best possible light when making an application for credit which would be scored and evaluated as to whether he was judged likely to repay, may now be subject to behavioural scoring as a prelude to any serious investment in tracing, legal enforcement and employment of bailiffs or other third parties, all of which will cost more money and add to the sum outstanding.

Behavioural scoring quite simply attempts to evaluate how the Debtor has behaved while a customer, both in terms of conducting his account and possibly also in combination with the evaluation of more recent credit reference bureau information about his payment of other Creditors. Debtors who behave in ways which resemble the behaviour of other Debtors from whom the Creditor has previously successfully secured recovery will be grouped into a cohort of "likely pays"; those who bear no resemblance to other Debtors with a record of ultimate successful payment will be grouped into a cohort of "likely non-pays". The Creditor will logically concentrate efforts on the "likely pays" and either sell or write off the "likely no-pays". Whoever has to deal with the "likely no-pays" will be aware of their measured low value and will be unlikely to invest much further effort in them.

> **Neural Scoring**
>
> *One of the types of scoring to identify target campaign groups such as likely pays is called "neural scoring", referred to above. This is a so-called blackbox approach, whereby as many characteristics as possible which are thought to be possibly indicative or predictive of a desired propensity, ie to pay, are fed into a computer programme. The programme looks at the combination of these various characteristics that are associated with either payment or non-payment and scores and then ranks individual cases from the most likely to be successful from the Creditor's point of view, to the least likely.*

Behavioural Characteristics associated with non-payment

Just as a hoverfly might try to make itself look like a wasp in order to deter potential predators, so an intelligent Hold-out may take care to demonstrate behaviours and characteristics which give the Creditor direct signals that they will not get paid and should give up trying to. A hold-out with assets, income and the means to pay will try to disguise or suppress these facts at the point of billing onwards. The behaviours and characteristics associated with non-payment and hopelessness for the Creditor can to some degree be controlled by the Debtor himself. This gives him power, influence and remote and anonymous input into the decision process as to whether to try to pursue him. He can to some extent lay his own trail to nowhere through the following attributes:

Lack of contact

There will be no acknowledgement by the Debtor that he is at an address or has received a letter or an attempted phone call.

Zero Cash History

A Debtor who has never paid anything whatever is much less likely to be converted to paying on enforcement than a Debtor who has paid any money, no matter how little.

No Phone numbers or email addresses

The hopeless never-pay is like the stone which gathers no moss, it has no handles to grab onto.

Female

Women can be harder to trace than men, perhaps because they have better social networks, or perhaps because they find it easier to find shelter at a new address.

No Forenames

An account held by C Smith is infinitely harder to track down than one held by Clive Smith.

Multiple Account

A multiple account has more than one customer. It may denote students, or transient workers, and very likely private rented accommodation. Such accounts are more likely to default at which point individual names may prove to be untraceable.

Age indeterminate

Demographic predictions about people's behaviour rely heavily on knowing how old they are. Are they likely to be students, or working with a family, or older living alone, or pensioners? If the computer model doesn't know its conclusions will be less reliable.

Private rented accommodation

Small private landlords are likely to be less data-hungry than public bodies or housing associations, more focussed simply on having their property rented out and unwilling to ask too many questions or apply preconditions which might affect their ability to do this - so long as their deposit is covered. They are unlikely to make any effort to validate a name or alias and are generally easily satisfied with references which might not bear scrutiny if checked thoroughly by a professional housing agency.

Value Limits

Although not a characteristic of the Debtor, the value associated with the Debt to be chased in association with the other characteristics mentioned here will affect the ranking that a debt will have in a scored list for collection. While many collection agencies like low value debts of less than £200 or even less than £100 in cases where there is a rich dataset about the Debtor, for Debtors ticking the above boxes debt values will need to be high to justify any pursuit – say over £1000 or £2000.

Obviously any debt of very high value – say over £10,000 or £20,000 will merit some further investigation just because of the relatively high value at stake. But the same principles apply. If there are no handles to grab on to, the subject being sought will be found to be slippery. There will be much less expectation of success at the outset of the pursuit and therefore less investment and intensity in the chase.

4.0

Attributes of the successful Payment Evader

WHAT'S IN THIS CHAPTER

What are the personal characteristics of someone who is likely to succeed in holding out against payment? Anyone wanting to resist payment for any length of time needs to possess these character traits or learn to acquire them. Just as a ship only needs a very small hole in order to eventually sink any would-be Holdout who cannot act in these ways is likely ultimately to be overwhelmed by his Creditors and be forced to pay up.

Attributes of the Successful Payment Evader

"Be assured that it gives much more pain to the mind to be in debt, than to do without any article whatever which we may seem to want."
Thomas Jefferson

While the principles of non-payment are simple, this does not mean that they are easy. Few indeed are those who can defy Jefferson's aphorism for any length of time, and while it may be relatively easy to acquire a debt, living with it is not to the taste of the majority of human beings: a fact which benefits the collections industry greatly in relieving sufferers of their bad consciences by getting them to pay up. Indeed, as we have already seen the collections industry actively works at instilling guilt, shame and fear into Debtors, seeking to introduce a moral element into the relationship between Debtor and Creditor.

"Ideas of morality are of course the invention of kings and priests, the haves and makers of laws and regulations to inflict on those below them who serve and prop them up"

Ideas of morality are of course, as we have seen, the invention of kings and priests, the haves and makers of laws and regulations to inflict on those below them who serve and prop them up. The moral and propaganda battle is almost akin to that between Deists and Darwinists. One side says rules should be obeyed because a higher authority has deemed it so and must be obeyed simply *because they declare themselves a higher authority*. The other side says that rules hold fast only so far and so long as they can be enforced in an eternal evolutionary struggle for the survival of the fittest. And let us be quite clear, the successful hold-out or payment evader needs to be very fit.

Getting away with not paying for goods and services demands a certain set of character attributes in addition to intelligence. One principle characteristic is to be unidentified: if no one knows that you have not paid, or if they don't know who you are or where you live, or how to get in contact with you, it is very hard to get you to pay – obviously.

Modesty

This is to do with modesty of ambition and of appetite. Perhaps the most significant reason why Creditors do not chase Debtors is that it is not worth it, particularly in terms of the amount of money owed. Most Creditors will not chase amounts below £25 but they will definitely pursue debts more than £1000 at least for some distance. The more a Debtor impacts upon a Creditor, the more definitely the Creditor will react and pursue the debt.

Sang-froid

The successful payment evader reacts coolly and with forethought and consideration before reacting to any communication from a Creditor. Do they have to respond to this demand? Do they have to do it now? What options do they have to buy time or to cast the pursuer off the scent? They think through each move and its potential consequences before making it. They never give up, they never despair, and they never allow themselves to be panicked into a premature reaction or capitulation.

Attention to Detail

The successful payment evader always reads their mail. They open dunning (debt-chasing) letters and note who they are from, including the department and name of the collector, they collate and maintain a record of all correspondence, they carefully note the dates of any planned action against them in order to be able to take counter-measures in due time. They definitely do not bury their heads in the sand and ignore incoming communications. This is the strategy of the ostrich waiting for the lion to approach, or of the rabbit frozen in the car headlights. Its outcome is certain surprise and wrong-footing by the Creditor.

Discretion

The successful evader is discreet. They do not boast of their achievements to friends and acquaintances, knowing that this will undermine their chances of continued success. The embittered ex-friend, the jealous acquaintance, the envious neighbour, the vengeful ex-lover are all excellent sources of information to revenue collectors in terms of letting them know where the Debtor is, how much disposable income they may have, what assets they possess and where, where and how to contact them and track them down...

> "The successful Payment Evader always reads their mail"

Equally undesirable are the admiring followers who display their flattery in the time-honoured manner of imitation, thus greatly increasing the source and manner of revenue loss to the Creditor and raising the profile of a problem which the Creditor may not previously have given much attention to. At worst, the Creditor may close whatever gap the payment evader may have been exploiting, thus removing the opportunity.

Creativity

> "The successful payment evader thinks ahead and anticipates the moves of their pursuers"

The successful payment evader thinks ahead and anticipates the moves of their pursuers. They brush down their trail and set false trails to lead pursuit away from them. They place barriers between themselves and the Creditor and use stratagems to delay and frustrate the hunt, knowing that all the while the Creditor must employ more resources to maintain the pursuit, adding cost all the time to an ever-aging debt and potentially to the neglect of chasing newer and easier targets. Who wants to chase a stringy old *goat* up a mountain, when fat *ewes* are sitting in the lower meadows?

Agility

Like the afore-mentioned *goat*, the successful payment evader is agile. They keep a distance between themselves and their pursuers and take care never to let themselves be surprised. Thus they will not answer a phone personally, but allow it to go to messaging. They will be in a position to physically remove themselves prior to any enforcement action at their residence. If surprised, they have the presence of mind to distance themselves from the pursuit, for example by refusing to accept the bona fides of a telephone caller and demanding written communication on headed notepaper, or the opportunity to call back the caller's head office "to mitigate against fraud". Caught on their doorstep they will evince a high degree of quick-wittedness and pretend to be a friend or relative or babysitter and will feign indignation or indifference to end the contact.

Endurance

They will also have the will and the endurance to maintain their defences over many months and perhaps years, during which time the number of their pursuers will likely have increased, but with early chasers already having given up. This goes back to sang-froid and having the temperament to maintain a battle of nerves over a long period.

Calculation

The successful payment evader will also be an excellent calculator of risks and probabilities, and be comfortable taking a risk position and sitting on it, and yet

_____

"The successful Payment Evader will be an excellent calculator of risks and probable outcomes"

_____

know when it is better to abandon it – just like the mountain goat sitting in a crevice until it is sure it has been spotted and then knowing when it is time to leap away to safety. Taking wild or unforeseen risks is something that will be avoided, precisely because it is dangerous and unpredictable in terms of behaviour. Impulsive behaviour is therefore foreign to the hold-out non-payer.

Moral Compass

The successful payment evader will be able to deal with equivocal ethical situations by interpreting matters to their personal advantage. Many who do not attempt to take things to their conclusion in holding out in the face of significant efforts by their Creditors to make them compliant share similar equivocal moral orientations, but do not have the fortitude, enterprise, cheek and daring to maintain non-payment. They submit to the moral superiority of the Creditor.

Role Play

Holding out against a determined Creditor requires a combination of all of the above including the ability to reinvent oneself in a different guise as a different character, and to do so consistently, holding onto the vital details under cross-questioning at successive encounters with the representatives of individual Creditors to be able to tell a consistent and credible story. This may include feigning health conditions, inventing lodgers or previous tenants or partners or indeed children; and also giving them a timely exit from the drama to suit the story, explaining their departure, temporary absence or sad death. All of this is of course fraudulent, but we had best discard moral outrage and simply be reminded yet again of Disraeli's declamation: " *Debt is a prolific mother of folly and crime*".

Simple but not easy

> "Few therefore are the numbers of those who have all the attributes to succeed as an inveterate non-payer"

Successful non-payers are likely to be those who make a strategic choice to be so *before* they have contracted or entered into a commitment for a good or service – taking them straight into the realms of intentionally seeking to obtain goods and services by deceit: fraud, although this may be very hard to prove so long as it remains an unstated thought. Be that as it may, they start as they mean to go on, rather than finding themselves in a disadvantaged unplanned situation and having to react to get out of it. Thus they will not have given information or intelligence about themselves at the beginning which they will regret having done later on.

They are very unlikely to be living the chaotic lifestyle of an addict, and not likely to be suffering from a diagnosed mental disorder. Such people are very unlikely to possess the attributes described above, although in their turn they are highly likely to fall into debt and ultimately to become known as calculable risk/reward returns to debt collectors. Because such people do not possess the complete skill set to be enduring non-payers, and will not be able to maintain non-payment for any length of time. They will not be able to renew their sources of credit and can be constrained in regard to their ultimate cost to the Creditor community. They will however consume a lot of time for Creditors, and at a point in time and as part of a *fallback strategy*, the enduring Debtor may be able to take refuge by hiding among them as a ledger item of "known uncollectables".

Few therefore are the numbers of those who have all the attributes to succeed as an inveterate non-payer. Most non-payers are amateurs and run out of road. They turn out to be might-pays who did pay after all, or couldn't-pays who have been bagged and tagged. This is good for them and their prospects of social rehabilitation, and to a certain extent comforting for Creditors, if also irritating to have to recognise, ie that the enduring non-payer is an in-exterminable but limited problem.

5.0

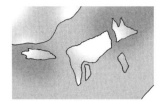

Career and lifestyle Choices For the Holdout Debtor

> **WHAT'S IN THIS CHAPTER**
>
> There are two fundamental types of Debtor, each with their own set of issues and opportunities. For both it is possible to acquire the capacity to become a Holdout Debtor, but the question of career or job will be key to the choices available. We look in some depth at a prominent real life debtor who succeeded to an extraordinary degree in evading his creditors, while being all the while under the spotlight of publicity.

Career and Lifestyle Choices for the Holdout Debtor

Almost no child, when fantasising about their future career, would dream of becoming a debt collector, and few school leavers would have this ambition either. Most debt collectors drift into collections work for want of a better choice. They do not generally set out to enjoy a fulfilling career chasing the desperate as well as the desperados. This lack of future intention they have in common with those Debtors who later find they need to have to evade their debts. Things just work out that way. But in certain subcultures and in certain families people do grow up in an environment where they feel outside "the system" and sense that they need to find ways to evade it and to exploit it where they can.

> "Almost no child when fantasising about their future career would dream of becoming a debt collector..."

By now it must be clear to the reader that successful payment avoidance is not a matter of happenstance. It requires the characteristics described earlier in Chapter 4 and it can be very hard work. As with the old Irishman asked the way to Cork: "*I wouldn't start from here if I were you*" is not a useful response to the question, how does the would-be non-payer organise their life to best fit them for this role? One can only ever start from where one is now, but it is evident that certain people are better fitted to be hold-out Debtors than others.

The Mighty Castle Dweller

Anyone deeply hooked into the modern consumerist credit economy with mortgages, insurances, hire purchase agreements, mobile phone contracts, credit cards and a career with a large company or government organisation

> *is ill-fitted to the "hunter gatherer" style of credit scavenging, more so if they have children committed to GCSE and A level courses in local schools and partners who also have high visibility careers. These are the "Mighty Castle" dwellers, living in houses in which they have equity – their mighty castles. They have no problem getting credit and sustaining it so long as they continue to pay regularly. But if they ever tried to hold out on paying debts off they are vulnerable to having Charging Orders secured on their houses, to Attachments to Earnings from career jobs which they cannot simply walk away from in order to evade involuntary repayment of their debts. They have too much invested in their next hoped-for promotion and in their pension schemes to make it ever worthwhile abandoning these perquisites.*

Indeed why would a "Mighty Castle" dweller ever need to resort to evading debts? Well, in fact their circumstances can change like everyone else's. They can be made redundant, fall ill, become separated or divorced, or simply lose money through poor financial management and find themselves struggling to keep up payments on revolving credit commitments. However, so long as they can see financial crises coming, they too can position themselves to minimise the impact of their fading creditworthiness and repayment ability. Times will approach when their fixed situation becomes less sticky, for example when children leave home to go to university, on retirement or redundancy.

At these times they can position themselves for the one-time coup, quietly liquidating their assets either by selling them outright or transferring them to trusted partners or associates before they physically remove themselves, possibly to a new jurisdiction outside the EU. They are most likely to succeed in doing so if they have maintained payments on all their commitments as they draw on credit lines to the limits, then suddenly disappearing to the utter surprise of their Creditors.

The Hunter-Gatherer

It is the hunter-gatherer lifestyle which is best positioned to take advantage of credit by suddenly disappearing. People who can choose to live in the black economy can evade not just their local Creditors and utilities but the rapacious clutches of the state agencies also. Those who can sell their services directly to the public and who have a skill which can be practised anywhere, in any country or culture regardless of language, are the best placed of all. They can work in Birmingham or Brighton, in Barcelona or Belize. Such trades might include hairdressing, manicurist, gardening, building and labouring, painter and decorator, security work, electrician, plumber, carpenter, car mechanic, chef, seasonal tourism worker...

There are hundreds, if not thousands of possible ways to make a living as a hunter-gatherer. All of these jobs have the additional benefit that they are suitable for self-employment. If a Debtor is self-employed they can re-invent themselves and their corporate identities in Protean infinity, finding new trade names, sheltering within new limited company structures, operating with a variety of off-the-shelf pay-as-you-go mobile phones and finding new email addresses to maintain their constant mutation and movement. At this point they also become a problem for government, which is interested in them for payment of National Insurance Contributions, Income Tax and VAT. Thus for the hunter gatherer non-payment becomes a habitual way of life and does not respect any Creditor who can be evaded, including governments.

> "It is the hunter-gatherer lifestyle which is best positioned to take advantage of credit by suddenly disappearing"

Contract workers are also well placed to be hunter gatherers: seamen, oil rig workers, procurement specialists and temporary workers. Given that contracts are of short fixed duration, these people are also always on the move, often from one set of rented accommodation to the next, often abroad. They can be resistant to *Attachments to Earnings* or indeed to tracing attempts by simply moving on. Furthermore, they can make it clear to their agency that if their details are passed on or the agent cooperates with any enforcement activity against them, they will simply leave the agency and find another one, perhaps even remaining with the same client, who may have gotten used to them and like them. Agents will thus often be tempted to turn a blind eye or deaf ear to requests for cooperation by government agencies for fear of losing the commission they enjoy from their client contract worker.

Debtors can also frequently take shelter in family businesses, run by a close relative who out of family loyalty will ignore court papers regarding an *Attachment to Earnings Order* or a *Deduction Order* from the Child Support Agency. They may even allow the Debtor to work casually, ie without being formally on the payroll.

To return to the world of the Mighty Castle dweller, many of these too have occupations which are eminently transferable and indeed desirable from countries seeking skilled immigrants such as Australia and Canada and to some extent the United States – notably and obviously English speaking countries. These people tend to have the added advantages of being well-educated, experienced in travel, in planning and executing complicated projects: such as emigration to a new country.

"Anyone who really wants to can indeed decide to move to avoid their creditors"

This applies to doctors, dentists, nurses and other health workers, but also to commercial professionals who have previously worked for large companies at home, completely tied in to mortgages. These days it is easy to transfer pension entitlements to external providers, even to those based abroad so as to take them further from the reach of potential UK Creditors. Cunning planning would imply this being done well before any impending pursuit for debt and before absconding.

In conclusion therefore, anyone who really wants to can indeed decide to move to avoid their Creditors. For some it is easier than others. Often hard choices must be faced and sacrifices made of friends, and jobs. But it is always possible.

Developing Capacity for Debt Hold-out

For the Hold-out with assets such as property, money in bank accounts, shares, pension plans and so forth, asset protection is a key consideration. All of these can be got at by Creditors if they can be discovered under a legal process such as a court-ordered *Oral Examination* - assuming of course that the Debtor will tell the truth, the whole truth and nothing but the truth when they are required under oath to declare all assets and sources of income during such an examination. If the Debtor has no assets, he will be safe from sequestration, but if he is seen to be deliberately transferring assets while under pressure from Creditors, this may be regarded as fraudulent and criminal activity and under certain conditions asset transfers may be held by a court to be void and affected assets thus able to be seized by Creditors.

The self-employed will find it easier to resist Creditors than anyone locked into a traditional career as an employee. The key assets of the self-employed are their skills and their customer base, neither of which can be seized and sold by a Creditor to raise money. They can reinvent their trading name, either in the same town or in another one; they can form a limited company and pay themselves no salary; often they can keep their money in cash. They are notoriously difficult to pin down. The ability which they have shown to become astute business people also equips them with cunning and knowledge that if they leave money in bank accounts in their own name, this can be attacked with a *garnishee order* obtained from a court after winning a judgement against a Debtor to scoop money out of the account.

In the ongoing Darwinian struggle between Creditors and Debtors each has grown to recognise the abilities and strengths of the other as well as relative areas of weakness and susceptibility. A Creditor knows when not to waste money and effort in chasing a Debtor of a certain perceived type. A Debtor knows when an amount outstanding is sufficient to make an informed and perhaps outraged Creditor determined enough to invest in legal enforcement. The strategy of the Debtor is for ever to appear to be invisible, inscrutable, bloodless to the Creditor, the strategy of *"Jackal and Hide"*

The Difference between a job and a career

*Upstanding citizens can have **careers**, but a debt Hold-out who has a need to move on frequently, will have a series of **jobs** instead. A career implies a static future, a ladder which needs to be climbed in one company or in a small number of easily identified competitor companies; anyone with a career is highly susceptible to a debt judgement being enforced by an Attachment to Earnings, whereby the court orders the Debtor's employer to deduct payments directly from his wages and to send them on to the Creditor.*

A job, by contrast to a career, is finite, it has no promise of an ascent to better things, very often no pension scheme attached to provide a further asset which may be attacked by a Creditor. People find jobs and leave them when something or someone better turns up; for a Creditor to attempt to secure repayment via Attachment to Earnings of anyone who merely has a job rather than a career is to invite them to move on again both in terms of the next job they do, and the address they do it from.

In terms of friendships, the Holdout will need to be charming, thoughtful and demonstrably loyal if he is to expect any loyalty in return. Those he trusts with his innermost secrets will be very few, perhaps no one person completely, but it is almost inevitable that he will need to trust someone for some of the time, for example to provide accommodation addresses where post may be received, somewhere to live anonymously when he needs to, someone willing and trustworthy enough to act as a banker by keeping cash and valuables for him, or as a nominee on a joint bank account, or as the formal owner of land, property, cars and other significant assets, offering evident legal separation from the affairs of the Holdout, so that these assets cannot be sequestered by Creditors.

"Uneasy lies the head that wears a crown" said Shakespeare's *King Lear*, expressing a King's dilemma in being unable to trust his nearest kin who might want to usurp his power. The same dilemma, albeit on a much smaller scale, faces the Holdout Debtor who needs trusted confederates.

The Advantages of Marriage and a little legal knowledge: Jonathan Aitken (ex-) MP

If the Debtor is married, his wife will be normally be seen to be associated with him and any attempt to transfer assets to her once he is being pursued by Creditors may be challenged at law, and the transfer ruled unlawful. But what if it is done quickly and the assets are no longer in the jurisdiction? An example of this being done successfully is that of Jonathan Aitken, former Conservative MP who was to be found guilty of perjury in an affair involving alleged corruption on his part while he was a Government Defence Minister.

Aitken reportedly owed £2.7 million pounds to The Guardian newspaper after losing against it in a libel suit over this matter in addition to owing money to other Creditors. It was widely reported in the newspapers that he transferred assets to his wife's name, disposing of four properties and pension funds plus off-shore accounts. During and after the libel action against him he was reported in the press as moving personal assets out of his home, and by that act also removing them also from the purview of Creditors. In August 1998, he and his then foreign wife Lolicia were formally divorced in Switzerland and she promptly took her assets out of the country, removing them from UK Creditors' reach should they try to question the propriety of the asset transfer. Meanwhile Mr Aitken had been reported as living on £11,000 a month, but now claimed total poverty. His assets had all "disappeared."

Jonathan Aitken went to trial at the Old Bailey in January 1999 and, previously notorious for citing "the simple sword of truth and the trusty shield of British fair play" in his defence, now pled guilty. He made himself insolvent and then declared bankruptcy before being sentenced to 18 months in prison. The point here is that, incredibly, he did manage to protect his assets from Creditors.

He had studied Law at Oxford and his early admittance to the ranks of the good and the great was assured by the fact of the attendance of Eamon Devalera, President of Eire, and the future Queen Juliana of the Netherlands who was to become his godmother, at his christening in Dublin in 1942, where his grandfather was the first British Representative to Eire. It is worth noting again the degrees and consequential steps of separation which Aitken managed to put between himself and his assets:

> 1) *He transferred his assets to his wife, a foreign citizen*
> 2) *She divorced him*
> 3) *She transferred the assets and herself to a foreign jurisdiction*
> 4) *He declared bankruptcy, cutting off any pursuit by means of civil law in the UK.*
> 5) *He went to jail where there was no point now further pursuing him to have him sent there.*
>
> *Even if a Creditor could have challenged Aitken and his ex-wife at law, what would prevent the assets being further removed or dissipated in the mean time? The end of the story is that Aitken as a converted Christian penitent was subsequently redeemed back into the ranks of the Good and the Great in being asked by then former Opposition Spokesman on Justice, Ian Duncan Smith, to lead a commission into the reform of prisons.*

In a more recent case a would-be property developer, Mr Kevin O'Kane of Northern Ireland , being pursued by Creditors for loss of their deposits on holiday villas in Turkey and also accused of allegedly continuing to lead a champagne lifestyle as he faced down 171 charges of obtaining money by fraud and deceit, found that he had an injunction placed upon him by his Creditors to prevent him of disposing of his assets. In this case the Creditors were able to act quickly and resolutely to prevent assets being transferred or liquidated so that they would remain available for any subsequent distribution process. Mr O'Kane had not studied Law at Oxford.

6.0

How Debt Collection Works

WHAT'S IN THIS CHAPTER

Within the ecosystem of credit givers and consumers, payers and non-payers there is a variety of roles adopted by the various participants. The Debt Path is a mechanism adopted by billing and collections organisations to herd consumers towards compliant behaviour. The intending Hold-out needs to know how the internal mechanisms of Debt Collection work in order to be able to anticipate and avoid these.

How Debt Collection Works

Debt collection is decidedly a science rather than an art, indeed it is a highly mathematical science which takes repeated empirical samples or "cohorts" of Debtor populations and tracks and records how they behave under given conditions. It is entirely based upon the probability of outcomes: "good", meaning that the Debtor will pay, and "bad" meaning that they will not. Debt collection is a process, starting with production of the bill or statement and ending with either payment or the decision to write a debt off as uncollectable or not worth collecting.

> **"Who the hell are these guys!?"**
>
> **Butch Cassidy and the Sundance Kid**
>
> *In the movie of the above name, our lovable jackal outlaw heroes are being pursued by a posse which is showing more determination than usual. They keep thinking they have thrown the posse off, only to see a cloud of dust some little way down the trail behind them. Eventually our heroes do escape by extreme means, but we don't want to spoil a good movie for those too young to have seen it yet. In the posse pursuit of debt collection, this feeling is exactly what the debt collection agencies try to achieve as a mindset in the Debtor: a sense of inevitable impending doom from a grinding relentless inescapable pursuit, carried out by professional and determined agents of good order. And yet Butch and Sundance got away on this occasion, as do millions of others every year.*

The debt strategist programmes interventions to take place at sequential stages in a "debt path" with a view to prompting customer contact and ensuring payment. Contact is a significant enabling objective based on the premise: "If you get contact, you get paid". This holds true in every case for the first segment of Debtors: those who will always pay when asked, who indeed form the large majority of any Debtor population. It is also largely valid for the segment of "Might pays".

Most "Might pays" will capitulate immediately upon being contacted. A lot of these have the ethic that they won't go out of their way to pay, but if confronted and asked, then they will pay. Other "Might pays" will take a deal more persuasion and indeed some of them start out believing that they can be successful "Won't Pays", only to be worn down by persistent contact and asking, fear of the threat of debt enforcement and a calculation that they will not gain by further delay.

For the true Hold-out "Won't pay", however, exposure to the Debt Path is a rite of passage which will be endured for each new debt based on a knowledge of the mindset of the collector: collection efforts will only proceed to the point of perceived diminishing returns. At some point, if the counter-strategy of the "Won't Pay" plays out as intended, the collector will lose heart, exhaust the budget available to collect that particular debt, be distracted by the availability of easier newer debts to collect using the available staff resource – and give up. Thus the Creditor:Debtor confrontation is a battle of wills. Is the determination of the collector to have his money greater than the determination of the Debtor to resist payment? From the Collector's perspective, to quote the ancient Chinese sage on war and strategy Sun Tzu:

> "For the true Hold-out Won't pay, however, exposure to the Debt Path is a rite of passage which will be endured"

"It is best if an enemy nation comes and surrenders of its own accord. To attack and defeat it is inferior to this... The best policy is to use strategy, influence and the trend of events to cause the adversary to submit willingly."

To this policy the Always-pay is susceptible as the Italian Army in the Western

Desert of the Second World War. They rush to surrender of their own accord. The Might-pay is more of a contest, but can still be overawed. The Won't pay is the true guerrilla, attesting to another of Sun Tzu's truisms:

"Invincibility is in oneself, vulnerability in the opponent... Keeping your own military in order, always being prepared for opposition, erase your tracks and hide your form, make yourself inscrutable to opponents... those skilled in defence hide in the deepest depths of the earth. Therefore they can preserve themselves and achieve complete victory."

The Zoology of Debt Collection and Debt Evasion

"Invincibility is in oneself, vulnerability in the opponent... those skilled in defence hide in the deepest depths of the earth. Therefore they can preserve themselves and achieve complete victory"

Given that this book depicts a Darwinian view of social order and Creditor: Debtor relationships, it is not surprising that an ecological metaphor springs to mind to populate the characters in the drama of collection attempts and payment refusal. Carnivores live at the top of a food chain mostly populated by herbivores, with omnivores somewhere in the middle, playing top and bottom against each other... The Always-pays are the **cattle**, almost longing to be milked at the end of a day of toil in the fields. Their udders aching with the cathartic urge to clean out their systems, cattle need instinctively to unburden themselves of any outstanding payment, by discharging it. For them it is in the nature of things that they simply want to pay; if a Creditor forgets to ask them, they will even write to remind him, just as cows wander to the gate of their field to meet the farmer leading them to milking.

Dogs or collections agents**,** dull, bullied and ill-paid lackeys, bark telephoned instructions at them as to what to do, and they willingly comply, because domesticity and the need to be milked has been bred into the DNA of cattle. They ultimately pay for everything; all other creatures benefit from them, them, particularly *dogs* and *hyenas*, because they provide the nearest thing to a free meal; the lion looks upon them approvingly, the *sheep* feel safe around them and will eventually follow them, while the *goats* and *jackals* can hide undiscovered among their thronging herd.

The big secret of the **Dogs** is that although they are exceedingly adept at barking down the telephone, they have absolutely no bite. Their Creditor principal almost never arms them with the teeth to follow through with any threat of legal enforcement. Their blandishments that if they are fed with money the credit record of the easily fleeced sheep will be restored are - at least in the short term and if limited to only paying the specific debt they are chasing - quite simply lies. Given that most Debtors who get to the stage of being seriously pursued by a Debt Collection Agency have multiple debts, satisfying one dog will not keep away the pack of his competitors for the pound of flesh of the sheep or cattle; indeed if a dog is part-paid it will definitely and with good reason believe it good business to come back and ask for more later.

> "The big secret of the dogs is that although they are exceedingly adept at barking down the telephone, they have absolutely no bite"

The *might-pays* behave like **goats,** who initially bound away when called to account, but more and more of them turn out to be **sheep**, who soon stop running and eventually tamely walk into the same pens as the cattle. Both can easily become prey to the commercial debt management companies who claim to work on their behalf to minimise repayments and seek to have large portions of their debts written off. In reality "Debt Management" and "Debt Repair"companies quite logically work first, second and third for their own commercial advantage and bleed the hapless Debtor of cash which he could better use to improve his own situation. The value that the Debt Management Companies claim to add can be had for free from the many Debt charities, so that they can be likened to the **vampire bats** of the Amazon, who suck the blood of lost sheep and cattle.

Arbiter of good order and the tax collector of last resort is the **Lion of the Law.** Unsurprisingly, his claws are sharpest when he is securing his own pound of flesh for HMRC, the Child Support Agency, Council Tax and other such obvious necessities for the maintenance of civil order. **Hyenas** in the personage of *lawyers* are always eager to snag an easy meal for little effort. **Ostriches** famously stick their head in the sand and don't want to know. They are a favourite prey for all predators and before they know it they have metamorphosed into **cattle** and **sheep.** In the middle of this menagerie, the **jackal** labours to maintain his freedom of movement, hiding while he can among the cattle, sheep and goats before they too are captured and he must make a nimble escape before the approaching dogs, hyenas and occasional lion.

Dogs abhor *jackals* because they represent the daring and freedom which was once the heritage of the *dog* before he chained himself to servitude, a mortgage and a pathetic little "career"; *hyenas* feel obliged to chase *jackals* from a professional perspective and out of fear of the *Lion*, but in fact are happy to be guided to a kill by the nimble *jackal. Hyenas* cannot catch the *jackal,* but they will eat at the feast he creates through his cunning by taking fees from the credulous Creditor client or penitent *sheep* alike. But the *jackal* must see that his appetite does not become excessive lest he evolve into a **big bad Wolf** or out-and-out criminal, who will destroy the entire ecosystem with his greed and loss of proportion. The *wolf* must be extirpated by the combined forces of *dogs, hyenas* and *lions* at all costs.

Life is not necessarily easy for the *jackal,* but so long as he knows his place in the ecosystem and applies his *"jackal and hide"* strategy consistently, he will, on his own, be too much trouble for too little value to try to destroy. *Jackals* will always be with us. In the wild they live in the savannah grasslands of Africa, where as small opportunistic omnivores they will eat anything from grass to insects to antelopes. They are also pack animals who rear each other's young and share their kills. It is hard not to find something to admire in their sheer determination and skill to survive their precarious lifestyle on the veldt.

There is an exception to this rule which we can call the **notoriety principle**. If an outlaw like Robin Hood becomes brazenly and iconically successful he becomes an affront to the professional self-respect of the collection organisation. The case becomes personal, indeed for many individual collectors, they derive much of their job satisfaction (these poorly paid dogs often depend on commission paid on successful collection, and tend to lead otherwise dull lives enlivened only by periodic group drunkenness at infrequent company social evenings) from demonising and obsessively chasing a particular Debtor who has attracted their attention, at the beginning often by the large size of the debt.

> "The jackal makes himself less visible than the sheep or the goat and thus escapes"

By attracting attention to him or herself in the eyes of the collection organisation, the Debtor becomes a challenge, and the successful collector a mighty hero, a slayer of dragons. It is not a good thing from the perspective of the Debtor to attract notoriety as his elevation from *goat* to *dragon* increases the likelihood of disproportionate resources being expended to enforce payment against them. The *jackal* makes himself less visible than the *sheep* or the *goat* and thus escapes.

The "Debt Path"

The debt path starts with a bill or statement on "Day zero". Collectors expect perhaps 70% of bills generated on a given billing date to be paid within a week or so. Sending out the bill or statement is therefore the first "intervention". The approach involves initiating a collection step or intervention, waiting for it to take effect, measuring the level of "drop-off" (from the original 100% by volume and by value of bills outstanding on day zero) achieved and then triggering the next stepped intervention. This is the siege cannon at work, but at this stage firing only loud dummy ammunition.

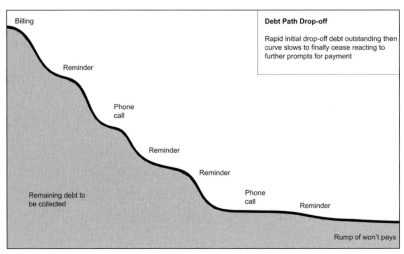

Billing

Debt Path Drop-off

Rapid initial drop-off debt outstanding then curve slows to finally cease reacting to further prompts for payment

Reminder

Phone call

Reminder

Reminder

Remaining debt to be collected

Phone call

Reminder

Rump of won't pays

Another useful analogy is that of speeding on the motorway. Nearly everybody exceeds the speed limit, although these days in traffic it doesn't make much difference in terms of absolute journey time because of the sheer volume of cars on the road and frequent hold-ups. The most logical strategy to shorten journey time is to join the back of a convoy of another three or four cars which are travelling at high speed. It makes no sense to be the first car in the convoy, and it is absolutely asking for trouble to overtake it. By not standing out from the crowd you can generally exceed the speed limit and get away with it.

So the debt path is a series of interventions which are designed to make the Debtor feel that they are personally being highlighted to pay their debt, that they are indeed in the spotlight and that evasion is hopeless.

Lettering continues, escalating in tone from " *payment now due*" to "*you may have overlooked the original invoice, can you please pay now – if you have already paid please ignore this letter*" an onwards to "*This matter is now urgent, if you have not already paid please do so now in order to avoid further collection activity.*"

"At the point where the curve of Debts outstanding stops falling, expectations of success are now fading very fast indeed in the mind of the Creditor"

Routine threats include sending doorstep collectors, loss of further credit facilities, and reporting to credit reference agencies which will pass the evil word not to lend the Debtor any further credit for mortgages, car loans, holidays or any of the other countless indispensable requirements of the consumerist lifestyle.

The more immediate threat to the Debtor is telephone contact, since it is routine to begin calling Debtors one week after the debt is due. If the Creditor has a mobile phone number or indeed a work number these are also favourite routes to obtain contact.

Each early intervention will progressively reduce the cohort of outstanding Debtors from a given billing run when on day zero 100% of cohort debt was outstanding, perhaps by 10% or 5% of the remaining balance each time.

When approximately 15% of debts remain outstanding some 4 to 6 weeks after initial billing, the easy-to-collect "Might-pays" have paid up and been eliminated from the action list. The vast majority of the remaining outstanding "Might Pays" have not been successfully contacted, ie the Creditor organisation cannot be certain that the Debtor is still residing at their last known address, or whether they are perhaps travelling or on holiday, or simply refusing contact.

Depending on the type of debt, some organisations – particularly utilities, where ongoing consumption can be expected to continue to increase the debt outstanding – will arrange for an initial doorstep visit. By this time the Debt Path (despite further repetitive messages flailing now exhausted admonitions, blandishments and threats through additional letters, contact cards, text messages, emails) is failing to secure any further significant downward reductions in the originally billed Debtor population, and the downward the curve has now flattened out to leave a residue of perhaps 5% of Debtors who still have not paid after around 10 weeks.

> **It is not necessary to be the best, just better than average**
>
> *Once upon a time an American and a Japanese tourist became separated from their tiger-watching group in the forests of India. A tiger approached from out of the bush, and immediately the Japanese put down his rucksack, found a pair of running shoes inside and began to put them on. The American shouted to him, "What's the point of putting on those running shoes, you can't out-run the tiger!" To which the Japanese replied urgently as he placed distance between himself, his companion and the tiger: " That's true, but I can out-run you!".*

Bitter experience will have shown the Creditor that it will now be very hard and increasingly resource and cash intensive to achieve further significant reductions. At the point where the curve of Debts outstanding has stopped falling, expectations of success with the remaining outstanding debts are now fading very fast indeed in the mind of the Creditor.

Debt Provisioning

Creditor expectations of collection success are reflected in the amount of provision for bad debt which they carry as an asset in their balance sheet. This asset is topped up as required from the Profit and Loss Account, ie it is a charge on profits, and company boards are very loath to accept that profits will be reduced. They only do so when they feel obliged to (in order not to make themselves criminally liable by misrepresenting the true value of their company). They show the debts which they chase their customers for as assets in their balance sheets – which they reasonably hope to convert into cash.

Recent debt will carry a provision charge of less than 1%. But when debt is older than say 6 months, it is not unusual for up to 25% of this to be provisioned as bad debt, ie the company is admitting to itself that it will only collect £3 of every £4 outstanding at this point. The older the debt becomes without successful collection, the less the expected percentage collection.

At a point in time – perhaps after 2 years – unless there are sound reasons for maintaining a specific debt on the balance sheet it will be written off. Does this mean that the debt ceases to exist from the Debtor's point of view? The answer is: probably not quite yet, but the heat will long since be off. When it is finally written off, all pursuit has ceased forever.

Contracting out debt collection

Perhaps the best thing that can happen to a would be hold-out Debtor in regard to an unsecured debt, that is a debt which is not protected or secured (from the Creditor or "Principal's" perspective) by an asset such as a house or a car, is that it is contracted out to a debt collection agency. Why? Because at the point where the debt is handed over to a third party, the Principal will regard the relationship with their customer as being over. They will stop further collection efforts. From now on the Debtor is dealing with "mercenaries" who are only interested in a proverbial quick buck. More than ever, by not encouraging them by any behaviour which indicates a "Might pay" attitude the Debtor can hope to educate the third party collector that investing any effort or cost in collecting will be a complete waste.

A letter from a debt collection agency is fantastically good news for a Hold-out Debtor? How so? Well, If the principal intended to litigate by taking the Debtor to County Court, he would do so himself: because this costs real money, he would want to be in control of the process himself and not hand his wallet to a third party contractor whose only interest is how much money he can make for himself. If the debt has gone to a Debt Collection Agency, or even better, has been sold for perhaps 5p per £1 of debt to a Debt Purchase Company, the Debtor can be sure that he does not need to pay because the DCA or new owner of an unsecured debt will not pay a penny in legal costs to enforce it.

> "A letter from a debt collection agency is fantastically good news for a Hold-out Debtor"

The process which now ensues is for debt to be contracted out as "First Placement". Under this arrangement a Debt Collection Agency (DCA) will take over all future contact with the Debtor. They vaunt their expertise to their Principal client at being able to secure contact and thereby payment as a skill in which they are paramount experts. Accordingly, the client generally leaves the precise methodology of collection to the DCA, including methods and and frequency of attempted contact, plus use of scripts (what threats and blandishments will be used).

No Cure No Pay Commission Contracts for Debt Collection

Almost always debt collection is based on "no cure, no pay", which means that the DCA invests effort in collection knowing that they need to collect to get paid. First placement debt is generally rewarded with around 15% to 20% of the value of the debt collected, and is contracted out in tranches of debts, ie lists of perhaps 1000 or more Debtors including the debt values, and all known contact information, addresses, telephone numbers, and email addresses.

After 3 or 6 months, the DCA passes back the majority rump of the debt they

---

are lucky to average a 15% success rate - which they have not succeeded in collecting to the Principal. The Principal will then contract out this rump again as "Second Placement Debt" and because the debt has already been raked over more often than an old gold mine, the reward for success will have gone up to perhaps 30% or 35% commission on payment.

After a further 3 or 6 months, the debt may be switched to another DCA one more time as "Third Placement Debt", this time giving the DCA a commission reward of maybe 50% of whatever they can collect. By this time the Debtor will have received dozens of letters, calls and texts; he will be thoroughly used to ignoring them, so any money received by a DCA at this point really has to be admired from professional point of view. Pickings are exceedingly thin, perhaps only 1% or 2% successful at this point.

Now at the latest, for the remainder of uncollected debt, the Principal is likely to write off the debt, abandoning forever any hopes of collecting any money against it. At least a year will have elapsed since initial billing, perhaps two. Maybe the Debtor has finally won?

Debt Sale

As a last resort – the debt having been farmed out two or three times for collection on a commission basis by a DCA – the Principal may decide to sell the debt. The buyer will be a Debt Purchase Company. This is probably a division of a Debt Collection Agency using precisely the same people and methodology in its "Debt Purchase Division" as in its main debt collection business which it carries out as an agent on behalf of third parties. This fashion has been imported from the USA, where it became popular

Triage

Triage is the process applied by medically trained armed forces personnel on battlefields. It is a dispassionate sorting of military casualties into those who cannot be helped, those who will survive without treatment until resources are available to treat them, and those who must be helped immediately if they are to be saved. Debt Collectors apply a similar process in terms of deciding which cases to prioritise for collection sooner or later... or perhaps let go.

"In the war of debt collection, the Collector needs to win: all the Debtor needs to do is to avoid defeat"

for the attempted recovery of credit card debt prior to the 2008 recession, and for a while lots of debt was being sold and bought in UK as well. Debt may be sold for around 3% to 5% of its book value, ie at a 95% to 97% discount, which reflects the expectation of both parties in the sale as to its collectability.

What does all this mean to Mr Grey, the Hold-out Won't Pay or *jackal*? Lots! The economics of Debt Purchase determines the methodology and strategies that Debt Purchase Collectors can afford to use to collect. Knowledge of the opposing general's strategy is the key determinant of success for the opposing guerrilla, for by knowing what his opponent is going to do he can take anticipatory action. In the war of debt collection, the collector needs to win: all the Debtor needs to do is to avoid defeat.

Debt collection agency processes

We have already looked at the mechanics of the Debt Path and seen how it seeks to maximise returns from a given tranche of debts which it starts off trying to recover at the same time. Although the collections industry has tried to federate itself and present itself as professionalised, there is no obligation for any DCA to join, indeed anyone anywhere can set themselves up as a DCA by applying for a consumer credit licence from the *Office of Fair Trading*. Providing that the Directors do not have previous criminal convictions it is a simple formality for anyone to receive a *Consumer Credit Licence* and thus set themselves up as a Debt Collection Agency.

Debt Collection thus continues to be pervaded by a culture of shadiness, pretence that individual companies possess a magic bullet or secret approach which makes them somehow different from their peers, that they work harder and longer for their client than the other guy. In reality, debt collection is all about repetitive methodology, combing, and fine-combing and combing yet again, persisting with a rain of letters and calls riddled with tricks to lure the Might Pay into contact and to scare them into making payment.

All DCA's regularly collect from the overlooked Always- Pays, who have perhaps been abroad or ill for several months. The more methodical and enduring collect marginally more from the Might-Pays, and almost no one collects from Mr Grey, the determined, intelligent and thoughtful Won't Pay or *jackal*.

Data Matching

One basic skill determines superior results for the more successful DCA: data-matching. Customer data are the fingerprints which enable DCA's to positively identify Debtors, to link them to addresses, to note previous dealings with them (successful or unsuccessful). The more fingerprints and clues that a criminal leaves at the scene of a crime, the more likely that the authorities will catch and convict him. This applies equally to the consumer in debt in terms of the likelihood of them being tracked down, successful contact made and then the psychological pressure being successfully applied to extract payment.

Data Sharing and scoring for collections

Increasingly, Collection Agencies, in terms of their activity as legal agents on behalf of their Principal-clients, are benefiting from the membership of their Principals in data-sharing organisations run by the large Debt Collection Agencies. In signing any consumer contract today, the customer invariably is agreeing to the vendor or supplier having the right to share information on attempted or successful fraud, and on overdue debt (black data), as well as on customer prompt payment (white data).

On the reasonable premise that customers' behaviours in terms of either regular good payment or alternatively doubtful or non-payment will be consistent across a number of credit relationships with different suppliers, all credit card companies, large retailers, insurers, banks and other financial services companies, phone companies and most utilities (except water, on which more later) share information every month with credit reference agencies such as *Experian, Equifax* and *Callcredit*. This provides participating members the ability to find out how new credit applicants - or existing late or non-payers are keeping up with credit payments to all the other data sharing suppliers.

If you show up as being a generally reliable or even intermittent payer resident at a "good" address, ie one at which you can be confidently shown to reside, then you will be prioritised as a high-probability "win", a Debtor who is worth betting on as a future payer, who will earn the collections agency at least 15% commission. You will get a lot of phone calls...

At the other end of the scale, if there is very thin or no other data about you at the address known to the DCA, if there are no Creditor relationships which show you as a good payer, then you are not such a good bet for a DCA to spend money on which they very probably won't recoup.

Debtors continue to be scored at each stage of the collection cycle, firstly by the original supplier who will retain high probability "wins" or customers he believes he can collect from for longer before farming the residue out to a Debt Collection Agency. The major difference between *Scoring on Application* and *Collections Scoring* is the inclusion of "behavioural indicators" to the former. Behavioural scoring factors in the age of the account, the value and age of overdue debt, payment history during the lifetime of the account, the availability of reliable personal and address data from data sharing groups and not least contact history. The more contact there has been with a customer, the higher the collection likelihood.

"If there is very thin data about you at the address known to the DCA... then you are not such a good bet to spend money on, which they probably won't recoup"

When a debt is placed with a Debt Collection Agency they may apply their own scorecard, taking into account the factors given by the Client – who will share all available data in their own interest – but also the question as to whether this is a first, second or third debt placement. A richer Debtor dataset, any evidence of previous good payment behaviour and any positive contact history all will promote the score of the Debtor to high collection probability, prolong intensive pursuit and increase the willingness of the DCA to spend more money on the case. But all DCA's are not the same, some are less sophisticated (and less successful than others in terms of collection) in regard to their access to data-sharing information and possession of internal scoring.

Churning and Burning

So the mindset of the DCA ,who will only be paid on successful collection and will get nothing for lettering and calling a customer who pays nothing, is to try to skim off the cream at the top of the milk and to waste as little cost and effort working what they perceive to be the whey at the bottom of the barrel. The financially successful DCA may persuade his Principal that he is working all accounts equally conscientiously, while in reality rigorously pursuing and spending money on those he believes he can collect from. (His Principal-client, on the other hand, nurtures the romantic notion that the DCA should be stand on the doorstep and hammering the door of even the most unlikely payers). If this sounds like very

"The financially successful DCA may persuade his Principal that he is working all accounts equally conscientiously, while in reality rigorously pursuing and spending money only on those he believes he can collect from"

encouraging news for Mr Gray, it gets even better. Thus the DCA will churn through his list of Debtors, showing particularly vigorous collection attempts for the first few weeks. Then he will be turning his attention to the next tranche and getting vigorous with them instead.

This does not mean that non-successful accounts are forgotten. All self-respecting DCA's load their portfolio of Debtors onto a "Debt Management System". This computer programme calendarises activity for every debt in the portfolio, including the next letter or phone call. These systems are particularly effective in recording contact details, agreements made with Debtors and due dates for promised payments. But they are not magical: if there is no contact or agreement they simply send out material into the ether, adding cost and no profit to the DCA.

Staying and Playing

Where accounts thought to be likely to unproductive are "churned and burned" in terms of attention and effort, the opposite is true for those cases where the DCA has found reason to believe that the Debtor acknowledges the validity and amount of the debt being pursued, where they are known to be economically active, employed or a house-owner and where there are recently validated contact details, particularly telephone numbers. In these cases, the DCA will be prepared to "stay and play". They will invest in repeated telephone calls and lettering, and worry the account like a dog with a bone – the more so if the Debtor has once made contact with them to acknowledge their existence.

Tracing Activity

Both the DCA and their Principal before them are at pains to assure themselves that their communications are actually getting through to the Debtor. If they get no response or telephone callback they will generally resort to tracing activity. Increasingly DCA's are gaining access to the rich data held by the Debt Collection Agencies which link consumer names to addresses and details of the loans, mortgages, mobile phone agreements, HP and other finance arrangements, and to some extent gas and electricity utilities.

DCA's can very quickly and cheaply key into a proprietary on-line Credit Reference Agency tracing system the name and date of birth of a Debtor to discover their last known address. The Credit Reference Agency systems will not give a result, however, if the date of birth is absent due to the very high probability of confusing the Debtor with someone else of the same name. By their very nature these systems are effective in finding people with an active credit profile, ie with numerous credit agreements and history of applying for credit.

If the Credit Bureau records have information that a Debtor is living at the address to which the Creditor or DCA have be writing to seek contact, the tracing report obtained will describe the Debtor as "living as stated". But what does this actually prove? Credit Agency systems are updated once a month and any data they provide is always at least 6 weeks old. And like everyone else, Credit Reference Agency data can be prone to error.

So the most that they can ever show is that a given individual was linked to an address 6 weeks ago. On the other hand if there are numerous credit agreements linking the individual to a specific address it is highly likely that the multiple cross-validating reports are probably correct at least at that point in time. For consumers who do not show up on a Credit Agency trace report, DCA's have a number of other – increasingly expensive – options. Many have an in-house manually based tracing function.

Telephone Tracing

The telephone is the primary non-system tool for tracing people, but often the DCA has to start from the position of not having any telephone number if their Principal has been unable to supply it to them. DCA's are able to cobble together large databases combining the British Telecom UK directory and the Post Office address file. Allowing for the fact that many numbers are now ex-directory , that BT no longer has a monopoly on landline customers, and that many people today no longer bother with a landline as they can use a mobile number, this is of limited use. DCA's also have no access as yet to the data files of the mobile phone companies. But there are many hapless Might-pays who will have supplied their telephone number to the Principal/Creditor on an initial credit or loan application so landlines remain a good source of contact for Might-Pays.

Tracing specialists spend their entire time trying to find people and tend to take a pride in this, often resorting to devious and cunning strategies, including ones which might not be in accordance with the Data Protection Act. Favourite tactics include calling neighbours if there happens to be a landline customer on a DCA nation-wide phone/address database as discussed above, who lives either side of or opposite the Debtor.

They will use *Google* or a similar search engine to find pubs or corner shops near to the last known Debtor address. Highly inventive and plausible tales are told of searches for a friend, relative, beneficiary in a will... As the British are anecdotally supposed to detest their neighbours, these enquiries can prove a rich source of information to the skilled trace agent, who will want to know the names of everyone living at a given property including the Debtor being traced, when he or she was last seen, what their personal habits are in terms of they are typically at home, who their employer is and their precise occupation.

A skilled and determined tracer can be very adept at positively tracing a subject who is then proven to be living at the address where they are suspected to be. Exceptions might be when the subject is living in a block of flats where neighbours don't see much of each other or indeed speak, where the subject does not drink in the local pub and does not give his or her name to the corner shop. Someone who is alert and does not want to be found will take such precautions. Might-pays generally do not, and they are generally successfully traced.

"Doorstep collection visits are very rare in the case of an unsecured Debtor"

If the telephone tracer is unsuccessful and the debt at stake for collection sufficiently attractive, the DCA or their Principal before them might even invest in a doorstep trace visit. These visits are expensive, costing upwards of £30 regardless of outcome so they are not undertaken lightly. For these visits to be commissioned by a Creditor Principal there generally has to be a very strong suspicion that a subject is at an address, that they are probably acting evasively and high confidence that collection can be negotiated or other enforcement steps taken to secure the debt.

Such visits are quite rare in the case of an unsecured Debtor. On the other hand for secured debts such as mortgages they are certain to occur; also for debts owed to gas, electricity and water companies. Debtor reaction tactics to doorstep visits will be discussed below under Doorstep Collection.

Truth, Lies and Threats by Debt Collection Agencies

It is the habit of DCA's to warn of dire consequences if the Debtor fails to make contact. They want the Debtor to admit that they have received correspondence, that they have had the benefit of the good or service for whose price they are being pursued, to declare willingness to pay, ideally to clear the debt immediately by a credit card payment; if not, to make an initial instalment payment with a view to clearing the debt within 3 to 6 months or earlier. Clearly if it is in the DCA's interest for the Debtor to oblige them in these ways, for the unwilling payer it is to their own disadvantage. It is to overcome the natural reluctance of the Debtor to accept that payment must be made that threats and warnings are made.

These can include:

"We have referred this debt to a doorstep collector who will shortly knock at your door."

For an unsecured Debtor (no security or mortgage has been given to the Principal): this is usually a bluff and an outright lie. DCA's cannot afford to share their commission with Collection Agents and controlling such third parties is a nightmare for them. Even if such an agent were to appear at your door, you are not obliged to open to them or to talk to them.

"We will refer this case to our legal department with a view to court against you."

Note first of all that such communications of legal action never say unequivocally: "We will definitely take legal action against you next week". Instead they are the verbal equivalent of foot-shuffling and merely say something like the phrase above or "you will now be considered for court action".

In fact DCA's NEVER undertake court action against Debtors referred to them on a commission-only basis.

"You will be blacklisted for further credit"

Firstly the DCA is not able to blacklist anyone. It is admittedly common practice for Principals of unsecured consumer debt such as credit cards, HP and other finance, storecards and retail agreements to report non-payment against a named individual, identified by date of birth at a known address. Such threats made by a Principal where the Debtor has signed a contract or credit application do need to be taken seriously. If any blacklisting were to have taken place, it has already happened by the time the debt has reached the DCA or Debt Purchaser and the Hold-out Non-payer will already have noticed any impact in terms of their ability to get new lines of credit in the same name and address as that of the debt now being pursued.

"Your house may be repossessed"

This could only ever happen in the case of a debt which has been secured upon a house with the Debtor's name on the deed of the property. It would require a court action in such a case , which the Debtor would be notified of and could attend to oppose the case. In the event of a normal unsecured debt such as credit card, HP or retail agreement, it is theoretically possible that a Charging Order may be sought by the Creditor, ie a charge or second mortgage (also sometimes known as a judgement mortgage) which would have to be discharged by paying out the Creditor as part of any sale process before the Debtor or his or her heirs could get their hands on the balance of any equity after the sale.

The prospect of a charge can be opposed by making an offer of an instalment plan at the County Court stage, requiring the Debtor to turn up at the Court and make the offer to the magistrate. He can also plead to have conditions attached to such an order, for example that it cannot be enforced before a youngest child reaches their majority.

For a house to be repossessed and sold would require an Order for Sale. This will be granted by a court to enforce a previous judgement for a mortgage which has been secured on a house as a condition of the loan. However, it is highly unlikely to be granted in the case of a previously unsecured debt which is small in relation to the Debtor's equity in the property. A hunter gatherer will in any case not be troubled by such a threat as he will not own the property in which he currently resides.

"You may be arrested and committed for trial if you do not pay"

This is false as a consumer debt is always a civil matter. It would be completely unethical for a DCA to make such a statement and they would be pilloried by courts, regulators and their Principals if they were ever to do so.

"We will continue to call you until you pay"

Neither the DCA nor their Principal/client may harass a Debtor with calls, specifically if the Debtor has written to them to state inability to pay and to request cessation. DCA's are not allowed to call Debtors late at night or in the small hours and can be reported to regulators. Their memberships of industry affiliated bodies withdrawn if it can be shown that they are doing this and they could even have their licence to trade withdrawn by the Department of Trade and Industry.

"We will add a collection/administration fee of £x to your account if you do not contact us by xx date to arrange payment"

The Debtor has no contract with any DCA and is not obliged to pay any fee that they may seek to administer. This tactic is another ploy to increase psychological pressure.

In sum, DCA's are in the business of spending as little money as possible to make a quick return. Their threats are invariably empty.

DCA Tricks

There are a number of tricks which DCA's will try in order to gain contact with an unwary, stupid or greedy Debtor:

The androgynous card

This may be a postcard or a greeting card which addresses the Debtor in a winsome and familiar manner. It will probably call them by their Christian name and it will be from a person whose name could be either male or female – like Chris or Sam – and will give a number to ring. The number will be different to the DCA or Principal's normal contact number and is known as a "campaign number". The DCA or Principal using this type of approach will know that all calls to it will relate to unsuspecting Debtors curiously calling to find out who Chris is. Can people really be so gullible as to fall for this kind of trick? Yes they can and yes they do.

The Purple Envelope

On the basis that reluctant payers do not open brown envelopes the collections industry has worked out that using other colours on envelopes may prompt more response in opening and responding to them. Such letters may well be addressed by hand and be franked with a normal postage stamp to increase their apparent innocuousness. On opening they may contain a mysterious and inviting short note from "Chris", or simply a challenging statement along the lines of "Gotcha!" from the DCA. It has to be said that most Principals are not sufficiently creative to use this type of approach.

The Text message from "Chris" or "Sam"

When DCA's think they have a good idea, they tend to milk it. This is because their repertoire is limited. It is along the lines of the androgynous card and the purple envelope.

The Phone message from "Chris" or "Sam"

DCA's can be persistent if unimaginative. Chris will be either a male voice if the Debtor is female, or a female voice if the Debtor is male. They will sound wistful and interesting and mysterious if they are any good.

The Competition Winner announcement

They probably learned this one from Nigerian scammers. Hold-out Debtors don't expect to win competitions or lotteries which they have never entered, or to receive notifications of parcels from people they don't know.

Insults, personal demeaning, attempts to use "guilt" as a ploy

The use of insults to undermine the morale of the Debtor, to make them feel guilt and remorse about their situation, which can only be redeemed by the act of payment, thereby setting straight the moral record, is one of the oldest and commonest ploys in debt collection. If a hold-out Debtor has determined a set refusal approach to attempts to contact or to persuade them to pay, it is not unknown for DCA's to resort to personal insults, for example about lack of personal honour, about being a liar, or not a decent human being... or worse!

This is to jar and unsettle the Debtor, to provoke and set them off balance, to make them so angry that they will just make that return call to get back at the DCA.... Exactly what the DCA wants: the DCA thinks that if he can get contact, he can get paid. So the more insulting and demeaning he becomes, the more desperate he obviously is for that contact, and the more disappointed and beaten when it does not happen.

Of course, it is illegal for DCA's to resort to personal harassment, and the Debtor is within their rights to take the case to the relevant authorities perhaps via the CAB. But to do so is to *engage*. It will almost inevitably lead the Debtor into having to discuss the fact of the debt and why it has not been paid. Is this helpful to the Debtor? Only if the case is so serious that a retaliatory attack would be likely to have the debt set aside. Perhaps such things happen in television scripts, but they cannot be counted on in reality.

"The DCA thinks that if he can get contact he will get paid"

The prudent Hold-out will take satisfaction from the obvious desperation of the Creditor to resort to such tactics, noting and recording them for later use if the occasion should arise. But they are probably best served if they wish to dishearten their pursuit by continuing not to be provoked, and to refrain from reacting as if there is no effect, or better, as if they had never received it, probably because they were no longer at the address.

Dummy Court Documentation or Disconnection Warrants

While the use of dummy documentation is unethical in terms of the code of practice of the Credit Services Association, the "guild" of Debt Collection Agencies, the Hold-out Debtor is not in an ideal position to ring them up to complain about it. Utilities have been known to use this approach, but a close inspection of the documentation should reveal whether the document really is a court document; in case of doubt, the Debtor can of course ring the court to find out if such a warrant has truly been issued; or they can have it checked out by one of the debt charities.

7.0

Debtor Tactics to Frustrate Debt Collection Agencies

WHAT'S IN THIS CHAPTER

The Debtor can buy time by creating delay and frustration for the Collector, eventually to the point where he will give up. This can be done by refusing contact so that the Collector will have the agonising uncertainty that he may be wasting time and money by trying to contact someone who is not there. Or the Debtor can make contact on his own terms in his own time and in the persona he chooses.

Debtor Tactics to Frustrate Collection Agencies

"When you do battle, even if you are winning, if you continue for a long time it will dull your forces and blunt your edge; if you besiege a citadel, your strength will be exhausted. If you keep your armies in the field for a long time, your supplies will be insufficient"
Sun Tzu: The Art of War

The contest between Creditor and Debtor as a military campaign

*The contest between Creditor and Debtor is very analogous to a military campaign. One has the seemingly all-powerful army, the other must resort to a guerrilla-style withdrawal. The Debt Collection Agency (DCA) has the problem described by Sun Tzu above. Sun Tzu was a Chinese warrior philosopher who wrote his seminal work, **The Art of War** more than 2000 years ago. It remains a classical work of strategy for all forms of conflict and competition today.*

The DCA has many citadels to besiege, all of them Debtors. He can only afford to spend so much time trying to overwhelm each opponent. Time is always against the DCA, it costs time to pursue the Debtor and the more time that elapses, the older and colder a debt will become, and the colder and flatter the hopes of the DCA to collect it. He can be exhausted by persistent holding out, and particularly if the likelihood of any victory he may wrest from the Debtor through the legal enforcement process can be made to appear to be Pyrrhic in prospect, ie that spending vast amounts of money on enforcement will yield no assets.

Step one – refuse contact

For a DCA to succeed, they need to find the Debtor, provide them with a bill or statement, get them to respond or acknowledge receipt, get them to admit that they accept the validity of the debt as genuinely owing by them, and finally get them to pay.

Debtor tactics involve non-cooperation in all these stages. By far and away the most effective tactic is to have the DCA think that their communications have not been received. The DCA is very anxious not to waste time, effort and money on a case which is not going to yield cash at the end. If they don't collect they don't get paid.

The factor most certain to frustrate DCA pursuit is for them to think that the Debtor is no longer available to receive a letter or to answer a phone call. Any Debtor who contacts a DCA to acknowledge receipt, or who picks up a telephone to announce that they, they Debtor, are at home at the address at which the DCA is trying to pursue them, is immediately and loudly telling the DCA: "*Yes, it's me and I am a Might-pay... all you have to do is to persist and to be a little creative and try hard, then I might very well pay you*". For the corollary of not investing in cases where there is no one to chase is that if money has already been spent on a case which turns out to be live and potentially available, then only by investing more effort to complete the chase can that initial investment be recouped.

Dealing with letters and written correspondence

An agile and determined Debtor does not allow himself to be surprised. Firstly he always opens all correspondence in order to know who is chasing him and how urgent or close the hunt is. That way he is less likely to be surprised by a doorstep collector or a court document which can be attended to and perhaps deflected or its consequences otherwise avoided.

Telephone Contact

Knowing that the telephone is the means most used to try to force contact, the Hold-out will resist the temptation to pick up a landline phone unless it is possible to see that a known and trusted number is calling, relying instead on listening to phone messages. DCA's will definitely try to contact at different times of day and must be anticipated calling even at unsocial hours – although they are not supposed to. It is very easy to spontaneously pick up a phone or a mobile or to react to an interesting or provocative or insulting phone or text message. While it is not thought to be currently technically possible for a text messenger or caller to be able to check receipt of their text or phone message, perhaps the best avoidance behaviour for a Debtor is not to open any messages from untrusted sources.

> "The Hold-out will resist the temptation to pick up the phone unless it is possible to see a trusted number"

Email Contact

It is easy for email-senders to include acknowledgement requests. The Hold-out Debtor will not open emails from anyone whom they do not know. They will certainly not send back acknowledgements of receipt to people trying to collect money from them.

Step Two – Remediate Contact

To be very clear: from the perspective of the Debtor, having to deal with unavoidable contact is an undesired fallback step from avoiding contact altogether. But there may come a point when either it is unavoidable to receive phone contact, or indeed some correspondence may have been received which indicates that enforcement action may be pending and needing to be addressed, necessitating a call-back, although by definition at this point the Hold-out Debtor will not be calling back to capitulate, but rather to fend off whatever action is about to take place.

Out of habit in answering calls the Hold-out Debtor forgets all previous notions of telephone courtesy. They never answer the phone by announcing their name. That way, even if they are surprised into picking up the phone they cannot be identified by the Debt Collection Agency which will always be at pains to assure that they comply with the Data Protection Act. This requires that they do not make any disclosure to a third party about any private data relating to a subject without their consent. A personal debt is very clearly within the scope of this Act, and a DCA will always routinely attempt to validate that they are talking to the right person at the beginning of every call.

"The logical tactic if unable to take a call is to deny that they are the person being sought..."

The logical tactic for the Hold-out Debtor if unable to avoid taking a call is to deny that they are the person being sought. If a "friend" or "babysitter" takes the call, they can at least relay who is chasing so that the urgency of any response tactic can be gauged in terms of previous debt chasing activity from that source. Perhaps the DCA finds themselves talking to someone who has just moved into the property and has never heard of the Debtor?

Step Three: False Trails?

It is not uncommon for Hold-out Debtors to engage with DCA's or Principals under an "alias" and to attempt to put them off the scent. The great risk in doing so is to make the pursuit of the debt a personal crusade for an individual collector, or worse a *"cause célèbre"* for an entire organisation. The last thing that a Hold-out Debtor wants is notoriety or fame as some kind of *Public Enemy* who must be eradicated in order for the honour of the company to be restored. This invites the spending of inordinate resources and going to extra-ordinary lengths to prove that no Debtor can hold out against the pride of the company.

The simplest and least offensive false trail, acceptable as possibly true by the DCA, is that the Debtor no longer lives at the address, and specifically that a relationship has split up, that the party has disappeared without trace after an acrimonious parting. Less is more in terms of the detail of such a tale. The remaining party is wounded, angry, suspicious and does not want to talk to anyone – unsurprising whenever these things are true.

A remark to the effect that the Debtor is *"Irish and probably gone back to Dublin"*, or *" gone back to sea"* gives an adequate flavour of hopeless elusiveness and should suffice to send the case back to the specialist trace process, which will take many weeks at least to run its course, during which time other defensive preparations can be made.

To embroider a detailed history might make the DCA suspicious as to why so much cooperation was being offered, or incredulous at a less than Oscar-worthy performance by someone who has not in fact been abandoned at all and cannot readily act their way into the role. Furthermore, it might compound any accusation of fraudulent behaviour – which could be construed as criminal, as opposed to debt-evasive behaviour which of itself is no crime – in the event that some other deception may have been involved in securing the initial credit for the debt, or in facilitating the build-up of the debt to its current value. Calls are routinely recorded both by Principals and DCA's and it does not make sense for a named caller to put lies on record and thus incriminate himself.

What if the Debtor or their accomplice were to simply drop a call from a DCA? Again, the individual collector would find this abrupt behaviour personally annoying, but also encouraging from the perspective that the Debtor was demonstrably uncomfortable enough to have to resort to this. So they become at once a challenge and a Might-Pay.

Feigning Compliance or holding out?

There may come a point when a Hold-out Debtor needs to pretend to comply in order to gain time to find other strategies with which to discourage and exhaust the resources of the hunter. This need not normally be necessary with regard to a DCA or Debt Purchase Company. Even if they have been unequivocally identified as living at a given address, all the Debtor needs to do is to continue to ignore requests to pay and to refuse to be dismayed by the rain of contact attempts and prompts.

The case will be forwarded for second placement and then for third placement by other agencies as discussed above. When this happens the Hold-out Debtor can rejoice in a minor tactical victory: a DCA has failed, and the one coming behind them, by virtue of their ever higher fee for success, has no great expectation of success either, and need feel no sense of personal challenge at the prospect of failing also. Even if the DCA does indeed resort to unethical tactics, to engage with them or to protest to an industry body would simply to invite the need to engage also on the central issue of payment of the debt which the Debtor is at pains to avoid.

8.0

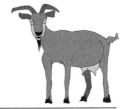

Getting fit for the Chase

WHAT'S IN THIS CHAPTER

Anyone proposing not to pay a significant debt needs to understand what they are getting into. We examine the difference between conditional credit, which is the norm for most goods and services, and unconditional credit which exists mostly for utilities. The decision to consent to credit scoring and data sharing is voluntary but far-reaching in its implications. Hence the need to understand the credit application process and the types of credit application fraud which can lead to a filing by anti-fraud agencies.

Getting Fit for the Chase

"If you think nobody cares if you're alive, try missing a couple of car payments"
Earl Wilson

The best place to start is at the beginning and this was never more true than in respect of later avoidance of debt payment. It is of course fraudulent to deliberately obtain credit with a plan beforehand not to pay. In the event that that this is done using untruths, then on the basis that these can be proven, the crime is clear. But how many people take on debt with no clear thought of how or when they will repay, without even having considered it, dazzled by the consumerist lure of " *Plenty! Easy! Now!* "? Is this fraudulent, or is it what the purveyors of "initial free credit" want the consumer to do in order to ensnare him later in high interest repayments when he does realise that he cannot easily repay as per contract?

These debt purveyors take on the calculated risk that among the *sheep* they snag into debt traps there will be the occasional *goat* or *jackal*: the intelligent Hold-out who has the end in mind at the beginning and whose every step is considered and taken with a view to achieving this end.

Brer Rabbit

There is a world of difference between being between helpless, hopeless quarry, being driven down by a relentless and efficient predator, and being a figure like the eponymous Brer Rabbit of childrens stories from the Southern States of the USA. Brer Rabbit is always able to anticipate the moves of Brer Fox to entrap him.

> *By analogy, at the outset the future Debtor has the initiative. The Creditor seeks to take control of a credit relationship by dictating terms and by gathering information about the Debtor which will be used to appraise how much credit they will be given, and later to pinpoint and track them down, to share data with other credit providers, and as a lever to pressurise the Debtor into payment. The future Debtor, now credit applicant, is therefore careful what he tells and to whom he tells it.*
>
> *It is perhaps too much to expect to enjoy the pursuit as Brer Rabbit appears to, but there may even be a satisfaction to be had for the wily jackal from eluding the best efforts of arrogant big companies stuffed with over-paid executives and dog-like underlings who assume that they are in control. While they believe that they are in control they will not undertake any radical and unpredictable action to endanger the status of the Hold-out Debtor.*

The basic strategy adopted by the credit applicant is to give future Creditors just enough information as they can get away with to gain credit and to do nothing at the early stages in what will soon become a deteriorating relationship from the perspective of the credit-giver. While the consummate Hold-out will be prepared to give false information to gain credit, taking on board the additional risks of early detection plus the likelihood of criminalisation and loss of credit standing in the persona used to apply for credit if they are detected, this is often not necessary to obtain credit.

Playing Defence with Unconditional Credit

Being given unconditional credit can easily but erroneously be equated with the biblical story of *"manna from heaven"*, whereby the Israelites awoke to find food on the desert around them. Arguably the manna was an unconditional gift, and would have continued to be forthcoming even if the Israelites had not repaid their jealous God with worship? In any case, unconditional credit does still have to be paid for, at least in the intention of the Creditor. However, it makes no good sense to waste something just because you think it is costing you nothing. Very high consumption for its own sake might just attract the attention of somebody, and attention is anathema to the Hold-out Debtor.

Being given unconditional credit means that you don't have to ask for it, no one asks your name, date of birth, address history or occupation. At the outset you are completely anonymous and you have a certain amount of control as to how and whether you surrender that anonymity.

Utilities

Water is always unconditionally available in any property, gas and electricity mostly are. Together these three utilities are very significant household budget expenses, often costing in excess of £2000 or £3000 per annum. They represent the classic "money for nothing" items of unconditional credit and it is generally possible to avoid paying them altogether. Failing to pay them is not illegal in a criminal sense in that it will not lead to criminal prosecution or a criminal record although protracted avoidance can frequently lead to crossing the line of legality. While there is no universal right to be given credit, the basic utilities of water, gas and electricity are deemed to be necessities for the maintenance of human life. Everyone has a right to access them, and most properties allow them all to be taken on the basis of credit, ie consumption prior to payment.

Road tax and Insurance

It is quite clearly illegal to drive a car without tax and insurance. The advent of the surveillance society has also made it more difficult. Police routinely deploy high-powered cameras which can read number plates and relay them to a computer which will match the number plate to the name and address of the registered vehicle owner, enabling follow-up and prosecution. But there are ways which these controls can be avoided.

Restaurants

Restaurants which require production and validation of a credit card before the diner sits down may well yet come into being, but for now they are almost unknown. The head waiter will undoubtedly give the diner a glance before deciding which table to offer them, or if he disapproves of their appearance, whether to offer a table at all, but by and large it is possible to take a table and consume all the food and drink one wants. Admittedly some inner-city pubs will usually want to hold a credit card behind the bar if one wants to "open a tab ", but in most cases they do not validate the card until taking payment at the end.

Rent

Rent is normally subject to paying a deposit prior to occupancy, but there are situations where no rent need be paid in advance... or at all.

Government

In the case of what the Government wants to collect from us in various ways, the difference is that they are not chasing for payment of goods and services we have individually specified, they are looking for money from us to spend in ways that do not appear to benefit us directly, and of which individuals might well disapprove. Only in the sense that the Government tells us we owe them is the "credit" we have received unconditional. And Government is perhaps the most rapacious Creditor of them all, seeking to put itself at the head of all the others to whom we may owe money and not stinting at creating fearsome "punishments", unique only to itself as the fearsome *Lion of the Law*, including jail and loss of driving licence or passport. And because Government has access to data above and beyond – but very much including everything – possessed by the Credit Reference Agencies, it is also in a position to be highly effective in tracking Debtors down. But again there are ways of evading payment to government agencies.

Preparing Defence with Conditional credit

Conditional credit applies to discretionary purchases to which there is no "right" of consumption. However, retailers are always keen to sell and to enable their would-be customers to afford their goods, just as banks and credit card companies need to have customers to lend to in order to trade and make profits. Anyone with a proof of address, who can demonstrate a source of income, and who does not have a history on the files of the Credit Reference Agencies which demonstrates poor payment performance, is likely to be able to get credit - for a credit card, for a mobile phone contract, for an unsecured bank loan.

The Etymology of Credit

The word credit derives of course from the Latin "credo", which means "I believe". This can be extended to belief in both the ability and the willingness of the Debtor to pay. Such credit always comes with conditions, notably name and address history to validate the identity of the applicant and terms upon which the credit must be repaid.

The longer the record of sound payment, the higher the demonstrated income, the better quality the domestic address of the credit applicant, the more credit they will be afforded. Indeed the irony of credit is of course that when one is wealthy and has no need of it, one is deluged with favourable offers including delayed repayment and low interest rates, even discounts off the purchase price and cash rebates. But for the honest and open credit applicant who is unfortunate enough to really need credit because their own funds are lacking, who has but little income and perhaps no long history of residence at a "good" address, no credit at all may be forthcoming. They are likely to be asked to pay in advance for everything they want to buy.

Making an Application for Conditional Credit

If one knowingly misrepresents material facts in completing an application for credit one may very well be guilty of attempted fraud. If detected one may be prosecuted, convicted and in extreme or repeat cases jailed for the offence. In addition to sharing data on their customers' ability to pay, retailers and financial services companies such as credit card companies, banks, unsecured lenders, utilities and telecoms companies also share information on names and addresses which are associated with attempted or actual fraud.

A name at an address which is associated with a previous *"application fraud"* notice will generate an exception report or warning flag at the point of credit scoring. Any such application will be screened with exceeding rigour and the chances of it being approved are in practice negligible. Intended non-payers have therefore a choice of telling the truth on credit applications or inventing plausible "facts" which will support their application: committing fraud.

Consent to Credit Scoring and Data Sharing

It is perhaps worth emphasising that a credit agreement is just that: the buyer and seller of goods and services both have the opportunity to agree on the terms of sale and of any credit being advanced. Normally this means that the seller's terms and conditions are obligatory, specifically for conditional credit applications. In other words, if the buyer does not accept the terms which a very powerful seller insists upon as a pre-condition of granting credit, no sale takes place, no credit is forthcoming and there is no agreement.

"The buyer does need to be very clear about the powers which they are giving to the credit granter at this point, because they are extensive and even intrusive."

But the buyer does need to be very clear about the powers which they are giving to the credit granter at this point, because they are extensive and even intrusive.

Implications of powers given to credit granter on application for credit

1) The credit applicant agrees that the credit granter, ie retailer, credit card company etc has the right to enter the credit applicant's personal data in an electronic system run by a Credit Bureau for the purposes of obtaining a credit score. In order to obtain this credit score, the Credit Bureau system will factor in the "quality" of the credit applicant's address (is it associated with a low or a high propensity to bad debts among other residents of the postcode area?), the age and sex of the applicant (to obtain a "geo-demographic" score which attempts to categorise the applicant with people of a similar age, sex, employment status) and also the payment history reflected back by other suppliers to the individual at the named address.

   For an individual "confirmed" at a named address this will provide a reasonably accurate probability for the credit grantor as to the likelihood of this particular credit applicant complying with the terms of their credit agreement and paying up on time.

2) The credit applicant also agrees to the use of his or her data to be shared with other retailers for credit application scoring purposes by them. In other words the payment history, yet to unfold, of how the applicant conducts the account which they are now applying for as regards keeping up payments is being approved for sharing by the credit applicant as party to the current credit agreement now being applied for.

3) The credit applicant further agrees that their data may be used for tracing purposes and may be shared with other credit grantors for this purpose. This allows contributing members of the retailer and financial services data sharing group to share data with each other as to the whereabouts of any common customer or Debtor who has signed up to this term.

4) The credit applicant agrees also to their data being shared for the purposes of fraud prevention or detection.

In other words at the credit application stage the credit applicant is putting into the hands of the credit grantor - soon to become Creditor to whom he or she owes money - the legal right to use very powerful data-sharing tools to detect any wrongdoing, to share it with others and to enable the Debtor to be tracked down by sharing the address data that can be provided by other credit granters if the Debtor should change address.

Defeating the Credit Application Process?

Applications for discretionary credit, ie for credit cards, loans, mobile phone agreements cannot in the aggregate be defeated by credit applicants who give full and accurate information in the sense that the credit appraisal system will give a reasonably accurate prediction as to the likelihood of applicants being able and willing to make payment. Someone with a hitherto good record, but now suffering problems, perhaps because of recent unemployment, will still very likely be able to gain credit due to their most recent presumably good payment behaviour; they may indeed apply knowing that they will struggle to re-pay, and succeed in being granted credit which they do not repay.

"In practice fraud is much harder to prove than theft, simply because fraudsters tend to put more distance between themselves and their crime..."

A change to "delinquent" behaviour, as non-payment is frequently called by Creditors, will result in all other new credit lines drying up about in a month or six weeks after payment for the new credit line has been missed. But for a credit applicant whose circumstances remain unchanged credit scoring does provide a good indication as to whether a Creditor will get paid. In order to get round the system, someone with a poor credit record or someone who is unable to more than two or three years continuous residence at their address can only succeed by deceit.

Overcoming the credit application process by Fraud and Deceit?

There are numerous ways in which credit applicants attempt to deceive credit application systems, all of them criminal in intent and in practice and all potentially punishable by a custodial sentence. In practice fraud is much harder to prove than theft, simply because fraudsters tend to put more distance between themselves and their crime than thieves or robbers who generally need to be present (not including cyber-theft) at the so-called "scene of the crime" in order to physically purloin whatever it is they intend to steal or rob for.

While criminals who are physically present at a crime risk being sighted, described and named; in the case of fraudsters, if they succeed, they are literally unidentifiable and even if they fail to get past the systems they are attacking, they still have not given away their identities and true whereabouts.

Most frauds are quite small scale. Few retailers or financial services companies will take the trouble to report them to police due to the significant time investment in preparing and filing a report which might be sufficiently robust to serve as evidence in any criminal case. Nor do commercial companies want to have their staff giving evidence in court unless they feel they absolutely need to in order to prove a point to deter a particularly painful form of fraud or trap an individual who has become to them a *cause célèbre* as described earlier.

Equally, the police simply do not have the resources to deal with large volumes of mini-impact crimes. A major nationwide fraud involving millions of pounds would be a different matter, but the fact remains that a small-time attempted unsuccessful application fraud is unlikely to result in a court appearance for three reasons: lack of follow-through by the Creditor, lack of prioritisation by the police, and difficulty of identifying and locating the perpetrator under their real name and current address, and linking the attempted fraud to them sufficiently robustly that they would be found guilty in a court of law.

"...the police simply do not have the resources to deal with large volumes of mini-impact crimes."

The statistics support this view. The number of successful prosecutions for fraud in the County Courts fell between 2007 and 2008 from just 14300 cases to 13200 according to Ministry of Justice data. Yet fraud cases reported to CIFAS (the Credit Industry Fraud Avoidance Scheme) were running at over 240,000 in 2009, an increase of 16% year on year. How many more fraud cases were detected or suspected but not reported, either because the companies affected were not CIFAS members, or the level of proof was too slight, or because it was considered pointless and excessively costly to report? And how many cases of fraud simply went undetected? The numbers do suggest that the odds favour the fraudster.

Application Fraud

Types of application fraud include:

1) *Naming a fictitious employer as a reference to demonstrate alleged employment status and potentially also income level.*

2) *Adopting the identity of a real person by discovering their date of birth and address – this is also known as identity theft. CIFAS reported around 100,000 cases of identity fraud attempts in 2009, half of which were successful from the perspective of the fraudster.*

3) *Empty house fraud, where credit applications are made from an empty property and goods directed there for receipt*

4) *Fraudulent application in a real consumer's name at their true address. This can lead to sophisticated and brazen attempts to anticipate a postman or delivery courier by "working in the garden" posing as the house-holder at a known time when delivery is likely to take place. A recent variant has been for a fake "postman" to turn up at a house where a mobile phone or other goods have been delivered to a named addressee at that house "in error" to collect the item, ostensibly to return it, but in reality to take possession for themselves.*

People also order goods in their own name and to their own addresses which they don't intend to pay for, sometimes after establishing a reputation as a good payer in a small way on credit terms which they honour. This is known as "long fraud" or "long day fraud". They know that they will destroy their creditworthiness at the point of non-payment, but make the decision that the return from this one-time coup will be worth it, perhaps combining numerous credit "purchases" from different suppliers or using multiple credit cards to credit limit at the same time, shortly before moving address. In this way it might be possible to amass debts which are not intended to be paid of hundreds of thousands of pounds if the deed is carefully planned.

Data-sharing on Fraud or potential fraud

The three major UK consumer credit reference agencies are *Experian*, *Equifax* and *Callcredit*. All three act as a platform for data-sharing on actual or attempted consumer frauds through CIFAS. This is a closed user group organisation based on the principle that members who contribute data to it are given access to view data provided by other members and it is automatically linked to the credit reference searches of the three agencies. Its data matching is based on name and address. For a contributing member carrying out a credit search of a named individual at an address if will flag the availability of potential fraud data availability:

Same name Same Address

This means for example that one or more members of CIFAS will have a record of the same John Smith, Date of birth 10/10/1961 at 15 Acacia Avenue Anytown AT10 1TU as the John Smith who is currently being checked on the credit bureau system by another CIFAS member.

Similar Name Same Address

If the Credit Applicant is James Smith at 15 Acacia Avenue Anytown AT10

1TU and there is a record of a John Smith, a J Smith or an Agnes Smith, the CIFAS flag in any of the credit bureaux searches would indicate a report under this heading. It would indicate a possible match or that potentially fraudulent activity had been reported by someone of the same surname at the same address as the applicant. Credit bureaux often assume, based on the terms and conditions enforced on companies offering consumer credit on new applicants, that people with the same surname at the same address are financially linked, unless there has been a notice given to the credit bureau of *"disassociation"*, for example by a parent of a wayward relative. The assumed association means that anyone of the same surname at the same address will be assumed to be linked financially for good or ill.

Different Name Same Address

If Samuel Jones of 15 Acacia Avenue Anytown AT10 1TU applies for credit at the same address where James Smith was associated with a credit fraud, then again this would flag a report to any CIFAS member company making a credit search of Samuel Jones at this address.

Impact of a CIFAS Report

The rules of CIFAS require that any member filing a CIFAS report must have a standard of proof of suspected fraud which would be of a quality to qualify as evidence to support a case for prosecution to the Crown Prosecution Service, whether or not the case is actually reported. (Most cases are not reported, based on the effort and cost to both the reporting company and the perceived low likelihood of the CPS seeing through an actual prosecution). The fact of a CIFAS report may not be used as a red-lining device to prevent anyone at an address which has been linked to fraud from gaining credit, and there are at least one million UK addresses which have had this distinction. However, it will inevitably lead to significantly increased rigour in the credit approval process, which is why fraudsters continue to find new identities and to move on to new addresses.

Increasingly credit reference agencies are using data on known frauds to create scorecards which correlate specific postcodes to fraud frequency at these postcodes, thereby identifying likely hotspots and cold spots for new applications to contain fraud attempts..

Refusing Consent to credit score and to share data

It is of course possible to refuse to consent to credit scoring and to data sharing. To do so in the case of an application for conditional credit would be to become an immediate "fail" with the result that the application would be refused and no goods or services forthcoming on credit. For goods and services which are initially potentially available on unconditional credit, however, the supplier will inevitably make attempts to capture data about who their new customer is, and often this will involve a credit scoring exercise.

> "It is of course possible to refuse to consent to credit scoring and to data sharing"

Given that the Debtor is already enjoying the credit facility in this case, they are of course well positioned to refuse to consent to data sharing and to credit scoring. This creates a significant problem for the supplier who will not be well-positioned to deal with such a refusal. It specifically refuses them the right to use the Debtor's data to be shared with other suppliers for the purpose of tracing, should the Debtor elect at a later date to leave the property without giving a forwarding address. This is a real benefit to the future absconding Debtor or "*Goneaway*".

Personal Guarantees

Certain Creditors will accept an ostensibly weak or high risk credit applicant in the event that they can receive security, typically including landlords and utilities (for example in the case that an applicant wishes to have a pre-payment meter removed and offers to pay by a credit tariff instead). Usually, the guarantor is a parent although it could be another relative or an employer. Using photocopying and scanning technology it is a simple matter

> *to forge a signature, an ostensible witnessing signature, and a letter with a solicitor's letterhead in order to create a credible-looking "personal guarantee". This is of course fraudulent and could be prosecuted if discovered.*
>
> *It is very difficult to enforce a personal guarantee in a court of law unless there is cast iron proof that the guarantor really did sign the guarantee in his own hand in front of a credible witness. From the perspective of the forger, having an ostensible "solicitor" witness a guarantee gives it the appearance of being genuine. From the perspective of the credit applicant prepared to risk fraudulent behaviour it is on the other hand generally straightforward to create documentation which appears genuine. Most retail organisations are not competent to check guarantee documentation effectively.*

Fake Leases and Rental Agreements for Proof of Residency

The same weakness as for guarantees applies to provision of forged leases demonstrating that someone has lived at a given address from a certain point in time. Leases and rental agreements are very important base documents for use in validating Proof of Residency and Identity for people who cannot be validated using a Credit Bureau on-line system because they have allegedly not been living at a named address long enough to establish a credit record there. These are very easy to create and the perpetrator is much helped by the fact that credit application processing departments in large companies do not generally invest much effort or training in fraud prevention.

The receipt and validation of guarantees and copy leases is usually performed only on an occasional basis by individual unqualified staff who simply do not know what to check and what to look out for as a potential anomaly. Incredibly, people attempting to deceive a credit approval process using fake documents very frequently fall down – despite the lack of awareness of staff – due to half-hearted, poorly drafted documents which have obviously been downloaded from the internet, or are obvious poor photocopies. Use of liquid eraser with manual pencilling in of names and dates is another very frequent give-away of very obvious fake documentation to even a casual reviewer. Careless mistakes like this cause an application to be immediately sidelined for attention by an experienced fraud management expert, leading to the unravelling of the attempted perpetrator's complete scheme. Even stupid policemen can catch very stupid burglars.

Loss of Control or Deliberate Fraud?

Of course, most Debtors who acquire multiple credit lines and acquire massive debts do not necessarily set out to not pay at the beginning. Even today, it is still easy to acquire multiple credit cards, paying off the minimum amount each month and using newer credit cards for cash advances to make these payments. The same retailers who hound over-burdened Debtors are those who bombard them first of all with offers for store cards, and offer payment holidays for large consumer durables purchases, followed by usurious interest charges when the payment holiday expires if the debt cannot be serviced.

However, those who lose control and find themselves deeply in debt are generally not well constituted to become Hold-out Debtors. The loss of overview and ability to keep pace with their increasing debts betokens also a lack of judgement and an absence of the personal characteristics of the successful hold-out which have already been discussed. Those who lose control are by and large current Can't Pays – at least they cannot pay every Creditor and in full – and certainly eventual Might-Pays. These people are the meat and drink of the collections industry; their haplessness, fecklessness, poor judgement and inability to plan cause them deep personal unhappiness, significant hardship, loss of relationships and mental health while enriching the Debt Collection Agencies and Debt Purchase Companies.

This population is literally a world away from the calculating fraud perpetrator who plans and thinks through their every move and tends to succeed to the tune of £30 billion in the UK each year according to the *National Fraud Authority*. Of course, the retail and credit industry factors these costs back into their pricing, with the bill ultimately picked up by the Always Pays and those Might Pays who for whatever reason do end up paying.

9.0

Jackal and Hide: Defending Against a Determined Creditor

> **WHAT'S IN THIS CHAPTER**
>
> It is firstly helpful to understand how organisations work and that behind that plate glass façade there is a great deal of chaos and incompetence. Poor understanding of the Pareto principle has been the undoing of many. For the creditor not to be sure who he is dealing with is an advantageous position which a Debtor may wish to hold on to for as long as possible. What techniques can a Debtor use to hold off a Creditor who knows that he is in residence?

Jackal and Hide:
Defending against a Determined Creditor

"Debts and Lies are generally mixed together"
Francois Rabelais

Debt collection lends itself to becoming a process. Large volumes of customers are billed on a given date and largish volumes of accounts become overdue and need to be chased for collection. The assumed intelligence behind the debt collection process "knows" that it will be dealing with large numbers of "Will-pays", moderate numbers of "Might Pays" of various hues, and a small number of "Won't or "Can't-Pays". It needs to politely engage with and prompt the Will-pays while at the same time giving a signal to the others that it means business.

Too aggressive an approach at the outset of the campaign to collect a tranche of outstanding debt and it runs the risk of upsetting and alienating perfectly good payers who may decide to take their custom elsewhere. Essentially the debt collection process is about progressively and doggedly convincing Debtors that payment is an inexorable necessity, it will inevitably have to take place, that there are dire and increasing costs of delay, and lingering penalties including social exclusion and sometimes even loss of abode or gaol for non-payment.

> **"Given that the individual Debtor is pitted against a steamrolling machine, the machine appears at the outset to be more powerful ..."**

Given that the individual Debtor is pitted against a steamrolling machine, the machine appears at the outset to be more powerful. It is resource-rich, possessed of marvellous search and trace capabilities, it has computerised records of its customers and programmes which segment them into types, and score them as to propensity to behave in certain ways, it can use "predictive dialling" engines linked to phones to repeatedly dial the Debtor's number; its debt collectors are trained on how to negotiate over the telephone to grind money out of reluctant payers using customised scripts to appeal to different kinds of people, and not least it has recourse to the might of The law. What can the individual do against this array of power?

The answer lies in the individual Debtor's very individuality and creativity, in their resourcefulness and determination. For by aggregating individuals into types or segments, and by treating individuals as being the same, the machine fails to anticipate and to understand and to react to differences in individual people. The Hold-out Debtor will hide among a crowd of Might-Pays, and seek to descend to the bottom of a hierarchy of prioritisation of those cases which might be seen as most likely to pay and most worthwhile to pursue. While looking from a distance like any other Debtor, he tries to make himself in every individual respect unattractive as prey for ripe and easy collection. Just as fish blend into a shoal, he will hide in the deepest centre.

And when the hunt becomes individual, he will disappear from the shoal into a remote and inaccessible crevice. He is in short inspired by all of nature's examples of survival technique: of sudden flight, of leaving a cloud of ink and confusion, of having a sting should he be approached too closely, playing possum, hibernating and re-awakening, changing from a maggot to a chrysalis to an unrecognisable butterfly... and he has no shame about mixing metaphors. The organisational machine was not designed for this. It cannot evolve as quickly, it does not have his speed of reinvention.

The Pareto Principle

Organisations are designed rationally and managed by accountants. They operate on the Pareto Principle or "80:20 rule", that is to say they are designed to deal with large volumes of similar events. According to this principle 80% of customers create 20% of the problems the corporation faces, and 20% of customers 80% of the problems. The temptation of the accountant is to create solutions for the 20% of customers creating 80% of the problems, because this is cost effective... and to hope that the rest will somehow take care of themselves.

How Organisations conspire to defeat themselves

In the past corporations were staffed by armies of people who carried out the same tasks for years, who became individually expert, not just at dealing with the commonest and simplest problems, but with those that cropped up infrequently. A high service standard was the outcome of a high staffing ratio. But in the new global economy with hotter competition and pressure on costs, high staffing ratios became unaffordable.

The accountants invented waves of money-saving projects to save cost and improve headline profit, usually by automating, "re-engineering" or "lean-designing" processes to take out cost and people, including the very experts who could deal with the exceptions. The gap was supposed to be filled by "contracting out" "non-core processes". Difficult, exceptional cases that could no longer be handled by the new computerised process routines, and for which the experts no longer existed, would now be dealt with by external contractors. Within a very short time organisations lost key knowledge about their own processes and customer behaviour.

Contractors were able to charge what they liked for doing what corporations had forgotten how to do – until the accountants decided that the contractors were too expensive and decided to bring the exceptional cases in-house again. At this point junior in-house staff (costing less than the old-timer experts of yore) needed to try to learn about these difficult cases from scratch, but by dint of their inexperience proved not very good at it. So corporations dealing with large volumes of customers in sometimes complex processes have continued to have hit and miss customer operations.

Attempts to fix things continue sporadically as one hotshot accountant follows the deemed failure of a predecessor to stem a thousand small haemorrhages of value and cost effectiveness and money by hiring in ace consultants from the big accountancy practices who turn out to be brilliant graduates who draw great charts on PowerPoint but don't have very much experience either. Customer service in large organisations continues to be poor, and rigid debt management processes are completely "hard-wired " into all the big-company Customer Relationship Management systems.

What does all this mean for the would-be Hold-out Debtor who seeks to play the system and to avoid payment? Well, a bill demanding payment is at the very end of a chain of processes which include design, production, sale, billing and distribution. If any of the elements of the chain are broken or distorted it means that the bill will pretty inevitably be wrong. Debt management and collection is a prime victim of corporate design malfunction. It means that there will always be opportunity for the creative, agile and determined artist of debt escapology to avoid payment. It means that opportunity knocks...

The Debtor as an unknown quantity

If the Debtor intends to evade payment at a restaurant or service station, his tactic will be to resemble other paying customers as much as possible – while maintaining anonymity. Where he or she has to appear in person they will do nothing to draw attention to themselves in terms of dress or mannerisms which tells the observer that they are nervous and uncertain and about to do something unusual. Wearing spectacles and a baseball cap may not attract attention where an obviously false beard certainly would. Obviously any such behaviour, accompanied by non-payment and flight amounts to fraud and theft – because payment for the goods offered by restaurants and service stations is required to be by cash or credit card, immediately subsequent to acquiring them. Perpetrators are routinely caught, tried and sentenced by the courts for such deeds.

Such is not normally the case with utilities however.

"The Occupier": Is there anyone there?

Life is less fraught with risk and danger of early pursuit, detection and arrest if the unknown Debtor is merely seeking to not pay for gas, electricity or water. Here the advantages lie with the Debtor: do they even exist? Gas, water and electricity utilities – which can easily consume over £3000 a year – routinely send bills to an "occupier" when they do not know who is living at a given property to which they have billing rights, or when they are not sure if it is occupied at all. At any one time around 3% of properties have the status of "Occupier" for utilities. From a UK household stock of around 23,000,000 that equates to 690,000 occupiers at any one time. This phenomenon is the equivalent of a permanent acute migraine for utilities which lose more money to Debtors flitting in and out of occupier properties than for any other source of bad debt. How easy is it for an occupier to maintain anonymity in a grey population of another 689,999 occupiers? Answer: how easy is it for a needle stay lost in the proverbial haystack? Easy.

Defence in Depth as Demonstrated by History

The over-arching strategy of debt defence is that of the Russian retreat, as practiced with complete success by technologically inferior Russian armies against two of the most determined and ruthless tyrants of the modern age: Napoleon and Hitler. In each case the inferior opponent fell back and withdrew into the mother heartland, drawing the enemy ever deeper into resource commitment, excessive cost in manpower and materiél, playing for time until winter came. In both cases the enemy withdrew, defeated in large measure by cold, exhaustion and resource depletion as much as by the courage of the defending Russian army. Two thousand years before the great strategist of oriental antiquity, Sun Tzu wrote in his short but seminal masterpiece, The Art of War: "The greatest victory is in the battle never fought". This translates to the Debtor who does not engage.

Local authorities will also routinely write to "The Occupier" of properties for which they are not receiving Council Tax if they do not have a named tenant. This lack of certainty of the existence of a real live customer at an address being billed to "The Occupier" is a major advantage to an intending non-payer living at the address. The Occupier becomes to all intents and purpose a phantom Debtor to whom energy utilities will send estimated bills which are based on the historic known consumption pattern of a given property. Over a period of two or three months the utility will send letters to the

"The occupier becomes to all intents and purposes a phantom Debtor"

"occupier" and may also dial the last known landline number of the property in case the previous resident elected not to take that number with them on moving out.

A meter reader is likely to call within a month or two and may be asked by the utility to report whether they believe the property is occupied. Utilities prioritise their enforcement activity on the value of an outstanding debt. Initially debt will be low and therefore will be accorded no priority for enforcement. Even after 6 months or so, if there has been no contact and no evidence that there is anyone there, the utility must reckon with the possibility that if they spend money to enter the property to collect the outstanding debt, it will be discovered that the supposed debt is "phantom debt" and the occupier account adjusted downwards. Money will have been spent and no debt collected, merely more administration cost to correct the books.

How much more sensible – on the surface – for the utility to prioritise addresses for enforcement where there is definitely known to be a genuine named Debtor in residence? For not only are the resources of each utility budget limited in terms of money and the availability of its field agents to do all the enforcement activity they are called upon to carry out, each company has internal targets for debt collection.

If they pay to obtain a warrant of entry and use this to install a prepayment meter for a £500 debt at a confirmed customer address, this will benefit their collection target at once. But if all they do is to establish that an estimated debt of £500 is unreal because the property was unoccupied, then they have collected nothing and used up resources that could have been spent better elsewhere. Hence, the occupier who is successful in retaining the illusion that the property is empty is much more likely to be able to avoid payment for a significantly longer period before having to resort to another tactic.

As to how this is done: for a flat dweller it is a simple matter to place a closed letter box on the door behind the letter slot, so that it is not possible for anyone to look through the letterbox for signs of occupancy. The letterbox will be left full of junk mail as if no one were there to empty it. They will not talk to neighbours so that they do not give away any information about their identity which a neighbour is only too prone to pass on. In the winter months and at night they will keep blinds closed and limit the use of lights if they have reason to believe that a debt visit is imminent. They will not answer knocks on the door which they are not expecting and will rely on taking answering machine messages to which they can call back if they choose.

If it is relatively easy in the case of a flat dweller to disguise the fact of their occupancy, this becomes more challenging for Debtors living in houses, but similar principles apply. The terraced house is easier than the semi-detached house because there is no garden to enter, and no risk of someone walking around the side of the house to see a dweller in the kitchen.

Large utilities continue to re-engineer their processes continuously and are apt to create new small errors as they try to fix large ones

The first element of defence in depth in the case of an occupier account is to maintain the doubt as to whether the property is occupied, and ideally to make it look as if it is not. In such a case some water utilities will stop billing entirely and occupier letters will cease. Gas and Electricity suppliers may also retain a category of "known empty" properties. Attention to these will be much less frequent, perhaps only a cursory visit every 6 months, so it is worth the effort from the perspective of the determined Debtor to maintain the illusion of emptiness for as long as possible.

Anonymous Debtor known at Address

Large utilities continue to re-engineer their processes continuously and are apt to create new small errors as they try to fix large ones, so it is always possible that an occupier account might be overlooked for a long time. Local authorities are forbidden to share data with utilities so the Debtor living in council or housing authority property ought in principle to be secure against their data being shared with Creditors.

If a Debtor plans to remain in a property for any length of time without paying for their utilities it is very likely that they will think it wise to contact their landlord to specifically understand the landlord's policy on data sharing and to give formal notice under the Data Protection Act to the landlord that they do not consent to their data being shared. If they are to do this, however, they will be likely to be paying their rent, otherwise they will merely draw attention to themselves for priority action to evict them.

If properties owned by a local authority or by a housing association are thought to be empty, however, it is often possible for utilities to gain the cooperation of local authority landlords to gain access to the property in order to remove a gas or electricity meter on grounds of *Health and Safety*. It is likely that a prior notice would be posted through a letterbox to warn of the immediacy of such an event, at which point the Debtor may decide to capitulate in terms of anonymity to become a known customer. In any case it could be at least a year before any such event occurred, during which time the Debtor could continue to enjoy free gas, water and electricity.

In the case of a private flat or house, the utility first has to detect who the owner is, which they can do via the Land Registry service for a fee. Gaining successful contact with the landlord can prove difficult however, and landlords often do not comply with requests for information if they are being paid on time, as they do not want to give access to a competitor for their tenant's cash. If the tenant may not have much money but is paying the landlord, why make it easy for a utility to enforce payment and thus possible leave the tenant short of the cash to pay the rent to them? An occupier of a property thought to be empty, can very often succeed in lying low and carefully benefiting from a supply of gas and electricity for a long time.

Potential Debtor Tactics

What options are open to the Debtor once it becomes known to the utility that there is someone living at the address where they are staying, but their identity is still not clear to the utility?

> **Must Read Processes**
>
> *It is possible for utilities to obtain Warrants of Entry from a magistrate based on the statutory duty of gas and electricity companies to acquire an independent meter reading at least once a year or if they can demonstrate that they need access for safety reasons, for example to deal with a suspected gas leak. Each utility will have a target for the number of properties which they must have a reading for in order to make the annual regulatory meter reading objective, which is one of the yardsticks they use to measure and demonstrate their efficiency and effectiveness to the Regulator, Ofgem or Ofwat. Generally towards the end of each year this might mean a rush of activity to obtain warrants of entry – again preceded by notices through letterboxes as a means of saving money for the utility. But because this activity is expensive and does not generally bring in any revenue (on the basis that there really may not be anyone living in most properties thought to be empty), utilities do not wish to spend money on this.*

Continue to refuse contact and hold-out until eventual enforced entry and installation of a pre-payment meter for gas or electricity?

This is perhaps the least logical tactic for any Debtor to take, but it is a very frequent default option for *Ostriches* who are too careless to read their mail or too frightened or apathetic to do anything to avert the situation. When the utility eventually gains entry using a court warrant, and if necessary with the assistance of a locksmith and the police, they will calculate the bill outstanding from the last secure meter read, either from one of their meter readers or from a previous occupant at the point of leaving. This value will be entered on a prepayment meter which will be installed to remove an existing meter allowing uncurtailed energy use.

In future the occupant will have to pay for their energy in advance, but in doing so will be obliged to pay off part of the historical debt which has built up. The utility may be allowed to take up to 60% of all monies charged to the meter until the debt is paid off, which means that if the Debtor pays £1 in future, they will only receive 40p worth of energy before the meter stops and automatically cuts itself off until the next prepayment amount is charged to it. Charging a prepayment meter will generally involve the Debtor making a cash payment at a *Paypoint* location, generally a petrol station or corner shop which may be several miles away and therefore adding time, cost and inconvenience to the price of home energy. Even worse, the energy tariff at which prepayment meters take payment may be more expensive in the range of prices which the utility can levy.

There has been talk of the Regulators allowing punitive tariffs for hardcore non-payers. This is justified by the fact that it is more expensive for the utility to administer and manage prepayment accounts than those paid for by direct debit, but it will have the effect of making life tougher for the generally poorest section of the community who default into having to pay for their home energy by prepayment meter.

This option therefore is to be avoided from the perspective of the intelligent Hold-out Debtor and by any intelligent Might-Pay also.

Capitulate by making contact with the Utility and Paying all that is due?

By making payment in full at what the utility calculates the debt to be (which may or may not be correct if they are relying on estimated reads, or data provided by the outgoing customer) it should always be possible to forestall the installation of a prepayment meter, so long as this is not at the point of entry under a warrant. A magistrate will not grant a warrant of disconnection (and reconnection via prepayment meter) if an account has been paid up to date.

Claim to have just moved in?

This is a tactic which any occupier can use. They choose a time at which to announce their presence to the utility and offer to become a normal customer.

The closer the wolf comes to the door, however, in terms of imminent enforcement, the harder this becomes. As the nominal debt of the Occupier account becomes ever larger, since the utility continues to bill based on its estimation of what may be being consumed, the potential value at stake means that the case will escalate in significance and visibility over time to the point where it may receive detailed attention from expert collectors who are not easy to deceive.

> "As the nominal debt of the Occupier account becomes ever larger, the case will escalate in significance and visibility to the utility"

It will become difficult to persuade a collections department over the telephone that the customer has just moved in – they will want to see some proof. They will normally demand to see evidence of the identity of the "new customer" such as a photocopied driving licence, passport or photographic employee id. In addition to confirming identity, they will seek proof of residency, ie a document which demonstrates how long the customer has been at their current address. This might be a copy lease or rental agreement, or for a home owner is could be documentation to support the purchase of the property or granting of a mortgage. As discussed above it has become increasingly easy for the focussed and determined "new customer" to forge such documentation.

At the point where the utility is satisfied with its test of documentation of proofs of identity and residency it will be prepared to close the existing Occupier account after having taken a meter reading to correct the outstanding value from its previous estimated value to an accurate cash value outstanding. At this point with no identified customer to chase for collection of any debt accrued up to the point of a new customer taking over the account, the existing debt will be written off and forgotten. For the Debtor in occupation who now starts off with a clean sheet and no debt on a new account, this is a clear win.

However, despite the typical lassitude of utilities in training their debt collection teams on how to check the validity of passports, driving licences and leases, for a Debt evader to send copy documentation does of course entail some risk. If detected it is an act of attempted fraud, and there is always the possibility that someone more experienced or intuitive or astute might just make the detection. Happily for the would-be perpetrator, a very good excuse is available not to have to send original documentation through the post on the basis that there is an unacceptable risk of it getting lost.

Dealing with the Field Visit from Utilities

Rather than take the risk of having copy forged documentation in the hands of the Creditor, the perpetrator may find it more expedient to wait until the visit stage, which energy utilities always carry out prior to applying for a warrant of disconnection.Utilities often use third party contractors whose sole desire is to earn money and to do a good enough job to be asked to do the next one. Instead of sending documents which provide evidence of attempted fraud if detected, the Hold-out may choose to simply show the documentation at the door when the Debt Collection Representative calls.

This Field Agent will be not be in a good position to tell whether the documents are valid or not, if the Hold-out does not give them fully into his possession and certainly does not allow them to be taken away or copied. He is very likely to get away with a truculent statement like: " I am showing you these documents which are about my private affairs and I am upset that I should have to do so. You have seen them so get out of my face and stop treating me like a criminal suspect". What will happen next is that the Debt Collection Representative will tick boxes in his Field Report to state that the Occupier account should be closed, and that a new account should be opened in the name and date of birth given by the Hold-out.

It is very clearly in the interest of the intending non-payer to refuse consent to credit-score for an energy supply is they have moved into a property where they are already able to access energy through a credit meter. Telephone agents will typically not have a script to deal with this eventuality and will become flustered. They can be put even more off balance by a caller asking them to confirm that the call is being monitored and that it is therefore on record that they do not consent to having their data shared with any third party.

A wily Debt Evader might then write to the utility asking for acknowledgement that their details will not be shared. Written correspondence with utilities is subject to inordinate backlogs and delays and can always be used to protract enforcement processes. The inevitably long ensuing delay during which the utility will have failed to give a satisfactory timely assurance that the Debtor's personal data will not be shared may then profitably be used as an excuse for non-payment "as a matter of principle" until this concern has been resolved.

Abscond?

If an unidentified customer leaves a property which is still classified as an Occupier Account the utility has no effective point of departure from which to pursue them. If they were an Occupier account with which no contact was made, and no evidence of habitation found on succeeding visits, then there is no proof that the customer ever existed. No trace enquiry can be made because no name is known under which to trace. The unknown customer who leaves an address will invariably have succeeded in getting away without paying. Customers who leave an address without prior notification are called "goneaways" in the trade. An unknown gone-away is a prince among deceivers who has escaped undetectably and scot-free.

> "The intelligent Hold-out Debtor as well as the intending absconder never reveals their date of birth to anyone, linked to an address from which they are enjoying credit."

Obviously the later the departure of the Debtor from a property where they are enjoying utilities for nothing, the longer the free credit which will never be paid for can be enjoyed and the higher the value of the debt which they will have succeeded in accruing and evading.

But the longer the occupier remains at a given property, the more likely that contact will be made with neighbours who will perhaps acquire information which could lead a doorstep visitor – and utilities are required by regulation to demonstrate that they have made every attempt at contact before asking a magistrate for a warrant of entry, so they will always send round a Debt Collection Representative in addition to repeated Meter Reader visits – to acquiring a name. And if the utility has a name it has at least part of the information it needs to start a trace, the other being date of birth. The intelligent Hold-out Debtor as well as the intending absconder never reveals their date of birth to anyone, linked to an address from which they are enjoying credit.

Attempt to change to a competitive supplier?

If the Debtor calls the existing supplier and claims to have just moved in and there is an outstanding debt greater than £100 on the current account at the address, then the existing supplier will always demand proofs of identity, leaving previous address and copy lease or rental agreement documentation. They will be sceptical about the validity of the Change of Tenancy and may be more than usually scrupulous in their checking. Trying to re-invent oneself as a new customer to a suspicious existing supplier is difficult.

If a new supplier receives an application for supply in a different name (ie a "different customer") to that given to the existing supplier, then the old supplier has no grounds for objecting to a Change of Supplier and Change of Tenancy at the same time.

If the Debtor calls a new supplier and asks to change supply the new supplier will be only too happy to take them on. However, the acquiring supplier is obliged to notify the old supplier via the transfer system operated by *National Grid* that the named customer has applied to transfer to them. The existing supplier has a 28 day "window" of opportunity to review their accounts and to object to the customer leaving if they have a debt greater than £100. Because utilities are forever trying to save costs, the debt objection process is frequently subject to work backlogs, and there is slightly less than even chance that such an application might be successful. If the case is not subject to backlogs or the careless processing that underinvestment in people in utility billing departments causes, then the account will be flagged for high attention and priority disconnection and reconnection to a perhaps punitively expensive prepayment meter.

If a new supplier receives an application for supply in a different name (ie a "different customer") to that given to the existing supplier, then the old supplier has no grounds for objecting to a Change of Supplier and Change of Tenancy at the same time. The only difficulty at this point is the creditworthiness of the "new tenant just moved in". Energy utilities have no right to refuse a supply to any new customer, but they can demand a prepayment of up to three months forecast consumption at the highest level of annual consumption, ie the winter months, when consumers can often take 70% of their annual energy consumption from November through to February.

Indeed, if there are exceptional circumstances – and one might be if the consumption address is flagged under a user group data sharing facility such as CIFAS as part of the credit scoring process with one of the three UK consumer credit reference agencies *(Experian, Equifax and Callcredit)* – the requested prepayment value can be as high as the putative new supplier utility wishes to set it, thus frustrating the ability of the would-be escaping defaulting Debtor to change supplier.

Any prepayment is held in a separate account at interest for at least a year, and it may be refunded at the discretion of the utility supplier if the consumer has paid on time consistently for a full year. It cannot be used as a drawdown account to pay for energy being consumed in the current year.

If the requested prepayment is not forthcoming, then the change of tenancy will not take place and the attempt to leave the debt behind with an old supplier will fail and the debt collection process of the current supplier will continue. From the hold-out Debtor's point of view it is therefore imperative that whoever applies to be the named account holder with the new competitive supplier has an unblemished credit record and at a different address.

Offer to pay in instalments?

Any Creditor will always demand payment of any overdue account in full. As trained negotiators they will always start any negotiation at the top, that is asking for their best possible outcome, but they expect to work down from this. From the point of view of the utility, it can take up to a year from a customer moving in until they get to the point in their "Debt Path" where they can schedule a disconnection of a credit supply. If they are far down this path, they will not want to abandon this process and the investment of time and growth in the debt value outstanding that it took to get this far.

If the debt has only been outstanding for three months and if there has not been a First Visit by a Debt or Disconnection Representative, policy instructions to the utility Debt Collection Agent on telephone will allow them to negotiate.

But if a warrant of disconnection has been applied for and if the Debt Collection Representative turns up on the Debtor's doorstep armed with a warrant and accompanied by a locksmith and a gas engineer from National Grid, then short of the householder being able to provide proof of identity and residency just before the current date (showing they have just moved in and are not the Debtor who is being proceeded against for unpaid energy bills) only cash payment in full on the spot will deter them from disconnecting the supply and reconnecting with a prepayment meter.

The named Debtor at a given address

Being the named Debtor at an address means being intended as the person to whom bills are addressed at the property. The consumer may have given an alias. They may have given no date of birth or a false date of birth. If they give their true surname, they may not give a Christian name or possibly just an initial. The less personal data they give to the utility the greater their chances of being able to move out, becoming a *goneaway*, whom the utility cannot trace and therefore cannot pursue for payment. Someone choosing to enjoy credit under an alias without paying it back may well fall into the category of fraud if they are successfully later named under their true identity and successfully traced and contacted by the legal process – subject to the burden of proof being delivered by any prosecution that the use of the alias was a device to obtain credit which would not have been forthcoming under the Debtor's true identity.

Returning again to the Law of Large Numbers: the more successful the single alias or repeat aliases at the same postal address are in running up large amounts of debt perhaps to multiple suppliers, the more likely that the dull Leviathan of law enforcement will stir and invest the significant time, cost and resource allocation needed to secure a prosecution. Well in advance of this, however, the CIFAS system referred to earlier will flag the potential for credit fraud at a specific address which has been associated with a reported fraud in the past.

Named Debtor of a Utility

Energy suppliers operate in a competitive market. That means that with the consent of their customers who asked to be supplied by them they nominate a property as being "owned" by their energy brand. They are charged for the energy metered as being used at each property and make their profit by charging the consumer a margin on top of what they pay. When a customer whom they have been supplying moves out, the current supplier retains "ownership" of supply at that property until and unless a competitor tells them that they are taking over "ownership", by signing a supply contract with a new customer.

If a new customer moves into a property they will normally give their name to the existing supply company. They might call the existing supplier directly, or write to them, perhaps through opening a bill or letter addressed either to the previous tenant or to "The Occupier"; they may give their change of tenancy details to a meter reader calling for a routine read; or they may take a phone call from a Debt Collector chasing an account under the name of the previous tenant.

A named customer cannot use the tactics of "The Occupier" if there has been contact with the Utility either directly or through one of its agents. The utility has a customer in its sights and will pursue for contact and for payment. So what can the Hold-out named customer do to avoid paying their energy bill? One primary strategy is that of procrastination and delay.

Setting the terms of supply: quarterly payment in arrears

If a named customer is able to demonstrate a good previous credit history, they have every reason to expect to be offered a credit tariff for gas and electricity, although the utility will invariably want the customer to accept Direct Debit terms, and will offer a cheaper tariff to induce payment by this means. If a new customer finds a prepayment meter at an address they have just moved into, they can demand to have it removed – and if they pass the credit score required this will be done. If they threaten to move to competition and agree to sign a direct debit mandate, they should be able to negotiate prepayment meter removal.

The Perils of Paying by Direct Debit

Direct Debit is a very impractical payment method for an intending non-payer, but for someone not intending to pay it is better than having to live with a prepayment meter. All major utilities today have access to the AUDISS paperless direct debit system whereby they can take customer instructions over the phone and set up a direct debit without the customer having to sign anything.

Previously a customer could agree to signing a direct debit mandate which would have to be sent out to them by mail. This offered opportunities to claim it had not been received, or that it had been posted and returned, but had probably got lost. Traffic back and forth along these lines could easily take a month before the customer then decided that they weren't happy signing direct debit mandates after all.

Indeed there is no reason that they cannot demand that all contact between them and their supplier be by mail. Perhaps they have a hearing impairment? Perhaps they have learning difficulties? The devious and astute will note that giving a valid email address invites the utility to pester the customer by using email as a channel of communication, and giving a valid mobile phone number will mean the Debtor in future being exposed to picking up surprise debt calls. They will in other words, be determinedly and old-fashionedly incommunicado via these new-fangled technologies.

_____

"The reluctant customer can still insert delay and obfuscation by demanding to read the terms of the direct debit mandate which will need to be sent to them by mail..."

_____

A highly plausible reason for a reluctant payer to refuse direct debit is by having healthy caution in regard to the risk of incorrect amounts being direct debited, or indeed being surprised by a large direct debit which might put a bank account into overdraft, attracting bank charges. Although the utility script will promise instant redress under a Direct Debit Guarantee, ie that amounts objected to can be recalled or placed in suspension, the consumer can simply refuse on the basis that they still don't trust the system, or have had a previous unhappy experience and resultant delays and frustration in having it fixed, so they simply won't do it.

If under pressure ground needs to be given, the intending Debt Evader will offer instead to pay by Standing Order. Direct debit is variable at the behest of the utility, that means that they control how much is taken out of the customer's account, and in the event of a price rise they will normally automatically increase the Direct Debit instalment value each month. This is not the case with Standing Orders, for which the customer sets the instalment value. This instalment value can only be amended on the customer's instructions.

Utilities may state that they no longer support standing order as a payment method, but this simply a ruse to induce the customer to accept Direct Debit. Standing Orders need to be set up by the customer with their bank, and the bank will send a copy to the utility. This leaves the initiative to make any changes, or indeed not to set up the standing order in the first place, with the customer. The utility needs to calendarise reviews to assure that the standing order has been set up, and then chasing activity to remind and induce the customer to follow through. All of this buys time for the customer during which they continue to consume unpaid for energy.

The Joys of Quarterly Payment in Arrears

From the perspective of the intended debt evading consumer, Quarterly Payment in arrears is the default payment mechanism which they are entitled to retain by Regulation (if they are lucky enough to have moved into a property containing a "credit meter") and is therefore from their perspective the King of all the payment methods. It was the basic tariff for energy utilities prior to the introduction of Direct Debit and remains the primary payment method of choice which all energy utilities must offer by regulation. If there is no prepayment meter in a property for which a new customer requests a supply from an energy utility, the utility cannot prevent the customer from insisting on payment by this method.

So what are the benefits of quarterly payment terms from the perspective of the intending non-paying customer? Firstly, they can avoid giving the utility their real name and the utility simply has to accept any name they give, or leave the account as an occupier account. There have been many Donald Ducks and Mickey Mouses as utility customers – although giving such a clearly false name alerts the supplier immediately that a game of intended non-payment is afoot. The customer has the freedom as to whether they supply a full first, middle and second name, telephone and mobile numbers, email address – or not.

While the utility obviously will not like it, the less information the customer gives the harder it will be later to trace and collect later on, or indeed to prove that any customer in attendance at a disconnection warrant entry is truly the same one whom they have on account as "J Smith" or "Miss White". The utility may well demand a prepayment from a customer whom they do not feel confident in as a negotiated response to the customer's stated intention to pay quarterly by cash – but they are unable to immediately enforce their demand for a customer who has "moved in" to a premise which the utility has registered with National Grid as being "owned" by them.

No magistrate will grant a warrant for disconnection and reconnection by prepayment meter on the basis that a customer has not supplied adequate personal information or indeed failed a credit score. There is a presumption of willingness to pay, and the customer has the opportunity to demonstrate their willingness and ability to pay by their eventual performance. That means, they get the opportunity not to pay.

Whereas a failed Direct Debit will be a clear signal of non-payment after an interval of at least one full calendar month from set-up, quarterly payment means that no payment is due for at least one full quarter. The intending non-payer thus has a least an extra 8 weeks before the signal of failure to pay is given to the utility, and of course at this point the "Debt Path" is just beginning. Failure to pay on time by a credit tariff may not be sinister from the perspective of the supplier, since payment may well be forthcoming a little later with or without chasing.

> "No magistrate will grant a warrant for disconnection and reconnection by prepayment meter on the basis that a customer has not supplied adequate personal information or indeed failed a credit score."

The population of customers who do not pay a quarterly bill includes lots of "Always Payers" who are simply late for whatever reason and "Might Payers" who just need more emphatic reminding. The intending non-payer who is on a "quarterly in arrears" tariff is invisible to the utility at the end of the first quarter after which they have failed to pay, hidden among the eventual payers. This is much harder for the utility to address than those customers who have clearly failed to honour a monthly Direct Debit or failed to honour a Standing Order.

There are other devices which an intending non-payer can use to make themselves even less visible which will be discussed below, so that an intelligent intending non-payer can expect to be able to defer any real need to pay for energy at a property with an existing credit meter (non-prepayment meter) for at least a year before needing to attempt a Change of Tenancy or switch to a competitive supplier.

Failed Credit Scores and Unconfirmed Customers

At the point when the intending Debt Evader eventually makes contact with the utility, which may be some time after living as an undeclared occupier or indeed under a false persona, they may find that the utility is unwilling to abandon an existing process for disconnecting a credit meter at the customer's address and replacing it with a prepayment meter.

Any intending Debt Evader who wishes to appear to be cooperating and compliant at this point (in their guise as a "new customer") may feel constrained to to accept a credit scoring process in order to seek to remain supplied by their current utility supplier rather than going at this point to a new one. After all, the UK energy utility supplier range is limited: while shortly after the markets were opened up to competition for domestic gas and electricity there were up to 20 UK energy suppliers, competitive pressures in the market have reduced this list to under10. Hence it might make sense for the intending Debt Evader to hang in as long as they can under the current supplier before moving on to one of the remaining nine.

As discussed previously, credit bureau scoring is based round applicants' personal identities – people are individuated by their full names and dates of birth – and also by their postal address, both current and previous. The credit bureau seeks to identify an individual at a known address for which the bureau has a stream of shared information by a number of credit suppliers (credit card, bank, insurer, telecoms, etc) all of which allows a clear picture of the applicant's payment behaviour over time, and up to the present moment, to be established.

As it takes a number of months for credit behaviour at a new address to become evident, and none can exist on the day that a customer moves into a new address, the credit score may based on the previous address which will have the desired data associated with it – if the address is a UK address and if it is a true address and if the applicant has been credit active and is on the Registry of Voters at that address.

Named Customer at Confirmed Address for Non-utility debt

Nearly all other items for which credit can be given demand that there is a named individual at a confirmed address. In the case of an application for conditional credit, eg. for a credit card or telecoms payment contract, this will simply be rejected if the applicant cannot be recognised or indeed fails a credit score threshold, or if the address cannot be confirmed as valid.

Services provided at home such as building, gardening or maintenance, very obviously link the Debtor to an address. Often a contractor will demand at least half of any agreed price to be paid in advance, usually by credit card, with the balance being paid on completion. Given that such people are often sole traders or one man operators and that there is usually significant personal contact during performance of the home service, most consumers will pay on demand at the end of the job. Only in the event of the customer failing to accept the quality or completeness of the work to be performed will they normally refuse to pay. In such circumstances and if the dispute cannot be resolved by negotiation, the debt will usually be passed to a debt collection agency.

Each Debtor will make a calculation as to whether to capitulate and pay up, or whether to continue to resist payment. Are they satisfied with the good or service which has been provided? Has the supplier treated them courteously and fairly? Do they feel they need to pay from a moral perspective? Will their reputation and their ability to get more credit or services delivered suffer if they do not pay? Is it worth the effort of resistance given the likelihood of ultimate success in the light of the value outstanding?

If after considering these issues and still deciding not to pay, what tactics can a known Debtor at a known address employ to delay and if possible evade payment entirely?

Raise a Dispute?

Payment is due under the contract of sale when a good has been received or a service performed. But what if the good is defective or unsatisfactory, or the service is incomplete or the service provider has caused damage in carrying out the service? In the case of a retail good or item of clothing or equipment, the normal procedure for a supplier who is owed money is to replace the disputed item with a new one on the basis of return of the offending item. In addition, it is now rare for a seller to part with a good without having first secured payment either via *Paypal* or by credit card. Sellers who will release the keys of a motor car on the basis of a cheque rather than a bank draft are rarer than hens' teeth.

It is of course perfectly possible to dispute an item paid for by credit card, but this will simply result in the debit for the disputed purchase being placed in temporary suspense pending resolution of the dispute. There will again be an expectation that a defective item will be replaced, or the transaction cancelled and the disputed item returned to the seller. Repeated attempts by a credit card holder to use a disputes as a way to avoid payment will clearly result in an investigation, likely to conclude with withdrawal of the credit card and possible blacklisting of the "buyer" for attempted fraud. There is an old Jewish proverb: "*Shame on you if you cheat me once, shame on me if you cheat me twice*". Banks, credit card companies and other financial institutions can all be assumed to have learned this cardinal principle. They will always detect repeated attempts to defeat their processes and controls systems.

> "It is much easier for a putative buyer to dispute the provision of a service as the conditions for completion are so much more difficult to define"

It is much easier for a putative buyer to dispute the provision of a service as the conditions for completion are so much more difficult to define. A motor either runs or it does not, but in terms of service provision how clean is clean, and how tidy is tidy? Contracts for provision of services generally allow for credit provision of at least 50% of the expected cost, particularly for small building works, decorating, gardening and landscaping. As a matter of commercial common sense, even an intending payer in good faith would be very ill-advised to pay in full in advance of any service being provided. Once a service has been paid for in full, any claim for incomplete service provision or damage caused will rely almost entirely on the goodwill of the service provider if it is to be satisfied, the recourse to law being very cumbersome, expensive and uncertain for both parties.

Using Disputes as a reason not to pay

Examples of the kind of disputes which domestic consumers raise about service provision and which they might consider a reasonable basis for withholding at least some of the price due might include:

- *Oil leaks on driveway from contractor vehicles*

- *Damage to lawns, flowerbeds, equipment, buildings windows*

- *Painting having been done in the wrong colour or splashing other areas than those intended to be painted*

- *The wrong plants removed or cut down, or plants cut down too much*

- *Damage to carpets, leaks causing damage to ceilings and floors*

It goes without saying that such disputes can be invented by the "dissatisfied customer" as a figment of their imagination, and access refused to the contractor to make good based on statements by the consumer of "broken down relationship", " lack of trust" or "refusal to have anything more to do with the contractor". The consumer may allege that they have had to rectify whatever these faults were themselves and make their own determination of the cost. They may indeed feel entitled to withhold payment due to stress and nervous debilitation caused by faulty workmanship. In many cases natural justice might suggest that the buyer has some right on their side. In others the fact of any of the above alleged faults may be difficult or impossible to prove or disprove after the event when the contractor has left the property, but before the buyer has made payment in full.

Disputes over building contracts are particularly common, due to allegations that the wrong materials have been used, the quality of the work is shoddy, the wrong finish applied, the dimensions are wrong, the builder is unreliable or unacceptably behind schedule.

It is in summary not difficult for a wilful buyer to find reasons to withhold payment. Particularly in the case of small suppliers this inevitably leads to anger and bad feeling between the parties. An aggrieved supplier may be tempted to go to law if no resolution is achieved, particularly if the buyer attempts to withhold all and any payment from him. A magistrate will at that point look unkindly at any purchaser who has withheld payment entirely. However, a dispute is by definition a stand-off between parties and not usually sufficient grounds to dissolve any remaining contractual liability on the part of the Debtor to pay at least something or to allow the Seller and Creditor to attempt to make good. It is thus very often the precursor and lever (on the part of the Debtor) for a negotiation, which may make it possible for the Debtor to secure the benefit of the contract at improved terms compared to the original contract.

> "A magistrate will at that point look unkindly at any purchaser who has withheld payment entirely"

Reduced Offer in "Full and Final Settlement"?

Thus a buyer who is reluctant but also very prudent may find it more politic to make some offer of payment, particularly to a powerful seller. This can be done in terms of an "irresistible offer" by paying by cheque, writing on the back of the cheque *"in full and final settlement"*. It might be accompanied by a letter along the lines of: *"I was very dissatisfied with ... because... However I am prepared to pay you £X. Yours Sincerely."* If the seller cashes a cheque marked in this way, the Debtor can argue that it is tantamount to accepting the fact of any amended contract whereby this payment completes the contract and no more money is due. Obviously, photocopies of all correspondence and particularly the front and back of any cheque marked on the back as being *"in full and final settlement"*, need to be retained, just in case the Creditor were to come back and ask for more money later.

At this point he can be told that under common law, he has already accepted a payment in full and final settlement, that the Debtor has retained copies of the proof of this and that he has no longer any case to pursue, he having accepted the earlier payment. At the very least the Creditor will need to take time to consider the legal implications, which may cost him more money.

And if the Debtor is later able to produce an appropriately dated letter stating that the cheque must only be cashed on the basis of the offer being accepted which he *alleges to have sent with the cheque,* (although perhaps no such letter was ever sent as it might have warned the Creditor not to cash the cheque) who is to prove that such letter was not enclosed with the cheque and either lost or suppressed by the Creditor? The Debtor's case will be strengthened by being able to produce a recorded delivery certificate for the postage of the letter.

The magic figure to offer in a dispute

A payment offered in the psychologically magical value of 60% of what is alleged to be outstanding in any dispute will carry the persuasive weight that it is a significant amount of what the seller wants to receive, that it is available now for no extra cost, and that the matter can then be closed and he can move on. An offered payment of 30% or 40% on the other hand may appear derisory and insulting, proof that the buyer is acknowledging that there is a debt to be honoured, and an incentive to win the additional 60% or 70% that is not currently on offer. The offer of 60% says to the seller: "You have got most of what you want, why not take it now?" As with the old psychological ploy of showing a seller cash in hand when making an offer for less than they were expecting, the remittance of a cheque with the offer may make the difference between acceptance and refusal.

Most contractors will have had to deal with disputes in the past and will have a sense of how hard they should push for full settlement. Offering them nothing at all is very likely to create such a sense of grievance, loss of dignity and outrage that they may be very tempted to incur the cost of going to court even if it means that they will be out of pocket.

The virtue of moderation

Here we have touched upon a significant strand in the philosophy of the successful non-payer: that of moderation. Just as it is not tactically wise for an occupier intending not to pay to remain in a property for an excessive amount of time on the basis that what they owe will eventually become significant enough in the mind of suppliers to make enforcement worthwhile almost at any price, so it is often politic not to try to pay absolutely nothing, but to pay at least something in order to try to close out a liability.

This is specifically the case when the Debtor is fully known and easily traced by the buyer, or indeed if he is vulnerable to litigation by virtue of career employment or ownership of fixed equity in a property. On the other had we can forget the nostrums about good negotiation being about "win-win" situations. Rubbish! Someone always gets the better deal, and it is invariably the better strategist who thinks through their position before committing themselves. To conclude by quoting Sun Tzu from the *Art of War* again:

"A surrounded army must be given a way out... show them a way to life so that they will not be in the mood to fight to the death and then you can take advantage of this"

Billing errors?

Factual errors on bills and statements are very commonly used in the commercial world to justify non-payment. Such errors can include pricing mistakes, incorrect quantities, the wrong tariff or VAT rate being applied, or the incorrect customer name being on the invoice. Such errors can generally be rectified relatively quickly and so do no more than delay pursuit of payment. While credit controllers will commonly ask for undisputed elements of an invoice to be paid, the buyer can generally use an expression of outrage to refuse to pay anything until the entire bill has been paid. At this point they are not refusing to pay, simply insisting that they will only pay when proper form has been observed.

Dunning or debt chasing activity will generally be delayed until the correct invoice has been produced, and what buyer achieves is simply delay, but with skill they can generally use lettering by post office mail to buy time. Stratagems can include writing to the registered address of a company rather than to the supply address, in full knowledge and expectation that there will be a delay while the letter is relayed to the correct internal addressee within the company. Writing to the customer relations department generally touches a sensitive corporate nerve as does writing to the chief executive or chairman. While such correspondence is in progress the Debtor can fend off credit controllers by referring to the ongoing exchanges without revealing full details to them.

From the perspective of the unwilling payer, claims of billing errors form part of a more concerted campaign of non-payment, being a temporary defence from which they will fall back to some other. In doing so they will be conscious that the initial goodwill and credibility with which the supplier deals with their complaint, once it is resolved, will inevitably harden into suspicion and prioritisation for collection and enforcement if necessary.

Special Needs?

It is very easy for a customer to state that they need large print letters and that they have been unable to read any of the mail sent to them thus far. Any regulated business – utilities, phone companies, insurance, banks – will fall over themselves in their attempts to be seen to be complying with legal requirements to assist customers with special needs. A particularly difficult issue to deal with from the perspective of any customer is if they can express to their supplier that they have learning difficulties and cannot understand whatever correspondence has been sent to them. (Obviously their communication to the supplier will be singularly unpolished, at least in appearance.)

Anyone with learning difficulties can then adduce a need to find a special helper or agency with all the attendant delays that this can imply. The adviser can then write on their behalf expressing outrage and threats of referral to a relevant ombudsman, the Office of Fair Trading, or a regulator for alleged failure to treat a customer, of whom they have been advised of learning difficulties, with due care.

Customers who say they have mental problems such as depression or addiction or who can allege that they feel that they are at risk because of the pressure of debts upon them – and often it is much more effective for there to be a dark hint of being "at risk" rather than to baldly state an intention of self-harm which may be seen through – will ring very loud alarm bells at any large company which values its image and corporate reputation. A tabloid headline: *"Disabled pensioner hangs herself after repeated by harassment for debts by XYZ Ltd"* would be a nightmare for any company with a significant retail presence. There is a known correlation between unmanageable debt and suicide. At least one severely indebted consumer in ten contemplates suicide according to reputable surveys. Any association with suicide is naturally disastrously bad for business, and collectors are also horrified by the idea that they may be part of someone's suicide story. The attitude of most collectors at this point will be: " *This is not what I am paid to do, it's not what I signed up for.*" They will get off the phone as quickly as they can.

> "Customers who say they have mental problems such as depression or addiction or who can allege that they feel that they are at risk because of the pressure of debts upon them.. will ring loud alarm bells"

But there are other reasons why Creditors need to be very careful about extending credit to people with special needs, particularly those with mental health problems. *The Office of Fair Trading's* guidelines on irresponsible lending make it clear that lenders need to take reasonable account of mental health problems including bipolar disorder when extending credit to people who they know to be afflicted.

A Cheque for £20,000,000.00

Mr Johnson owed Bellevue Banque some £500 as an unsecured loan. Following contract out to a Debt Collection Agency and some persistent lettering and call attempts, all of which had been unanswered, Mr Johnson finally broke cover and sent in a cheque for £20M to the DCA. Their Head of Collections took one look at the cheque and closed the case as uncollectable on the grounds that Mr Johnson must be insane and that to grapple with someone obviously deranged would be bad for business.

Can't Pay?

Particularly at a time of economic hardship for consumers UK retail companies are all too well aware that there is a large and growing population of Can't-Pays, people who genuinely are no longer able to pay bills because they have lost jobs, perhaps lost entitlement to benefits, and who truly are at their wit's end as to how to cope. What more convincing reason not to pay a debt than to be able to truly state that one simply has not got the means to pay?

> "A genuine Can't pay will take calls from Creditors and will simply tell them that they have no means to pay and no prospects of being able to do so in the near future."

The analogy in nature might be with animals which advertise themselves to predators as having a bad taste. One such example is the *fire-bellied toad*. It has bright red and orange colouring to warn predators of its identity and the fact that it can ooze a foul-tasting, slightly poisonous foam if attacked. A Can't Pay does not need to hide, they go out of their way to advertise the fact that they are unappetising, and as a result predators leave them alone.

They will undoubtedly be asked to provide proof of this, but simple apathy will be enough to make unsecured Creditors prioritise richer fare. The true Can't pay will have many symptoms of despair and depression and the very gifted Hold-out will be able to think their way into this role on the telephone acquiring a strained voice, harsh breathing, abrupt sentences full of non-sequiturs and dark hints. They may also appeal to the humanity of the phone collector asking them *"What would you do in my situation?"* Any collector so callous as to continue to prompt for payment can be angrily dismissed with accusations of inhumanity, double-standards and being *"just like all the rest"*.

The intelligent chameleon "Can't pay" will make themselves a written script, just as the collector does, reminding themselves of the key points of their cover story – the collector will be looking for gaps, inconsistencies and self-contradictions to overturn the credibility of the story they are being told and to be able to break into an "Aha! Gotcha!" moment when they hope to demonstrate to the Debtor that their scheme has been penetrated, seen through and collapsed – and continue to parrot these repeatedly until the collector becomes tired and ends with their final threat of imminent enforcement.

For the "Can't Pay" at this point, a tired expression of resignation and acceptance of what may happen accompanied by a firm statement that they still won't be able to pay in any event, will be an effective closing. This may prompt the collector (who will in every case have to fill out a brief call report of customer contact on the customer computer record for other collectors to see) to be pessimistic about future collection prospects and thereby help to condition the collection effort to be abandoned. Being a Can't-pay is the best reason in the world from the point of the Creditor to abandon collection efforts.

> "Being a Can't-pay is the best reason in the world from the point of the Creditor to abandon collection efforts."

Creditors are all too aware that Can't-pays exist, they just need to convince themselves that an individual Debtor fits into this category. Persistent non-payment combined with contact acceptance and repeated assertions of inability to pay over a long period of time are a combination of factors they find most convincing – provided they receive no contradictory evidence such as CAIS data showing ongoing payment to other Creditors.

Obviously enough, furthermore, if the address at which the Debtor resides shows the Land Registry that they have title to the property either in terms of single or joint ownership, a plea of "can't pay" will not satisfy any Creditor who has paid the fee of £15 or so to access the Land Registry record, now available online. Demographic scoring of postcodes will enable the Creditor to take a view as to whether property in a particular postcode is likely to be housing authority rented, occupied by private owners or private rented accommodation. Search engines such as *Google Earth* enable a collector to access a satellite image of any UK property, sometimes to a sufficiently good level of quality that the make of car in a driveway can be ascertained. This information can add to lifestyle analysis data derived from shopper surveys of postcodes and ultimately from supermarket loyalty cards.

If a Debtor with equity in a property, in other words value owned by them which exceeds their proportion of any secured debt or mortgage in that property, is known to have such equity then a plea of "can't pay" will not hold, although it may buy the Debtor some time.

Ignore?

As for the previous item, if the Debtor is a property owner they cannot realistically ignore debt pursuit at an address owned by them for any length of time. They may or may not be able to do it if they are in the process of selling, but need to be aware that Credit Bureaux now offer members of their data sharing groups a service whereby they score addresses that are likely to be for sale, and even take data from estate agents.

However, ignoring a bill is a time-proven strategy for delay and is used very successfully by short term tenants who know that for utilities and most unsecured credit it will usually take around a year from date of billing for a consumer debt to get to the point of litigation. In-house collections debt paths for most consumer debts will last approximately two months, and each farmed out collections process (first, second and possibly third placements) will each last at least 3 months. Mobile phone companies are leading a trend to shorter in-house collections processes of less than one month, but the Debtor can still expect at least 6 months of a chasing process from external DCAs.

It needs to be continually re-emphasised that the longer that the collector receives absolutely no acknowledgement of receipt or echo of awareness, the more discouraged they will become, the more likely are they to switch their attention to more recent cases where at least they are getting some response.

> "It needs to be continually re-emphasised that the longer that the collector receives absolutely no acknowledgement of receipt or echo of awareness, the more discouraged they will become"

Particularly for a Debtor who knows for whatever reason that they have time on their side, appearing to ignore collectors completely is an ideal strategy from their perspective. Even better from the perspective of the Debtor is this costs nothing but cool nerve and calculation.

It is of course possible that a determined collector may decide to take legal action. This too can be dealt with and need not be a catastrophe for the reluctant payer. It will be discussed below.

Pretend to abscond?

It is a common stratagem for Debtors to pretend to have gone-away when they have not, and collectors are very well aware of the practice. They will use proprietary credit bureaux data sharing information (known as *CAIS* – Customer Account Information Sharing, by *Experian*, *Insight* by *Equifax*, and *Share* by *Callcredit*). Essentially these all use the same customer data provided by credit card companies, retailers, finance houses, banks, telecoms companies, insurers etc to match an individual by name and date of birth at a given address and to match also their recent credit history at that address, refreshing and reporting the data each month. Credit history at an address is very much akin to an electronic fingerprint giving strong indication that a subject is resident at that address.

The more credit relationships a Debtor has in terms of credit cards, mobile phone agreement, mortgage, bank account etc, the more data there is that will be reported each month to link them to a specific address (as well as indicating their continuing payment performance). It is therefore pointless and hopeless for a Debtor with multiple credit relationships at a given address to pretend to abscond while remaining in residence unless they give these all up at the same time as "absconding" and by stopping payment break the link to themselves at that address. This "all or nothing" strategy means that they will then have to contend with multiple collectors trying to locate them at their last known address.

The Hapless Camper

In September 2010 Weymouth resident Steve Morris was widely reported in the press as having lived in his shed for 12 months to avoid bailiffs who had fixed an eviction notice on the front window of his house and eventually changed the locks on his house, thinking it empty. Under pressure by phone, mail and attempted doorstep contact, he withdrew into his shed with just a microwave and a tv for company, sleeping under a worktop in order not to allow any light emission at night.This worked so well that he was unsuspected by his neighbours, who eventually called the police, believing he had disappeared.So pretend-absconding can be done successfully even in a semi-detached house with neighbours next door, even allowing for the accessibility to the garden that a semi-detached location provides for visitors to undertake a full inspection front and rear of the property. It is worth emphasising that he appears to have enjoyed the benefit of continued electricity supply for the whole year (to run his tv and microwave), showing yet again how slow and inefficient the utility disconnection process continues to be.

They are most likely to succeed in maintaining the fiction of their departure without trace (or traceability elsewhere) in cases where they live at a shared address in which they have no equity with a willing, committed and trustworthy collaborator. This might mean a property lived in by multiple tenants, including people sub-letting with or without the knowledge of the landlord.

Given the high cost of rentals in major cities in the UK which can amount to the entire after-tax income of a low paid manual worker, the only way in which many such people can survive economically is to share accommodation. Private landlords tend to be aware of this and turn a blind eye in the knowledge that they at least will get paid their rent (although wear and tear will be higher than normal) and if needs-be they can easily evict the named tenant for breaching a primary term of the lease, which is that the tenant may not sub-let.

This nether-world of sub-letting and multiple occupation is an insoluble nightmare for Creditors and indeed for the all-intrusive credit bureaux. Such people come and go with alarming frequency, they are often foreign with little or no local credit history and the use of aliases is very high.

Associated benefits of a live-in Lover

The other classic case where a Debtor can succeed in pretending to have gone away is that of the live-in lover. This happens frequently in both housing association and in private rented accommodation, and to the despair of the moneyed classes with mortgages, ordered lives and sharp-eyed spouses, such people have a tendency to change partners almost as often as they shop at the end of season sales. Live-in lovers or common-law spouses who do not have financial association with each other, ie they do not have mortgages in their joint names, or joint credit cards or hire purchase agreements, cannot be made responsible for each other's consumer debts. If the live-in lover has no credit agreements, is not on a voter's roll at a given address, and does not broadcast their domestic arrangements or even their real name to neighbours, post offices and pub landlords, then they are to all intents invisible and non-existent to the financial world.

They are like the wooden-framed canvas covered mosquito fighter planes of the World War II, invisible to enemy radar. Thus, a live-in lover who succeeds in acquiring lines of credit at their accommodation address can pretend to have gone away if their partner will maintain the fiction. This is normally done in response to a dunning or collections chasing letter by marking mail "no longer at this address" or "address not known" and returning it. If the live-in lover is still in residence this is of course a lie. They may be making themselves guilty of the crime of assisting another in the commission of a crime, but the balance of the burden of proof and the infinitesimally small risk of prosecution and conviction are in their favour

Note that in the case of gas and electricity, both the Gas and Electricity Acts state that all persons in a property who benefit from the energy supply are liable to pay for this supply, ie as *"deemed customers"*. For someone to state that the customer named on the electricity and gas bill has gone away without forwarding address will beg the question by the utility as to how long the person making this report has been resident at the address. The utility will then demand payment in full for the energy consumed since they admit (or can be proved by fact of credit applications or payment history at this address) to have resided there.

A very common way in which people pretend to abscond is to use a series of aliases. There is nothing illegal in using an alias *per se*, or indeed in changing one's name by deed poll. However, credit agreements are quite likely to have a clause requiring the applicant not to suppress material facts to the agreement, and if an applicant were to sign such an agreement and indeed suppress facts which might otherwise result in their credit application being refused if revealed, they would undoubtedly be guilty of application fraud. As stated earlier, this did not prevent fraudsters making around 60,000 known attempts at application fraud reported by CIFAS in 2009, of which 1 in 6 succeeded.

Really abscond?

As the story of Steve Morris , as reported above, demonstrates however, simply pretending to abscond in the absence of reinvention of oneself in an alias as a "new customer" is only a short term tactic. To stretch it to a year, he had to resort to considerable discomfort, and in the end, in the absence of any forward plan, he was discovered. So what happens in the event of sequential multiple alias use?

Noting that for the 270 major High Street retail lenders, retailers, insurance companies, telecoms companies and utilities who are members of CIFAS, the fraud prevention data sharing user group, any credit application linked to an address at which a fraud has previously been reported will be automatically flagged for rigorous vetting, it is unlikely that credit can continue to be obtained and not paid for at a given postcode address using a series of aliases. Quite quickly new credit applications will be refused at an address which has been previously linked to poor payment compliance; at an address where a fraud has been reported credit availability is likely to be even less.

> "Serial non-payers need to move on to new accommodation every six months to two years depending on their circumstances"

Hence, just as rolling stones gather no moss, so do serial non-payers find that they need to move on to new accommodation perhaps after 6 months to two years depending on their circumstances. It helps them greatly if they are living under short-term rental agreements, and indeed such people have a tendency to live lives which involve short term jobs and short term relationships as well as short term tenancies. This makes it easy to break out and move on. It may well be the need to find a new job, or the move away from a relationship that has become burdensome which prompts people in debt to move, just as much as any pursuit for an existing debt or desire to start afresh in a new location with new opportunities for seeking out credit at an address untainted by previous poor credit history.

10.0

Dealing with the Legal Process

WHAT'S IN THIS CHAPTER

Is the law fixed and immutable, or is the courtroom a Gigantic Gambling Casino? What strategies are available to a Debtor defendant? The statistics on numbers of summonses issued versus the incidence of monies actually being paid out make for revealing reading. Debtors who look to a defence of unenforceability or to a strategy of attacking the Creditor by counter-suing receive perspective on the realism of such gambits depending on their circumstances. Not least we also consider the options for "guerrilla warfare" and the significance of a county court judgement.

Dealing With The Legal Process

If I owe you a pound, I have a problem; but if I owe you a million, the problem is yours.
John Maynard Keynes

Keynes was a Nobel Prize winning economist, and what he meant with this quotation is that with regard to very large debts the lender has to take the question of repayment very seriously, the question being: can and will the borrower repay? But the first part of the quotation implies that the question of repayment for low value debts needs to be taken seriously by the Debtor. We might beg to disagree with the logic of this in the context of the decision as to whether a Creditor will use legal means to pursue the outstanding consumer Debtor. A Creditor will very certainly be prepared to resort to law to recover a million pounds, but realistically for less than £500 he is unlikely to be bothered to get out of bed, although his bluster might say otherwise.

> "Anyone owing low amounts of money to non-Government unsecured Creditors will virtually *never* be taken to court as a means of attempted recovery"

If I owe you a pound I really don't have a problem: you do. I simply don't need to repay you if I don't want to. You would have to spend much more than that to make me pay and it simply won't be worth it to you... Anyone owing low amounts of money to non-Government unsecured Creditors will virtually never be taken to court as a means of attempted recovery.

The Law in regard to *civil debt* is basically concerned with bringing two parties together to mutually accept the facts of the case and to lean on them to fulfil the contract that exists between them. The supplier, now become Creditor pursuing an unpaid debt, needs to demonstrate that they did have a legal contract with the Debtor which they the supplier have conscientiously fulfilled in terms of product or service quality, completeness and price demanded.

The Law expects that the Debtor will be brought to reasonably accept the fact of completion of his part of the contract by the supplier/Creditor and will therefore consent that it is right and proper that he the Debtor should now be willing also to complete his own side of the bargain, completing the contract by making payment. Thus there is an implied assumption of consent to the process by the Debtor. As we have seen, the Always-pays completely buy into the consent paradigm. If they are satisfied that the supplier has honoured his part of the contract, they consider it automatic that they must pay.

To deal with Might-pays, the Law fluffs up its leonine mane and is prepared to roar and look fearful and menacing. *Sheep* and *cattle* will always panic at the sight of a legal letter from a solicitor which threatens county court action. But as anyone who has been lucky enough to observe lions in the wild will know, *jackals* will not flee in panic at the approach of a *lion;* they will withdraw to a safe distance, observe and await events. Herbivores are creatures of the herd; they can be shepherded and corralled in mass numbers. Carnivores need to be opportunists, they are independent thinkers capable of reacting intelligently to events, or indeed orchestrating events to suit their purpose; panic is not part of their repertoire. So it is with the Hold-out or *jackal*.

The *lion* will not expend the effort to chase *jackals;* it knows it won't catch them. Yes, it will snarl and keep them off its kill, but both parties know that it is in the natural order that they keep a certain distance from each other. The *jackal* does not challenge the dominion of the *lion*, and the *lion* tolerates the *jackal* to subsist in its proximity because the effort to eradicate him, factored by the difficulty in catching him and the very limited real competition for resources that exists between them both mitigate towards effective toleration; so if there is a war between them, it is a phony one. This is the fertile territory for the strategy of: ***Jackal and Hide.***

"This is the fertile territory for the strategy of: *Jackal and Hide.*"

Basic Strategies for legal defence

Litigation Preparation for the Castle Dweller

If the Debtor is a castle dweller with a strong keep (equity in his property, if it is allowed to strain this metaphor) then he is certainly fixed for now in his circumstances. He will have access to cash by liquidating some of the equity if need be, but his opponent can easily assess probable equity. How? If the Creditor is a major retailer, bank, insurance company, utility or finance house, he certainly has access to credit bureau shared data and he can see if the Debtor is paying a mortgage and how much each month. He can find out who is on the deeds to the castle as titular owner, when the dweller bought it and for how much, by paying the online Land Registry Service around £15 as a search fee.

The military wisdom of Sun Tzu

The ancient Chinese military master strategist Sun Tzu suggests that it is best to be first on the battlefield because you can choose your ground; let the opponent come to you, rather than going to him; never fighting with your back to a river, instead covering your back with high ground. But first look to your own troops, equipment and resources: what are you capable of? Do you have the stomach for a protracted campaign? Are you indeed able to choose your ground or are your circumstances so fixed that you are prey to events and completely exposed to the moves of your opponent?

Staying on the internet, he can use *Google* to see a photograph of his house; he can use estate agency websites to see how much it is currently worth. With a combination of all of this information he can work out how much a house has appreciated by since purchase, subtract the approximate mortgage value based on the monthly repayment figure and calculate rough net equity. The mighty castle dweller is transparent to this type of Creditor. What can he do?

How does a solvent Debtor with equity in a property evade debt?

Remembering that any attempt to transfer assets when being actively pursued by Creditors will very probably be set aside by the courts, the castle-dweller with a strong keep can:

- Transfer assets to a spouse, then divorce, but before defaulting on any payments to Creditors.

- Transfer assets to a limited company, ideally with other trusted shareholders, again before defaulting on any payments to Creditors.

- Remove treasures from within the castle keep to a safe offshore location, if possible one with strong secrecy laws.

- Invest in and pay the premium for legal insurance in order to be able to afford any later legal attack strategy.

- Understand potential legal loopholes which may emerge at the outset of any legal agreement, eg re having an opportunity to read small print, being mis-sold payment protection insurance which is rolled up into the credit being granted; being given time to consider agreements before signing; being formally given a cooling off period during which the agreement may be cancelled; the APR being correctly calculated and quoted at the right places in the agreement as per the Consumer Credit Act

- Scrupulously keep records of all documentation received at the outset of any credit agreement and any subsequent correspondence.

Litigation Preparation for the Dweller of a "Crumbling Castle"

This Debtor has little or no equity in his property; no strong keep representing value which he can liquidate. In its way, this can of course be a strength, specifically in regard to unsecured Creditors such as credit card companies, utilities and retailers. What point in setting up an expensive siege to knock down the doors to an empty treasury, or at least one that will have been emptied by the secured Creditors such as mortgage holders before the unsecured Creditor can look to whatever small portion might be left?

Any Debtor with title to the property in which they dwell cannot easily afford to demonstrate ignorance of the communications of their Creditors. Certainly a Debtor with equity has good reason to fear a charge being placed on their property if they do not attempt to treat with their besiegers. In the case of a property owner with little or no equity, they will obviously prioritise payment of the secured Creditor, ie the mortgage holder: unless they are prepared to face the fairly certain consequence of an *Order for Sale* and eviction, they may well calculate that in circumstances where they cannot easily escape by simply leaving the property, they must capitulate to the secured Creditor.

Of course if the castle is entirely ruined in the sense of the owner occupier having negative equity, in other words owing the bank more than the property is worth, they may well choose at a point in time to simply walk away, leaving the keys to the secured Creditor. The debt will of course attempt to follow them unless they can either bankrupt themselves or successfully disappear, most effectively of all by moving abroad.

"The Hunter gatherer who has been prudent... has the simplest path"

With regard to unsecured Creditors, the dweller of the ruined castle who has a cool nerve may still choose to (appear to) entirely disregard them, but only in the sense of not communicating with them. He will do this calculating that when it comes time for them to decide to litigate against him, they will use the existing intelligence available to them from credit bureaux to give up on any prospect of litigation. He may at a later date choose to appear in person at a court hearing to offer a modest repayment plan; if he can make a case that he is indigent but willing to pay what he can; and if he can excite the sympathy of the magistrate in terms of his health, mental ability to deal with his situation or the existence of a dependent family, then a magistrate would likely be very loath to grant such an order for an unsecured debt.

Preparation of the Hunter Gatherer

The hunter gatherer who has been prudent enough not to disclose detailed identity and trace tags to their Creditors and maintained the flexibility to simply break camp and move on has the simplest path. Being elusive, grey and mobile, his preparation is to keep track of the communications of all of his Creditors, trying if possible to orchestrate and coordinate enforcement activity where he must by making late contact and attempting to fob enforcement off, eg by promises to pay or token payments, until he is ready to leave. As with the *jackal* timing its move away from the approaching *lion* or *hyena* the hunter gatherer will not be quickly or easily panicked or frightened into giving away his position or into defensive action including flight.

> "He will calculate at all times what it is costing the attacker and for what likely reward"

He will stand his ground against feint attacks, calculating at all times what it is costing the attacker and for what likely reward; he will be supremely accomplished in putting himself into the mind of his attacker, affording the Creditor enough or so little information as to influence his opponent's calculation to arrive at a conclusion that it is not worth continuing pursuit through litigation. In the event that a Creditor does maintain his pursuit to the relatively unlikely outcome of a CCJ, the hunter gatherer's very mobility in leaving the property and not allowing himself to be traced to his new address will mean that the CCJ will adhere to the old one. It will become less evident to a new credit granter that the John H Smith appearing at 15 Smith Street is the same Henry Smith against whom a judgement might be registered at 10 Acacia Avenue.

In similar vein, the hunter gatherer will take pains to avoid his Creditors knowing who his current employers are, thus frustrating any attempt to apply an *Attachment to Earnings* by way of enforcement attempt. Or he will change employer repeatedly to remain one jump ahead of the Creditor; equally he will use a different bank for his new wages should the Creditor have earlier been aware of bank details, such as having to be recorded on a credit application. As we have seen, hunter gatherers have jobs where castle dwellers are more likely to be fixed to careers and long term employment.

Pretend to ignore?

Appearing to ignore legal notices is something which a Castle dweller may consider ill-advised; however, it has been successfully used as a device initially up to the point of a *Judgment by Default*. At this point the Debtor can write to the court declaring that they had not previously received any court notices and asking for the judgement to be set aside. They may be asked to explain that they had been abroad or temporarily living elsewhere in a peripatetic capacity with no opportunity to have mail forwarded; they may have been ill or had a breakdown which rendered them temporarily incapable of dealing with their affairs. GP's, particularly young and female ones, tend to be idealistic and ready to side with a patient with a credible history of problems leading to mental incapacity. Often they can be prevailed upon to write a suitable letter to extenuate the behaviour of a cunning and dissembling Debtor.

To re-emphasise what has been said earlier on the subject of ignoring debt pursuit: the prudent Hold-out Debtor will never ever ignore what his Creditors are doing. The Might Pays may do it for a time until the worry of pursuit and enforcement becomes unbearable, and the Can't Pays whom he might wish to be counted among will ignore debt pursuit; the Hold-out will always know who is after him for what, when to expect the next step, and what he plans to do to combat it.

"...the prudent Hold-out Debtor will never ever ignore what his Creditors are doing."

Attack! Attack! Attack!

This is essentially the approach recommended by Stanley Hilton in his book *"To Pay or Not to Pay"* written for an American readership. Hilton recommends, as a lawyer who gets paid to represents Debtors in suits against their Creditors, that Debtors invest in getting their legal retaliation in first. They can do this by finding loopholes in the credit granting process, whereby the Debtor has perhaps not been accorded his full rights under consumer law. For a Debtor with deep pockets, steely nerves and a positive appetite for vertiginous risk this approach may recommend itself. Smart lawyers may indeed have ways of turning up flaws in the execution of credit granting and collections processes, and indeed of ingratiating their client with a sympathetic judge.

Experience in UK courts shows that it can, however, be ruinously expensive to attack with full-on litigation. It is easy to spend well over £25,000 just in getting to court in a defended case, and with absolutely no assurance of winning. As Mr Hilton fairly concedes: " *A courtroom is nothing more than a sophisticated gambling casino".*

What would Sun Tzu recommend? The tenor of all of his strategic wisdom is actually very strongly against engaging in unmeasured and unnecessary risk.

Of course it is entirely possible that the Creditor's suit is flawed, that the *elephant* has a massive limp. Thus, a pragmatic approach in the UK context might be for the Debtor who thinks they sense some flaw in the arguments of the Creditor – and we must really expect that large retailers and finance houses will have usually have learned and systematised their processes to avoid the repeat of earlier process mistakes – to contact the *Citizens Advice Bureau* (*CAB*) or other debt charity. Volunteers here are very well trained in the basics of consumer and debt law, sufficient to give a good sense of whether a Debtor may or may not have been so badly handled by a Creditor that they might successfully pursue compensation.

If so, the involvement of the *CAB* in the case should be sufficient to achieve by their representation of the client vis a vis the Creditor some significant amelioration in the amount of debt for which they are being pursued. Foolish the Creditor who would choose to go to court in a case supported by the *CAB* for the Debtor. On the other side, the CAB will not support what they would regard as cavalier behaviour of refusal to pay a debt which is legally due if it can be seen that the Debtor is solvent and perfectly able to pay.

Websites such as *www.consumeractiongroup.co.uk* from time to time contain threads or blogs which suggest conditionally admitting liability to pay a given debt but subject to proofs of various statutes being adhered to including *Unfair Trading, Irresponsible Lending, Consumer Credit Act* etc. Any Debtor who feels inclined to adopt full-frontal confrontation with a Creditor in the glare of the court's power can check out these strategies for themselves. But he had better be prepared to account for his own behaviour. He might ask himself: would any sane *jackal* start an argument with a *hyena* to be presided over by a *lion*?

Debt Unenforceable under the Consumer Credit Act?

Lord Bingham summarised the problems with enforcing against a difficult judgment Debtor as follows: 'As many a claimant has learned to his cost, it is one thing to recover a favourable judgment; it may prove quite another to enforce it against an unscrupulous defendant. But an unenforceable judgment is at best valueless, at worst a source of additional loss.' (Société Eram Shipping Co Ltd v Cie Internationale de Navigation [2003] UKHL)

A complete cottage, or better, slum industry has grown up in the UK with the advent of Claims Management Companies (CMC's). Some 200 of these companies out of a peak population of around 3000 were said to have been disbarred by licence withdrawal by the Office of Fair Trading (OFT) in 2009. Many CMC's charged up to £500 simply to "review" a debt case, whereas any of the debt charities such as Citizens Advice Bureau (CAB), CCCS or National Debtline would have done this to a professionally reliable standard and for free. CMC's purport to find loopholes under section 77 to 79 of the Consumer Credit Act 1974, specifically demanding to see a "true copy" of an original credit agreement within twelve days of asking and upon the payment of a £1 fee. Starting with a judgement given in October 2009 by the High Court in the Case of BRS vs McGuffick, the courts have been showing their displeasure at claimants alleging that a contract might be void because a debt was "unenforceable" under the Consumer Credit Act.

The Office of Fair Trading has given a comprehensive clarification of the relative rights and responsibilities of Creditors and Debtors in terms of the enforceability of debt under the Consumer Credit Act, and this can be easily found on a web browser to provide full detail. At the heart of the issue of enforceability is the ability of the Creditor, or whoever now owns the original debt, to provide a "true copy" of the relevant agreement; notably this does not require that the true copy be an exact photocopy nor need it have the signature of the Debtor upon it. It is sufficient for the agreement to be reconstituted containing all the relevant terms which apply to the original agreement. This appears to allow some leeway for a Creditor to allege that an agreement was signed and executed when in fact it was not, but the wording of the OFT on this point is arguably preachy, woolly and unhelpful!

Logically, therefore, it might appear that the way forward for a consumer who alleges that they never signed a document would not be to state that it was unenforceable, but that there was never any agreement or contract and that they have no relationship with the would-be Creditor. The circumstance in which this might very well occur would be if the alleged Debtor's name and details had been used fraudulently by a third party as part of an identity theft fraud. However, the debt-refusee might have to be able to stand up to some pretty robust cross-questioning in court to defend this position, and would want to be aware of the significant criminal penalties for lying to the court. If it were to be shown that they had benefited personally from events, say by proof that monies from the alleged Creditor had passed through their bank accounts, they would surely be standing on very insecure ground.

What remaining advantages are there to alleged unenforceablity?

If an agreement is shown to be void, as if the Debtor had never incurred any liability, this is possibly the best outcome: they can notify Credit Reference Agencies (CRA's) to correct their credit record by deleting any negative information which would impact future ability to secure more credit. What if the agreement did exist in law, but is declared by the courts to be "unenforceable" , ie in circumstances where the Creditor or his successor to whom he has sold a debt is unable to provide the definition of a true copy of the agreement defined by the Consumer Credit Act and clarified by the OFT?

Well, it does then appear to be true that the Creditor will be unable to obtain a *county court judgement* or an *enforcement order*, so that the Debtor really won't have to pay. However, the contract for the debt remains valid, so the Creditor is entitled to report the Debtor's account as being in default, damaging their credit status with the CRA's. One benefit the unenforceability does confer, should the Debtor be prepared to go all the way to County Court with the risks of additional cost awards against him, is time, perhaps up to a year.

Conclusion on the Attack-Defence Strategy

The specific attack-defence that a Debtor was mentally incapacitated at the time of credit granting and that the Creditor would or should have been aware of this and therefore was guilty of irresponsible lending would seem to be one of the more fruitful of these possible defences in the UK. But on the whole, a reliance on attack as a means of defence without encouragement by the CAB or other debt counselling charity that the Debtor may have a valid case appears to this writer to be unlikely to yield great rewards other than perhaps a delay before an even more vigorous onslaught by a Creditor encouraged both by the fact of engagement by the Debtor, and by the paucity of the arguments being brought to bear as an excuse for non-payment.

Guerrilla War?

If our ancient military Chinese master strategist Sun Tzu had been a Hold-out Debtor we can be confident that this is the path he would have taken to avoid payment. The basic tactic is of delay, seemingly ignoring all communications only to later claim not to have received them, to frequently change address in order to be impossible to serve court papers upon; to make last minute token offers of payment or even to appear suddenly in court having just made up some payments; to attempt to negotiate or accept a repayment regime in court, only to break the repayment plan shortly thereafter... In sum it is to wear down the determination of the Creditor, all the while adding to his costs in the calculation that he will eventually give up. If the value at stake is small, say less than £1000, this is much more likely to succeed. Tactics include:

1) Making use of the *Human Rights Act* to require that any court hearing is relocated to a court convenient to the Debtor. This can be done by simply writing to the court in question. It is particularly useful when confronted by a summons which has been mass produced at *Northampton Bulk Issuing Centre*. It forces the Creditor to come to a court inconveniently located for him, and at extra cost.

2) Notifying the court that the Defendant means to appear to represent himself followed by a last minute request to the court for a re-scheduling due to the defendant's illness in a defended case. Most family doctors will easily be persuaded to write a note certifying that the Debtor was unwell and unfit to attend court.

3) Involvement of a Debt charity to assist the production and endorse the veracity of a *Common Financial Statement* (CFS) by the Debtor, showing the ability to pay only a very limited monthly sum of say £5.00. This will be supported by an offer to pay such a sum. The magistrate is very likely to accept such an offer, thereby freezing payments at this rate for the future, and excluding the rolling up of any additional interest or fees which the Creditor might otherwise seek to add to the debt.

4) Subsequent missing of payments, prompting a return to court, with payments resuming shortly before the court date, and an explanation of new difficulties being made to the court when it eventually sits.

5) Absconding: the party piece of the hunter gatherer

6) Part-settlement. Most guerrillas eventually come in from the cold in the

real world. A settlement in which you win most of what you want in order to stop the war is still an outcome very much worth having. This applies particularly to Castle-dwellers and those with fixed roots in their homestead.

Capitulate?

The Won't Pay who is now feeling worn down to a Might Pay could try offering a lump sum payment to the Creditor even during or after litigation in full and final settlement. An offer of even 10% of the sum outstanding at this stage, again supported by a plausible story as to why no further payments can be expected, may be enough to persuade the exhausted Creditor to settle. The money may have been an unexpected small lottery win or horse race win. It will never be the proceeds of a new job, otherwise the Creditor will naturally demand more to be paid over time.

The reasons why no more money can be expected might typically include family breakup, terminal illness, redundancy and unemployment. Sometimes these reasons are true and can be milked or exaggerated; at other times they are simply a fabrication. But if an offer is accompanied by a cheque marked "in full and final settlement"; if it is sent by recorded delivery and copies kept; if it is sent shortly before the Creditor's year end when he will be struggling to meet annual collection targets – then it might well work.

Of course capitulation could always be payment in full of all arrears plus any rolled up fees. That is down to the choice, the energy and the appetite of the Debtor for settlement as opposed to continued withholding of cash which he might feel sits more comfortably in his own pocket.

"Who's afraid of a CCJ?"

It has commonly been said in the "credit industry" that the only significant *County Court judgement* (CCJ) imposed on a Debtor is the first one; one CCJ will undoubtedly stain a credit record enough since, after allowing one CCJ to be

"...such has been the spread of data-sharing access across retail that poor payment performance alone is today likely to be enough to condemn any credit application by a named and confirmed poor payer..."

inflicted on him, a Debtor will be ruined in terms of future credit, so why would they care about a few more CCJ's obtained by other Creditors? A CCJ is in the so-called public domain, so that credit granting organisations who are not in data-sharing groups such as CAIS will still have the benefit of the CCJ to impact the credit score, securely weighting it down to drown in the sludge of rejected applications.

However, such has been the spread of data-sharing access across retail that poor payment performance alone is today likely to be enough to condemn any credit application by a named and confirmed poor payer of credit cards, hire purchase agreements etc to rejection of any new credit application. The CCJ is therefore now arguably redundant for this purpose.

CCJ's as a Numbers Game

Yet approximately 2,000,000 summonses are issued each year in England and Wales, approximately 80% of which are for the recovery of debt. Half of all money claims are processed "in bulk" via *Northampton County Court Bulk Issuing Centre*. In the sphere of the County Court the Pareto law holds true yet again: only 14% of summonses end up in court to be defended. Approximately 1,000,000 cases or 50% of all summonses proceed to *judgement by default*, ie the Debtor does not respond to or defend the Summons, thereby making an effective admission of liability by their lack of challenge and giving the plaintiff the right to seek to enforce the judgement. But by their non-appearance they also leave a massive doubt in the mind of the litigant as to whether they can be located at their last known address and enforced against.

This might help to explain why only around 10% or around 100,000 of judgements against individual consumers are "satisfied", ie paid so that the litigant Creditor gets his money. Thus by inference: of around 2,000,000 summonses issued by Creditors each year in England and Wales just 5%, that means 1 in 20, end up "satisfied". Even if we assume that all of those judgments cancelled were paid in full (which they are not since the reported statistics include those cancelled because they were made in error or set aside because

> "...large numbers of Creditors give up after issuing a summons."

of some legal objection by the defendant) this would add just another 2% or 3%: ie at best roughly 13% of summonses can be seen to end up with the Debtor paying off the Debt to "satisfy" the judgment.

From the point of view of a gambling Debtor, how good does a game look where 87% of the time the Creditor issues a Summons against him which turns out to be completely ineffectual? But we have not yet considered what happens to the 50% of summonses which do not get as far as the stage of judgement. The answer is that a small number – perhaps 1 in 10 of the 50%, or 5% or the initial summons population – will undoubtedly pay on summons. These are the Might-pays who have had enough: they did not think that the Creditor would pursue them all the way to litigation and now they believe that he will see it through to the end, and knowing that they have vulnerable assets, or are simply worn doubt with fear and guilt, they pay.

So let us revise our estimation and suggest that total payers from the initial summons population rise to 18% paying. The other side of this coin, though, is that in that vast gambling casino which is the county court enforcement process, large numbers of Creditors give up after issuing a summons. Like the bluffer in a

> "...But before we get too tied up in the mathematics of this discussion let us simply conclude by stating that the odds of a Creditor firstly suing and then secondly getting paid are slim..."

poker game, they pay some initial stake, a final desperate throw of £85 (at time of writing) for a last blustering threat – which they cannot afford to follow up.

Thus, with a roughly 82% probability of not being paid as they issue a summons, this calculation looks terrible from the Creditor's perspective, but it gets worse. One very large British energy utility only can afford in terms of its historical budget to litigate against 5% of its "Delinquent Final Debt" customers, in other words, customers who have left the property where they had a contract with the "large British Energy utility" and are known to be at another address where they have resisted blandishments to pay. Can it be possible that such utility customers have an average chance of 5% x 18% = 0.9% of being taken to court and having money squeezed out of them? But before we get too tied up in the mathematics of this discussion let us simply conclude by stating that the odds of a Creditor firstly suing and then secondly getting paid are slim.

The costs of County Court Litigation to the Creditor

The average value of a County Court Judgement in England is around £2000. Costs to reclaim this can of course be added to the value of the debt being pursued and recovered from the Debtor – in the very small number of cases where debts are actually satisfied! Up to the point of payment the Creditor is simply adding to his problem by quite literally throwing good money after bad. Costs to pursue a £2000 Debt will be as follows according to Her Majesty's Court Service Leaflet EX50 on Court Fees as at time of writing:

Civil Court Fee:	*£85*
Hearing Fee	*£100*
Application for a Warrant of Execution	*£55*
Bailiff fee for unsuccessful enforcement visit	*£60*
Cost at risk prior to bailiff collection:	*£300*

Any rational Creditor – and this includes the flinty-hearted finance directors of large utilities, retailers and financial institutions who have to justify salaries in excess of £500,000 per annum – is going to think twice or three times before spending another £300 on a debt of £2000 which has taken well over a year to get to court since first becoming "delinquent", during which time the Debtor has shown all the persistence of the Hold-out, a true *"Jackal and Hide"*. Add to this the time having to be spent in the Creditor's Collections and Legal Departments, time spent briefing solicitors and the solicitor's fees. This will double the average cost at risk from £300 to £600 on an average debt of £2000. The costs become astronomical, unaffordable, crazy... It is a mug's game.

The county court process is thus a watershed event for both the Creditor and the Debtor. Costs are incurred, certainly for the Creditor, but potentially also for the Can Pay Debtor. It is a poker game in which the faint hearted, and those who know they hold poor hands will throw in their chips. Has the Hold-out done enough to convince the Creditor that he has a winning hand?

To turn the tables on the Clint Eastwood figure in the now rather dated *"Dirty Harry"* movie: *" Do YOU feel lucky, Punk?"* This question is now one for the pursuer rather than the pursued. But it is only the Hold-out *jackal* who keeps his nerve. The Might-Pay *goat* has by now panicked and paid more or less on behalf of the Hold-out; after all the costs of litigation and bad debts has to be recouped by retailers and utilities from those who do pay. The *jackal* thus eats from the flesh of the *goat*, although he has had no part in killing it!

Yes of course, the successful Plaintiff who has won his case can apply for an order to obtain information from a judgement Debtor (what used to be known as an *Oral Examination*) for a fee of a further £45, for example to find out if and where they are employed or what assets they may have. But does the now rather subdued "winner" of the court process really believe that by the time the Debtor is obliged to show up in court they will have left their assets available for easy collection? Or that they will continue to stay for any length of time in an employment which they may be forced to disclose? **"Is the Debtor behaving like a *sheep* or like a *jackal,* are we confident to proceed, or had we better give up now?"** Thus the cost of £65 to apply for an Attachment of Earnings is probably more money which will see no return.

> "The Emperor's clothes are at best so skimpy and threadbare that they would disgrace the modesty of a Bangkok Ladyboy."

One ends up wondering why large companies even bother to litigate – and there is one very large water company in England which is known not to, despite what its debt dunning letters might state. At this point we are yet again back with Simone Weil from the first pages of our opus: *"pour encourager les autres"*, large Creditors with a significant stake in the economy need to be seen to engage in a certain amount of litigation to enable them to continue to trade and make profits.

They therefore engage in token litigation to put the fear of God and of the *Lion of the Law* into the hearts of the Might-Pays lest they ever infect the Always Pays with any cavalier ideas about the need to be seen to pay: *"The payment of debts is necessary for social order".* Let it be said quietly: the Emperor's clothes are at best so skimpy and threadbare that they would disgrace the modesty of a Bangkok Ladyboy. The Hold-out knows this, and it is best for him that the Might-pays don't, because if everybody thought the same way the Creditor/Debtor ecosystem would break down. Shhh!

So in practice, many Creditors who pursue a case as far as Judgment, give up at this point. They have made their point in the sense that the CCJ will attach to the name of the Debtor at his last known address and he will be unable to gain more credit from that address and with that name. Those Creditors who do go the whole way do so only based on very sound intelligence: they use further behavioural scoring applications to determine if a given Debtor fits the profile of others who have paid after Judgement has been achieved. The Hold-out has already taken great pains not to look anything like this profile. So who's afraid of a CCJ now?

High Court Proceedings

Almost by definition the type of Debtor who will find his case appearing for hearing in the High Court will be a Castle Dweller, someone with sufficient standing to have been able to incur credit of excess of £5000 as an individual debt. However, so-called Regulated credit agreements under the *Consumer Credit Act 1974*, which usually means instalment credit agreements whatever their value, are always heard initially at County Court level and will only proceed to the High Court on appeal.

"...the defending Debtor will need to have very deep pockets and a strong belief in his case if he is to proceed"

While the types of evasive defences already described would apply to Debtors who might fall under the remit of the High Court, if things have got this far it is likely that the Debtor is "on the hook". The Creditor will know where he resides and have confidence from his own intelligence that the Debtor has the means to pay. He will be living in fixed circumstances and will inevitably have had to engage a lawyer who will explore in detail any of the possible legal wrinkles in terms of particular statutes which may have been breached by the other side in his particular case.

With lawyers involved in both sides, serious legal costs can be expected to be incurred – possibly £50,000 for both sides, with the loser having these costs awarded against them. As lawyers will inevitably require to be paid while the case develops, and again this can take a year to get to court, the defending Debtor will need to have very deep pockets and a strong belief in his case if he is to proceed. The matter now comes down to the legal rights and wrongs of the case as they can be proven in court and the Debtor is now locked in a cage with the *lion* and various *hyenas*. He had better not be a *jackal* at this point, but a big enough beast in his own right to put up a stiff fight by hiring a barrister-*hyena* of his own.

CCJ Removal

Commercial agencies offer to remove county court judgements on payment of a fee, and may like to suggest that a Debtor's record can be simply "cleaned up", so that they can start to take credit again with no public domain history on record of previous defaults. An intelligent Hold-out will recognise such agencies as simply more poisonously rabid *vampire bats* intent on sucking out his vital juices without delivering very much in return. In fact it is possible to challenge CCJ's under limited conditions, as follows:

1) If a Debtor can demonstrate that they were unaware of a hearing, having been incommunicado due perhaps to hospitalisation or being abroad travelling, they may well succeed in having a court set aside a judgement.

2) If the Debtor can demonstrate that they did not receive a *default notice* from the Creditor, 21 days in advance of a court hearing, again they can apply for the CCJ to be set aside.

3) If they can allege mistaken identity or identity fraud, then again they can ask for set-aside. In this case, they would state that someone else had used their name and possibly their address to gain credit; however, the burden of proof may lie with the alleged Debtor eg, to demonstrate that a signature on an agreement was not their signature.

Where a CCJ has been made on a Debtor for a proven debt other than for the above exceptions, it is in fact only possible to have it removed by paying up and then paying the court a £10 fee for a certificate of satisfaction which can be sent to the credit reference agencies along with a request to have it removed from the individual's credit record.

11.0

Defying the Physical Siege

> **WHAT'S IN THIS CHAPTER**
>
> Collection agents may appear in various guises, but with subtly differing objectives and powers to achieve these. What options does the Hold-out Debtor have in dealing with a Doorstep Collector? The roles and powers of bailiffs, Utility Debt Representatives or Disconnection Agents and Doorstep collectors are summmarised.

Defying the Siege

One of the threats most feared by Debtors – and which debt collectors play on by exaggerating the probability of this ever happening – is the knock on the door. There are three very different individuals who might call:

- Doorstep Collection Agents

- Bailiffs

- Gas and Electricity Disconnection Agents

More on Dealing with Doorstep Collection Agents

"Doorstep collectors will try to time their visits to accord with when the subject may be expected to be at home"

Debt Collection Agencies and Debt Purchase Companies will virtually never at their own expense engage a Doorstep Collection Agent to visit a Debtor in an attempt to collect. On the rare occasion when such an Agent is engaged, he or she is paid for by the Principal directly. This is because it is expensive and hit-and-miss to visit non-compliant Debtors at their homes. Doorstep Collectors are always self-employed and unlike DCA's generally do not work on a commission basis. They are usually paid a base fee of at least £25 for each customer they visit and may also gain some commission in the event that the customer pays. (The reason for the base fee is that customers very rarely pay and it would be uneconomic for them to work on a commission only basis). So they are paid for simply turning up at an address, and sometimes in stages they receive additional fixed fees if they can make contact, obtain a forwarding address or get information from neighbours.

Doorstep collectors may work a fixed neighbourhood if it is in a densely populated area, but they frequently have to travel many miles from home to a distant Debtor. In such cases they try to amass a number of accounts to call on which are close together and which make it cost-justifiable for them to travel so far. Their clients usually ask them to make at least three contact attempts including daytime, evening and weekend. Depending on the known circumstances of the Debtor, whether a parent with a school-run to attend to, a shift-worker, or someone working nine to five, they will try to time their visits to accord with when the subject may be expected to be at home.

Fortunately for the Hold-out Debtor, Doorstep Collectors usually do not visit each Debtor address three times, simply because it is too costly for them, despite what their contract states. Some even resort to using the phone to avoid visiting at all and can be treated to all intents and purposes like another DCA.

"Doorstep Collectors have absolutely no power to force entry, no right to seize or constrain goods, have no powers of arrest or any legal power whatever"

Doorstep Debt Collectors are not the same as Neighbourhood Lenders, who routinely visit every other house in a run-down city street each payday evening to collect £10 and £20 loan repayments. They may also work as bailiffs, who will be discussed separately, but in terms of their role as Doorstep Collectors, they have no powers beyond those of a DCA, ie to ask a Debtor to open their door to discuss payment of an alleged debt.

Doorstep Collectors have absolutely no power to force entry, no right to seize or constrain goods, have no powers of arrest or any legal power whatever. The Debtor is not obliged to open their door to a Doorstep Collector, nor to talk to them. They cannot prevent the Collector from perhaps taking a photograph of their house or flat (to prove attendance to their Principal who pays their fixed fee) or from attempting to talk to them through a letterbox.

Given the cost of engaging a Doorstep Collector, this is only likely to happen in

Refusing engagement with Doorstep Collectors

For a would-be Hold-out Debtor to engage with a Doorstep Collector simply creates exposure to a confrontation and to making themselves available prey. Best from the perspective of the Debtor who does not intend to pay to simply ignore the door-knocking and to be "not at home", and even if confronted by a Collector waiting on a doorstep, to simply step past them and close the door. There is nothing to be gained from rudeness to anyone acting in a collections capacity.

the case of a large unsecured debt which the Principal believes that the Debtor is likely to pay without being forced into court. This might be because the Principal has information that the Debtor is asset and cash rich and that it would be easy to enforce a judgement in the event of successful court action. But in that case why would they not simply proceed directly to initiating court action by issuing a summons?

In summary then, a DCA will not engage a Doorstep Collector as they may end up paying him for a fruitless visit and simply add cost to a zero commission for failed collection. A principal will probably not want to fund this either. In those cases where the debt value and the Debtor's perceived ability to pay might merit committed pursuit, their interests would invariably be better served by court action.

Bailiffs

Bailiff avoidance is discussed in **Part Two.**

Disconnection Agents

These are also discussed under in Part Two, in this case under **Gas.** If armed with a warrant which they must show to the Debtor they do have a legal right of entry and will be supported by the police in this if necessary.

12.0

Flitting

WHAT'S IN THIS CHAPTER

What are the signals for the Hold-out Debtor that it is time to move on? He will plan his move carefully to avoid pursuit and detection, working out which destination will provide the best combination of escape, security, rapid acclimatisation and opportunities for future prosperity and wellbeing. Awareness of how pursuit will take place will be of assistance to him in making his arrangements. The idea of living abroad will have very strong attractions for a number of reasons. But the stories of two very contrasting escapees, one current and one from long ago, illustrate the dangers to the Hold-out of under-estimated risks and becoming complacent, but also the success that boldness and ingenuity can deliver.

Flitting

"Afore ye go"

The intelligent Hold-out Debtor will be aware of the level of pursuit which they are receiving from various sources, and will be keeping records of correspondence from Creditors. If they intend to leave their place of accommodation to avoid Creditors, they need to decide what trigger event might prompt the move; how to be ready, when to go; how to make the move; and where to go. For the first of these decisions, they are helped in that credit industry believes that it is best practice to tell the Debtor what will happen next if they do not pay so there should be plenty of clues. However, as we have seen, much of what Creditors warn of is bluff and bluster and need not have any significant impact on the decision when or if to go. The following statements will not worry the Hold-out unduly as he can read between the lines as to what they really mean:

"We will pass this account to a debt collection agency to collect" :

"You've beaten us so far with your intransigence, and we hope that the DCA will be more effective than we are, so you can expect more letters and calls from a different source who is driven entirely by trying to get easy money. Given that we keep reducing the commission we pay these agents, they aren't going to keep throwing good money after bad if they see no signs of you acknowledging them or allowing them to have contact. We will not be surprised if they can't collect either, so you are well on your way to getting away without paying".

"We will ask one of our doorstep agents to visit you to discuss payment"

"This is most likely just a bluff on our part because it is so expensive for us and we usually can't afford the expense unless you have given us reason to hope that a doorstep call might prompt payment, but we hope that it will scare you and worry you anyway about the potential embarrassment of neighbours finding out that debt collectors are on your trail. If a collector does call, we know you probably won't open your door to talk to him and he certainly cannot force his way into your property or take any goods. But we are relying on your ignorance and hoping you will now be panicked into contacting us."

"We will pass this account to our Legal Department/Solicitor for action"

If the debt being pursued by the Creditor is has been secured, typically a mortgage loan against a property, then clearly such a warning is no idle threat. In such a case the dunning letter warning of this sanction will usually be quite specific, for example about action being taken to repossess the asset. Debtors do quit properties under threat of repossession and disappear, but generally only where there is negative equity, ie the debt outstanding to the mortgage lender exceeds the likely sale value. Where there is real equity still in the property, ie after sale, including costs of sale and legal costs incurred by the lender there would still be money left over when the mortgage was paid off from the proceeds for the Debtor, then there would be no economic incentive for the Debtor to leave the property early.

Where the debt outstanding is not secured, then a single instance of pending legal action would not normally comprise a sufficient threat to incentivise a Debtor to leave their property to avoid it, even if it meant a County Court judgement and ensuing bailiff action were inevitable. Most threats of legal action are mere threats and not followed up on. See also the section below on the Process.

Other threats do need to be taken more seriously.

"This is a warrant of disconnection for your energy supply"

Again, a warrant of disconnection will at worst involve a prepayment meter being installed which will consume up to 40% of any cash paid into the prepayment system against outstanding debt, giving only 60 pence of energy for every £1 paid in. If there has been as yet undetected theft of gas or abstraction of electricity, either by manipulating or by-passing meter, then a disconnection of the existing meter and reconnection of a prepayment meter will very probably reveal this.

For many Hold-out Debtors, the installation of a prepayment meter might well be a sufficient trigger to make it economically worthwhile to leave property, particularly if other debts have mounted up at the address and there are now a number of county court judgments on record. This might particularly be the case for people who are flat dwellers, with few possessions to encumber them – the proverbial rolling stones gathering no moss – no children at local schools or other networks tying them into a specific area.

"This is an order for sale on your property"

Assuming that this is a genuine court document, it does need to be taken extremely seriously. If a *charging order* has already been granted as the result of a court judgement, then the order for sale is very likely to succeed. Eviction will almost inevitably follow and it only remains for the Debtor to decide whether to wait this out; or if they are unlikely to receive any equity balance in cash after the sale, because there is no equity in the property, they may choose to disappear anonymously in order to avoid future pursuit; there will doubtless be other Debtors in addition to the charge holder who is forcing the sale.

Each Hold-out will decide for themselves what the trigger to move will be, depending on their individual circumstances, the number and value of debts they are trying to evade, the degree of pressure they perceive, considerations for family and friends, and not least opportunities which may present themselves to move on, all of which combine to suggest: " Now the time to go approaches".

"Having obtained a judgement against you we have appointed a bailiff who will clamp your car and may sell it if you continue not to pay the amount outstanding plus all fees"

As with the enquiry on "how to get to Cork from here", this is not a good place to start from. Bailiffs will indeed clamp cars and may have them removed and sold. However, this tactic is always carried out by surprise if a Creditor has gone to the expense and trouble of obtaining a judgement. They are unlikely to warn a Debtor that he needs to take care to hide his car for fear of it being clamped or towed away, hence a Debtor who has been notified of an *Enforcement Order* being granted against him by the court as a follow-up to failure to pay on County Court Judgement had better look out.

Making the Move

If the Goneaway is prepared to break the link with schools, jobs and temporarily at least with friends and relatives by moving further away, they will have a better chance of remaining undetected and thus avoiding continued pursuit by their Creditors. This may enable them to reinvent themselves and to gain new lines of credit and start a new cycle of debt build-up and avoidance. If they are able to move not just to a new district but to a new country, they have every chance of escaping all their Creditors entirely – particularly Government in the form of HMRC, DWP and Child Support Agency.

Key Considerations for the flitter

There are some key objectives for the Debtor involved in "doing a flit". Firstly, there needs to be a significant consideration or value at stake to justify the cost and upset. This may mean holding off certain Creditors for a period of time until the Debtor is ready, perhaps entering into repayment agreements and making some instalment payments. There needs to be a destination which is convenient yet secure. The credit industry is very aware that most movers remain within just a three mile radius of their point of departure – to be convenient for schools, ongoing jobs and networks of friends and relatives. This can make it easy for Creditors to trace the gone-away.

Hunter gatherers can find new anonymous lives in the tourist industries within the EU, where they will be able to maintain many of their benefits such as health care; or they can move outside the EU to places like Turkey, Cyprus and the Far East. Fortress dwellers can buy new property and lifestyles in the same places, but taking note of the fact that Credit Bureaux such as Experian do trade in numerous different countries, and that cross-border legal enforcement within the EU is only likely to increase.

If assets are to be sold, this will be done quietly. Creditors are increasingly alert to the risk of Debtors absconding and not only do they employ scorecards to predict possible flitters, which may pre-empt attempts to gain charging orders, they can also contribute to intelligence services provided by the credit bureaux from large estate agents as to which properties are on sale, using computer based matching with their database of Debtors to highlight anyone who may be about to sell-up their Mighty Castle.

"Neighbours and schools will not be told of an impending move and family, friends and certainly children will also be kept in the dark"

Mighty Castle dwellers who are able to keep up instalments on their debts prior to the point of departure may not attract so much attention as those whose payment record has been intermittent. After all, moving house is a perfectly legitimate and common thing to do, and the Always-pays provide the cover under which the intended long-day fraud perpetrator can disguise their intentions.

Houses of those in debt and under pursuit already will be sold privately or using small local agents. Neighbours and schools will not be told of an impending move and family, friends and certainly children will also be kept in the dark as to the details of a new destination. Indeed any information given outside the closest coterie of trusted family and chosen associates may be active disinformation to put later pursuers off the track.

After the Move

Creditors trying to trace and chase the Goneaway will be relying on the hope that if he remains in the UK, he will make fresh credit applications under his existing name and date of birth. He will try to ensure that none of his family applies for new credit agreements, particularly for catalogue debt for house fittings, carpets and curtains at the new abode. Not least this will be because there will very likely be a "financial association" recorded by the credit bureaux between himself and other members of his family, so that any credit activity by them may lead to a search for him at their current address.

He may instead use a new alias and even seek a new national insurance number as part of the re-invention process. There are around 77 million National Insurance (NI) numbers in the UK which has a population of just 49,000,000 adults, and government admits detecting around 500 people using false NI numbers each year. The number they do not detect is by definition unknown... More likely the arrived Goneaway will try to live at a new address as an "occupier", not announcing his arrival to the local council for council tax purposes or indeed to the utilities. He may be able to start a new credit/debt cycle all over again.

How the most wanted man in England disappeared

In 1667 a notorious outlaw and renegade against the settlement of King Charles II, the self-styled Colonel Thomas Blood - shortly to become even more famous as "the man who stole the Crown Jewels", having kept moving around in Ireland, Scotland, Holland and England during a series of quasi-terrorist assaults upon the crown and its servants – ambushed a prisoner escort near Doncaster to free one of his associates being taken to York Assizes for trial and certain execution. He did this before reappearing three years later to kidnap his old enemy from Ireland, the Duke of Ormonde, erstwhile Lord Lieutenant of Ireland, at Piccadilly in the very heart of London.

Despite being wanted for reward throughout the kingdom and being disadvantaged in terms of being easily recognisable for his oversized thumb and large nose, not to mention a wife and 6 children in train, Blood managed to reinvent himself and live under the nose of the law. Changing his name to Dr Allen he set himself up as a medical apothecary in Romford in Essex just 14 miles from London, living an apparently quiet life and increasing the number of his brood while tending satisfactorily to the medical needs of his neighbours. This was a man whose prior knowledge of medicine will have been gained from tending his animals on his estates in Ireland.

What has Colonel Blood – described as "the Seventeenth Century's most wanted man" to instruct us on about being a successful gone-away for debt? Well, while not primarily on the run for this reason, he is nonetheless a classic case study of the characteristics of people who can successfully defy the conventions of society and the Law for years. Blood was bold, completely unpredictable as to what he would do next and where, he was brave to the point of a recklessness which was his undoing through a poorly planned escape from the Martin Tower in the Tower of London where the Crown Jewels were held; creative and discreet in managing to continually reinvent himself and live anonymously for years as a wanted man, completely unsuspected by his neighbours; loyal to the point of death to his associates who repaid him in kind helping to support and protect him and maintain his anonymity; quick-witted, charming and credible to the degree that he was able to negotiate a pardon and re-award of his estates in Ireland and a pension for life from his bemused sovereign , the Merry Monarch Charles II.

The modern gone-away by contrast, does not need to fear for his life if caught. But he does need to be able to find a new job and new accommodation. He will not be able to provide references for either without betraying his new location, and so will likely invent these, using accommodation addresses and false histories to be supported by trusted associates pretending to be previous landlords or employers.

Anyone trying to avoid unwanted contact with a Creditor will be wise not to be on a mobile phone contract, let alone have a landline in their name. Mobile phone companies are all highly sophisticated and advanced in their memberships of anti-fraud networks such as CIFAS and the Gone Away Information Network (GAIN) and are active contributors to online payment performance data sharing programmes run by the credit bureaux. They share "white" data - payment performance, name and address data for customers paying for their contract in full and on time- as well as "black" data (information about poor payment performance) with other members.

Using Pay as you go Mobiles

Anyone with a contract phone who pays on time to maintain a clean credit record with their mobile phone company or indeed with any other major retailer or credit provider) will still have their data shared with other members seeking to trace them. So instead of a contract phone, the intelligent goneaway will buy a pay-as-you go phone at a supermarket or computer or stationery store, topping it up with cash when required.

This way their phone remains for ever anonymous and they can take it with them and use it at their new location with impunity – provided that they have not used it previously to contact their pursuers. Increasingly the flitter needs to consider the possibility of geo-positioning technology being used to pinpoint their new whereabouts. Currently this facility is used by the police in serious crime cases. Tomorrow it may be a commonplace trace tool.

It makes life easier for tracers if the Goneaway has an unusual name. A common name such as that of the archetypal "John Smith" is a real headache by contrast. Simple aliases can be used for it such as Jo, Johnny, Johnnie, Jack, Jackie, any of which can be used by a Goneaway even supported by existing id under the name of John Smith and likely to be accepted by new Creditors. If forced to continue under an existing id, the re-emerging Goneaway can refuse to supply their date of birth as a matter of personal privacy, this being particularly credible in the case of women. However, in the case of an unmarried couple, often the id of only one will be used at a new address, with the other being used next time so that the primary recent Debtor always fails to appear as a live credit applicant.

Creditors will actively search for Goneaways usually for no longer than three to six months, and will usually write the debt off at the end of a year after they close the account with no contact. At this point active pursuit is over. For higher value untraced debts, however, some Creditors may be willing to pay the credit bureaux for an ongoing alert even several years after the original account closure due to customer disappearance. But this is unusual as most Creditors are unwilling to commit to an ongoing spend on a written off debt on the basis that it is likely to amount to quite literally throwing good money after bad.

Starting over

At the point of arrival in a new property, the Hold-out has metamorphosed into Goneaway in terms of his account status at his old address as discussed above; but he has also become a "new tenant" at his new address with all the choices this brings as to who he is, when or if he decides to make himself known to utilities as a new customer at this new address, and if so, what starting meter reads he will declare. If he declares himself in his old *id* and applies for new credit, he will not only fail to obtain it based on poor payment performance at the old address, but draw attention to himself as an absconding Debtor at the new address.

If he applies for conditional credit in an unknown alias, he will by definition have no positive credit history and he is likely to either fail new credit checks or only gain very limited credit. He may have to resign himself to living in the cash economy without a bank account and jobbing for cash in the black economy. Or he may rely on another associate or relative using their credit and banking facilities on his behalf. Or he may invent a new identity.

> "The surest way to escape all one's Creditors is to move abroad"

The Big Flit – Going Foreign

The surest way to escape all one's Creditors is to move abroad. While it is theoretically possible for Creditors to pursue the Debtor abroad - and this is probably easiest in developed Commonwealth countries such as Canada and Australia, or in Eire – for a UK Creditor to contemplate the costs of tracing an absconder abroad, get to grips with a foreign legal system and deal with foreign untried lawyers to enforce a claim, is a potential nightmare. If the sums involved are eye-watering, then obviously they would swallow hard and look at their options.

But for sums of £5000 to £20000 even to go to court in a defended action in UK is a large and uncertain step. Creditors may pass a trace/collect case to a foreign or international debt agency, but these collectors too are generally paid on commission. They may buy a debt for single pence in the pound, but they are unlikely to commit any of their own funds to litigation unless they have a clear view of the Debtor's assets.

By definition, anyone who has successfully disengaged from the UK and moved to another country is mobile; having moved once they can move again. If found the Debtor will be subjected to the usual heavy bombardment of threats, but in the EU if he denies or disputes the claim in a statement to a court, the Creditor will be unable to enforce a *"European Payment Order"*, needing to resort to the local country's home legal enforcement process.

The least attractive territories for Creditor to choose to pursue a Debtor will be those with connotations of international pariah status, eg Northern Cyprus, Iran, or parts of South America. Distant holiday melting pots such as Thailand, or Turkey or Morocco, outside the EU, will also be beyond the view and the reach of nearly all Creditors.

What do long-run flitters do to disguise themselves and secure their tenure at their new destination? If entitled to another passport, perhaps an Irish or Indian one, they will apply for it before leaving and use this on their travels. Although it may be mandatory to register arrival at destination, as it is still everywhere in Germany, they will not do it. They may choose to make a marriage of convenience and to take the name of their spouse.

If they take a job working for a friend abroad, say in a café or a boat hire business, they will be off the payroll. They will avoid having large amounts of money in a local bank account, choosing where possible to bank in a third country, eg they may live in France but bank in Luxemburg; or they may place their money in the account of a (very trusted) friend or lover; or have property in the name of their local foreign spouse and manage their lifestyle so that they have no personal assets to attack.

"Cross-border data sharing between Creditors has not been systematised as yet by the credit bureaux"

Cross-border data sharing between Creditors has not been systematised as yet by the credit bureaux, so an application for credit in a foreign country should not require UK credit history to be divulged. Thus it should be possible for an absconder to start again with a clean sheet in the new country.

In order to make as clean a break as possible and depending on the level of pursuit they expect , the intelligent absconder may break all links with his old existence, including networks of acquaintances and use of old email addresses. They will not return to the UK to live for at least five years, and even if they do return, they will not bring assets back with them.

As the case below shows, however, it is another matter entirely if one disappears because one is guilty of a crime and wanted by the law. Avoiding a civil debt in a foreign jurisdiction is regarded by the authorities in quite a different light to being suspected of a criminal offence, in which case extradition to the country of origin is a racing certainty.

A Case History in Nearly Disappearing very well: John Darwin

By definition, it is not readily possible to cite a case of someone who has succeeded in becoming an absconder or Goneaway. For one thing they cannot advertise the fact since it would nullify all the work they had done to disappear. In the words of the joke: "*I can't tell you how I did it or I would have to kill you!*" (to maintain the secrecy). Secondly, in the case of people like Lord Lucan, suspected of murdering the family nanny and disappearing to avoid the consequences, the very reason for their successful vanishing act could be that it is real and not an act. Lucan may have killed himself by drowning so that there is nothing to learn from his story. If he did not kill himself, he would have much to tell us, which we will never learn because he must keep his anonymity intact.

In 2007 John Darwin, previously presumed dead, also (first clue) by drowning, turned up alive and well in Panama. He had been "dead" since 2002 as part of a fraud designed to relieve the pressure of unsustainable debts incurred in purchasing buy-to-let flats. The fraud worked to the extent that insurance policies on his life which he had taken out with the intent of committing fraud did pay out after his disappearance, even though he was alleged to have drowned as an experienced kayaker in perfectly calm seas.

He was caught after a picture of him was found by " a member of the public" and forwarded to the *Daily Mirror* and the Police. It turned out that Mr Darwin had lived in a secret bedsit, reminiscent of a 17th Century Priest's Hole at his house in Hartlepool for three years before making the move to Panama. Apparently, as someone used to the outdoors he became extremely agitated over time at being cooped up and took to nocturnal wanderings in the streets around his home, even being recognised by an acquaintance who, luckily for him at the time, did not report him.

Darwin had been a maths teacher, then worked for a time for Barclays Bank , next as a prison warder, then trying to get rich by buy-to-let property speculation. These occupations may seem quite unconnected and indicative of someone struggling to find their path in life. But they obviously provided a school for a budding fraudster and insurance scammer. The maths teacher Darwin was calculative, introspective, able to formulate plans and strategies. The prison warder also must have had much time to ponder, especially on the crimes of inmates and how they could be better committed. No doubt he had illuminating conversations with the wards he was guarding. Finally, the stint in Barclays Bank will have added some insider information on fraud, finance and money laundering techniques.

"Darwin was undoubtedly successful for quite a while, evincing some real criminal 'talent' "

Here Darwin was growing from egg to caterpillar. His disappearance and self-inflicted incarceration may be compared to a pupae phase; while his emergence in Panama and collaboration with a programme on reinvention in Panama was the fatal butterfly stage.

Darwin was undoubtedly successful for quite a while, evincing some real criminal "talent". He could count on the loyalty and discretion of his wife, and not least on her resilience and ability to play her designated role as grieving widow and accomplice in crime. He built his secret home hideaway, unsuspected by the world. He cultivated his kayaking hobby as an eventual vehicle for a credible disappearance.

He took out life insurance policies with the intention of disappearing to enable his wife to fraudulently claim on them. He even managed to acquire a passport under the name "John Jones" (note the use of a very common surname) by using the identity of a deceased baby born in Durham around the same time as his own birth, itself a criminal offence, but one which went completely undetected. He chose a suitably obscure hideaway in selecting Panama as his long-term hideaway.

But he made disastrous mistakes also, which led to his downfall. He firstly overestimated his own ability to continue to live quietly in the hidden bedsit and committed the first fatal error – which amazingly went unreported – of being recognised in the street. Boredom and frustration would contribute again to his downfall. Hadn't he learned to cope with these in those long hours as a prison warden?

The move to Panama without his wife was well planned in the first instance, but the loneliness of separation became a great strain for them both. In addition, the money she came into must have been a source of speculation and envy among her neighbours. The bust is reported to have come when an acquaintance became suspicious of her financial transactions when she decided to emigrate to Panama, and suspected her of emigrating to be with her husband. (Who ever emigrates to Panama from the UK?) This could have been avoided if she had sold up ostensibly to make a new life for herself by renting a property in another UK city for a while, avoiding her new neighbours and leaving behind the network of curious old ones.

> "He must have been a very gaudy British butterfly set against a drably exotic background in Panama"

She could have then started a new life with a new bank as an unknown. Perhaps she might have rented a home in France for a few months and then joined her partner in crime. Meanwhile Darwin's frustration, alone in Panama, vented itself in his having an extra-marital affair. This too was a disastrous error, as someone in the triangle was always likely to be angry, disappointed, potentially vengeful.

Then the utter hubris – the fatal tragic flaw of classic tragedy, but in this case perhaps more farce than tragedy since no one actually died – latent in Darwin's character showed itself, when the aggrandising dream seen earlier in his failed bed-sit speculation reappeared quite literally with his participation in a video showing people how to move to Panama, with him figuring as a prospective hotel owner. He must have been a very gaudy British butterfly set against a drably exotic background in Panama, conspicuous and very easy to spot as being out of place. This was deeply unintelligent behaviour for someone supposedly trying to escape detection.

One wonders if some part of him wanted to be identified as "the failure who succeeded." If so, his calculative abilities had betrayed him again. Perhaps he had not been such a great maths teacher either, explaining why he left the profession?

So in conclusion in our examination of this fascinating fraudulent disappearance, it is plain that aside from all meticulous planning, if the absconding plan itself is flawed it will likely fail. If the absconder does not possess the supreme attributes mentioned earlier as those of the successful Hold-out; and if they do violate some of the key Does's and Doesn'ts (*"doesn't let neighbours know what he is doing"; "doesn't betray those close to him"*) then small wonder that this nearly clever fraud, for reportedly just over £160k, ultimately failed.

But when John Darwin was released from jail not all the money was recovered... perhaps it was worth in then?

13.0

Dealing with Government

WHAT'S IN THIS CHAPTER

While it is important to stress that it is widely illegal not to comply with requests for payment from Government agencies, the fact is that many of these are actually very inefficient at collecting revenues and enforcing their will despite the draconian powers they possess. Government appears to be a very strong creditor at first glance but is in fact beset by a number of significant weaknesses which suggest that its collection efficiency may decline over the next years. Notably if Government can no longer afford to send recalcitrant Debtors to prison its credibility as a Creditor is likely to be greatly diminished.

Dealing with Government

The Mighty Lion

Playing Ducks and Drakes with commercial or retail Creditors is one thing, but governments insist on being taken seriously, so much so that they reserve for themselves the very toughest deterrents for non-compliance, including loss of driving licence, loss of passport, and jail. The very premise of parliamentary democratic government is that the citizen hands over taxes in order that government will spend them wisely for the benefit of the population as a whole. As the early American revolutionaries put it in the 1760's: "*No taxation without representation*", the corollary being that if you pay taxes you should get at least some of what you want from the government.

The UK Government is strongly of the opinion that it does provide adequate representation as a consideration for the taxation it imposes and therefore is quite insistent on fiscal rectitude and propriety on the part of its citizens. It does not take lightly the refusal to acknowledge or to pay debts; indeed to demonstrate to the world's financial markets that we are not like the Greeks, that we are creditworthy in the international bond market and that the National Debt can be safely added to by further foreign loans. It cannot afford to.

The Principle of Consent (on Government's terms…)

In a parliamentary democracy, there is a least a pretence that the citizen has a real influence on how much tax they are charged and what the proceeds are spent on. Yet recent widespread cuts in government spending and increases in effective taxation (eg by withdrawal of benefits) arguably have been dictated more by the international financial markets than by the citizen.

Dodging Tram fares in East Germany

In the Worker's Free Democratic Republic of East Germany (an oxymoron of ambitions if ever there was one) trams were the simplest way of getting around the inner cities as very few people were "free" enough to possess a car. These trams were plastered with signs saying: "If you don't pay your tram fares, you are cheating yourselves!"

The logic was that as everything in a communist "democracy" (which was in theory "ruled by the people" but in reality the fief of a few hundred "Bonzen"{privileged few}) belonged to the people, why would the people try to cheat it? Alas the very necessity of putting up such signs demonstrated that there was in fact a significant problem of fare-dodging against the government owned and run tramways systems. Could it be that some human beings are simply hardwired to dodge Creditors including governments everywhere?

But unilateral proposals by government to arbitrarily cut the rate at which pensions and benefits will be increased to allow for inflation, show yet again in recent history that in fact an elective dictatorship determines what benefits and costs the citizen faces in the UK. The UK Government recently announced that private occupational Pension schemes which had been paid into by savers over a career lifetime (on the basis that they would be increased in line with increases in the consumer price index which measures inflation) were to be made retrospectively eligible to be changed by Company pension providers to provide lower benefits based on a new lower inflation

"Governments also find ways not to pay..."

increase mechanism.

The Retail Price Index measure of pension cost inflation was to be set aside to allow use of the Consumer Price Index. In this way private pensions, which were contracted for by employer and employee tens of years previously, and were completely unfunded by Government would become worth much less, perhaps a third less at the end of a pensioner's life as the value of the pension was gradually eaten away by real inflation. In this way Government thought that it could more easily make public sector employess accept the loss of their own inflation proofing mechanisms. This was not in any manifesto, the electorate was not given the opportunity to vote on it. Governments too find ways not to pay...

To reprise the earlier theme of the morality of payment or non-payment by a Debtor to whichever Creditor: perceived unfairness surely strains the principle of consent, whereby the citizen is supposed to cheerfully and cooperatively hand over taxes, to a government he knows is doing the "right thing".

When the number of public servants earning over £200,000 per annum is shown to be in the hundreds, obscene salaries much higher than this continue to be paid by the BBC, funded by the licences of the poor, and the money is spent by the billions in pointless wars , why would the taxpayer who sees their own covenant with Government broken by that Government not waver in terms of their own continued consent to pay?

> When money is spent by the billions in pointless wars, why would the taxpayer who sees their own covenant with Government broken by Government not waver in terms of their own continued consent to pay?

The Thatcher government was demoralised and effectively broken by the widespread citizen revolt against the Poll Tax in the 1980's. The Hold-out Debtor is not politically motivated, however and he certainly does not want to become part of a general wave of payment refusal. As Simone Weil intimated, if everyone tried not to pay, the economic system would collapse, engulfing the Hold-out also. The Hold-out only can succeed if he is in a very small and unnoticed minority, supported in macro-economic terms by the behaviour of all those who do pay. Can he succeed against mighty Government?

The Increasing Strengths of Government Collections

We have already described how Government has the severest punishments of all rapacious Creditors for wilful evasion of payment. Allied to this is its increasing adoption (twenty or thirty years behind the retail and financial services industries) of data sharing applications developed by the credit reference agencies in tandem with its primary customers. Government muscles into the data-feast like the worthy British *Lion* chasing away *leopards* from their kill.

Government now takes all the data feeds it can, but like the *lion* it dominates and shares with no one. This is as it should be under the Data Protection Act, for while consumers of credit everywhere have universally consented to data sharing by the retailers that provide the credit, they have not had the opportunity to be asked by government whether they might agree if their benefit claims history or tax arrears details may be shared with third parties in the credit industry.

"Government has the severest punishments of all rapacious Creditors for wilful evasion of payment."

Debtors everywhere should be heaving a sigh of relief, because the dataset which the Government possesses on all its citizens is of truly terrifyingly Orwellian proportions. The Taxman expects by right to know who our employer is, where we bank, what our current address is. If we refuse to supply this information we may be guilty of tax evasion, which is a criminal offence, carrying a jail sentence. The retail credit industry has no such rights, however, but would be delighted to receive the information from government as it would make tasks such as tracing, furnishing *garnishee orders* and *attachments to earnings* so much easier.

From retail and commerce government is fast learning how to apply scoring and predictiveness algorithms using vast amounts of data on the known attributes of known "pays" and "no pays" to identify which of its Debtors it is most likely to be able to squeeze successfully for payment. The most recent wheeze has been to propose identifying spending patterns from those on benefits to determine if claimants have been living a spending lifestyle inconsistent with being on benefits. At first glance this may appear terrifying – but perhaps only to the guileless who are unaware that they have already signed up for their data to be shared in this way when they applied for retail credit.

In addition to adopting data sharing practices from the private sector, government is now sharing data between its various agencies. The DVLA can identify addresses of registered keepers of cars from the registration plate; like HMRC it has a massive register of names linked to dates of birth and addresses. Anyone who legally owns a car or is legally employed is known to these agencies and their data is available to any other government agency. Moreover, HMRC data on income can be shared by other Government agencies to determine ability to pay, details of income producing assets, identity of employer, bank details and telephone numbers.

The TV licensing agency has a database of millions of names, addresses, telephone and mobile numbers as does the Department of Work and Pensions. Government has the right to access more data linking Debtors to addresses and assets than any other Creditor. They are also recruiting people from the private sector with debt management and collection skills to use these assets to improve government collection performance. It is therefore reasonable to assume that overall the efficiency of Government in collecting debt will improve, particularly in extracting money from the Might-pays, including some who were convinced that they were born Hold-outs.

The Ongoing Weaknesses of Government as a Debt Collector

And yet , and yet... HMRC was recently reported as needing to write off £1.5bn debt older than two years and to have a backlog of 7,500,000 cases dating back three years. This difficulty no doubt prepared the low moral ground for their policy decision to seek credit card payments where available from tax Debtors, thus pushing people into a position of exchanging an interest free debt for a credit card debt which will cost the Debtor interest.

Government's weaknesses in terms of collections ability are in fact many, grave and set to increase. The determined and intelligent Hold-out still has many aces to play in the evolving game. Start with the fact that many Government Agencies appear to merit contempt.

How Top UK Civil Servants Live it up on Taxpayers' Money

Government Money collecting agencies are top-heavy with would-be Napoleons who live in eye-wateringly expensive accommodation in the most desirable Office Parks in the country, able to pick their own personal office furniture suites which can cost into six figures, ensconced several days each week in a conference room far from their home office, planning a tomorrow that never comes.

These armchair generals spend taxpayers' money, jetting up and down the country several times a week in business class or travelling First Class by train and being put up in smart inner city boutique hotels. They have largely never collected a cent from a customer in their lives themselves.

Let us look a little closer, for example, at the *Child Support Agency*. In 2007 it either collected or **arranged** (i.e. didn't actually collect but claimed credit anyway) £883M at a cost of £520M In other words: **It costs 59p for the CSA to collect £1 of child maintenance!** If this sounds shockingly inefficient it should be remembered is that this is the overall cost, ie including debt that is easy to collect from the "Always Pays" who pay from day one by direct debit and never miss a payment. Collecting debt from those who really don't want to pay must therefore cost more than the debt itself. To be plain: for hard to collect debt, it therefore costs the CSA more than £1 to collect £1.

This cannot be sustainable in a climate of cuts and the need to demonstrate value for money. Would it not be cheaper as a use of taxpayer funds to merely accept the money from those who volunteer to pay, then simply pay the maintenance owed by non-payers directly from CSA funds, using cash saved from largely abandoning debt collection and paying off most of their collectors?

To be plain: for hard to collect debt, it therefore costs the CSA more than £1 to collect £1.

A survey showed that 50% of collectors in one government agency hated the work they had to do, asking people who they felt could not afford it for money; these people did not want to confront Debtors on the phone. Government debt collectors are demoralised. To quote Machiavelli from *The Prince*: *"There is nothing a prince must avoid more than at once being disdained and hated"*.

The next weakness that government has to contend with is that of economic weakness. If government is to cut spending by 20% then less people will need to do more work, or alternatively less work will get done. Those people will have to contribute more to their pensions and will be expected by government to continue to set an example in pay restraint, all the while having to be anxious about having a job at all.

Backlogs – the key indicator of an organisation which has lost control of its processes – must inevitably increase, and with this increase in the age of cases to be dealt with the quality of data and with this the likelihood of successful collection can only diminish. The anger and frustration of government debt collectors will increase, their motivation will drop, their expectations of successful collection from a populace reeling under the impact of increasing unemployment and therefore reduced ability to pay will also drop. What will happen to their performance? How hard will they really try to prise money from the debt Hold-out?

The third weakness of government is its need to be impartial, ethical and honest. Where a DCA will cream a collections ledger, churning and burning, government needs to be seen to apply effort to all its Debtors. This dissipates its effort, making it less efficient. Unlike DCA's government has not found a way to incentivise its own debt collectors by paying them commission: it needs to be fair (read: equally unimaginative) to all its employees, so if all of them cannot be incentivised, then none can. Incredibly, government debt collectors are not even measured in terms of individual collection performance as this is seen as unfairly singling out people. Management is not prepared to challenge the unions on this key element of effective performance management. In sum, there are more reasons to expect collections performance from government stagnating rather than improving.

"Against all of this background it is very possible for the Hold-out to be agile and ahead of the game."

A fourth and equally helpful weakness of Government from the perspective of the Hold-out Debtor is the extreme slowness and lack of agility of Government in recognising change and being able to adapt effectively to it. On the basis that good government means governance dominating all other considerations of effective project management, things get done very slowly based on yesteryear's best insights, to be rolled out late, working at best partially and then set in concrete for years thereafter. Against all of this background it is very possible for the Hold-out to be agile and ahead of the game.

Squaring the Government Circle

What this means for a Debtor displaying the characteristics of the Hold-out is that the heat will be taken off them: Government will decide they are not worth chasing. It will give up and they will have succeeded in escaping this hitherto most tenacious of Creditors.

So the strategy wizards in government have to contend with falling staff numbers and budgets, growing numbers of people struggling to pay, and the prospect of ever increasing **backlogs** of work which is growing old, stale and deteriorating in quality and accuracy of Debtor information. What will they do? They will rush to their new-found friends in the credit reference agencies to try to highlight those cases which are most likely to pay based on individual Debtor payment performance history for credit cards and retail credit.

What this means for a Debtor displaying the characteristics of the Hold-out is that the heat will be taken off them: Government will decide they are not worth chasing. It will give up and they will have succeeded in escaping this hitherto most tenacious of Creditors. They will send the occasional letter to Debtors who are lowly ranked as likely payers, perhaps placing them under "Debt Surveillance". This monitors credit application activity and use of credit cards and other debt facilities to identify any increased use of credit including white data showing ability to pay.

Hence someone not pursued hard for debt now could be contacted again in a few years should they be giving signs that their circumstances have improved. But even this surveillance service costs money which government will be ill-fitted to afford. A hold-out Debtor with basic knowledge of how behavioural scoring works may well be able to avoid paying. In other words if they consider what behaviours are consistent with non-payment, they can present themselves to be scored as no-hopers.

A further straw in the wind for the Absconder is that Government Debt recovery departments are likely to set a trend of disbanding their specialist tracing units, relying instead on collectors to carry out their own tracing as part of their "day-job", and looking to increased inter-Departmental data-sharing and on traditional credit reference agencies' online trace capability. This is likely to lead to a fall in the skill level being practiced in tracing; and even more it will lead collectors to focus on the easy trace cases. Old-fashioned tracers who traced full-time all day every day might take a professional pride in tracing the hard cases. The pressured collector will let them go.

Non-compliance versus Non-payment

Rebel figureheads have tended not to prosper when confronting English governments head-on on home turf through the ages. Wat Tyler as a leader of the Peasants' Revolt of 1381 – refusing to pay a poll tax widely seen as uneven and unfair on the poor – and having been tricked by the King into believing his demands were being met, was quickly put to death. Government ministers regularly pledge to make examples of those who try to defraud the Queen's coffers. Hence naked tax evasion is a crime, punishable by a prison term of up to 5 years in the case of a serious tax fraud, and we do not recommend it.

> **Beware the example of Admiral Byng!**
>
> *Brazenly cocking a snook at Her Majesty's Government Agencies invites them to be brutish and nasty to salve their personal pride – "pour encourager les autres" as was said to be the reason why Admiral Byng had to be hanged as a scapegoat when the Dutch fleet successfully marauded in the River Medway, inflicting a bruising defeat on the home fleet in their own backyard in 1666. No one can be seen to succeed in defying government authority. Otherwise, authority has no authority, and we are back yet again to Simone Weil.*

But failure to pay is not the same as evading payment. People who owe HMRC money, having fairly complied with the requirement to declare all their income, and then fail to pay do not necessarily go to jail. The CSA has the power to jail non-payers, but in 2010 just 40 people were jailed out of a CSA caseload of 1,300,000. A mere 95 people had their driving licences withdrawn as a result of failure to pay the CSA. If a pensioner goes to jail for non-payment of council tax, the event is so rare - and usually to make a (fair and logical) political point that Government-determined state pensions are failing to keep up with the price rises of Government-determined services - that it becomes National news.

" failure to pay is not the same as evading payment..."

> **It is simply too expensive to sent Debt Evaders to Prison**
>
> *The problem the Government faces in deciding whether to imprison people for crimes associated with non-payment is that it costs £41,000*

to keep someone in prison for a year. That equates to £223 per day. Justice Secretary Kenneth Clarke described the interminable rise in the UK prison population as "unsustainable" and declared: "We will not abolish short-term sentences, which are an important tool for magistrates, but I do want to provide the judiciary with alternative sentencing options so that short sentences are used only when necessary".

Taken together with the abandonment of plans to build 4 new "supersize" prisons and the announcement of an impending "rehabilitation revolution", all of this is code to suggest that very few people will be sent to jail in future for socially relatively inoffensive offences such as not paying tax, or child support or indeed council tax. After all, Government is the first to recognise that when people are in prison they not only cost the Government money, but the prisoner can no longer earn money for his family and is likely to be jobless when he comes out – all of this adding to costs for the Government.

A final simple fact is that if a Debtor moves abroad it will be very difficult for any Creditor including Government to pursue them unless they can be accused of a serious crime.

How mighty does the Lion of Government appear now? Will he chase little mice owing him a relative pittance down their underground warrens during the course of an economic winter, or will he concentrate his resources on hunting down the big beasts of arch-criminality instead?

In conclusion, the Law requires that Government Creditors should be paid promptly. The law must be obeyed. And yet not everyone will pay, even if they ought to. And not everyone can be enforced, some will escape. Among them will be Hold-outs. We do not applaud, endorse or recommend this inevitable outcome; it is a simple fact.

A final simple fact is that if a Debtor moves abroad it will be very difficult for any Creditor including Government to pursue them unless they can be accused of a serious crime. How many people have been extradited for non-payment of child maintenance, or indeed for unpaid taxes? Is this something people are talking about in the pubs, clubs and launderettes across the land?

14.0

Students!

WHAT'S IN THIS CHAPTER

Students hardly require to be reminded that they contain among their ranks some of the most prolific Debt Hold-outs as a proportion of the overall population. They possess a constellation of attributes which places them in a unique and an ideal position to exploit credit and avoid payment. Why is this? But they need to be aware of the consequences of crossing the line from abusing the system to out-and-out felony.

Students!

"Debt is a prolific mother of folly and of crime."
Benjamin Disraeli

Even those abused and ill-fed *dogs* who squat day after day in dusty dunning (collections) departments (actually they tend to be football pitch-sized metal and glass sheds lit by fluorescent light) , chained to their desks and telephones by fear of being cast out to become starving *street dogs,* forced to wear a headset which makes their head sweat and itch, monitored by telephony software as to how much time they spend logged onto the phone and how much actually talking – even these dull denizens of debt management know that students comprise some of the most devious, creative and successful debt Hold-outs since Portia defied Shylock.

> "Students comprise some of the most devious, creative and successful debt Hold-outs since Portia defied Shylock. "

What a one-time incredible opportunity for these supposed financial *ingénues* to capitalise on the fact of having more than one address, previous good credit standing, complete mobility, likely multiple occupation at their credit address, ie lots of suspects to hide among in the game of *Whodunnit*, no assets for a Creditor to seize – and the Dionysian boldness of amoral gifted youth! Not only that, but if and when they are ever brought to book they can count on the fondness of the court for youthful indiscretion, the sort perhaps, that saved a young Richard Branson from jail, though no student he, when charged with fraud for evasion of VAT on records sold in UK rather than exported as declared.

The young are apt to ignore the assets they were born with and to look with envy at the possession of their elders, who perhaps have lost the inherent bounty of the new born. Not only is nearly everyone born with health, vitality and perhaps even good looks; intelligence comes free as well for those lucky enough to be endowed with it. Least regarded perhaps of all by the young, because they never think to question it or even count it a benefit, is their good name and reputation, their as yet unblemished credibility.

This foundation upon which credit-worthiness is built, the belief in the good intent of another, starts off with everyone quite literally "in credit". Americans were first to see the value of a good credit record and are known today to assiduously tend to theirs, seeking regular copies and being ready to challenge and correct any errors or misinterpretations of fact which could jeopardise their ability to gain more credit.

Thus students too have the advantage that they can apply for credit, which they actually intend to discharge by paying it off, at their home address. Even today, despite the best efforts of Tony Blair when he was in power to shift working class kids off the dole statistics and onto media studies courses at ex-polytechnic "universities", the parents of most students are likely to be in the so-called *AB socio-demographic grouping*, more likely to be living in owned accommodation and in a postcode associated with a good credit rating. This address information is the cornerstone of the philosophy attributed to the credit reference agency Experian: "*You are where you live*", and is likely to qualify the young student for an early good credit rating at their parents' address.

"...home address information is likely to qualify the young student for an early good credit rating at their parents' address."

This is the ever feckless and recurring generation which leaves on lights, lets taps drip, leaves windows open and the gas central heating on at full blast. At home the parents pay the utility bills and doubtless attend to switching off excess appliances, but the habit formed there can carry on regardless in the student abode: because students can be both relaxed and elastic in their payment morality.

They can afford to be because they are among the most mobile users and abusers of credit on the planet. Not least they can be relaxed because, like the young Richard Branson when he had to make restitution to Her Majesty's Revenue and Customs for his crime of VAT fraud, they too are generally able to turn to the bank of Mum and Dad to rescue them from what otherwise would very likely have been a prison sentence in Branson's case.

So gas, electricity and water are at grave risk of successful evasion in a student household. If they ever have contact with utilities, students will often therefore disguise their occupation – if this epithet does not sound too strenuous a synonym for a stint at university. Utilities will frequently apply a postcode "red-lining" approach to accommodation which is known to be in an area inhabited by students. They may even employ door-knockers to enrol the unwary with their real names, occupations and home addresses.

Is Donald Duck a real name?

The fact is that no one actually needs to give their real name to a utility; indeed aliases such as "Mickey Mouse", "Donald Duck" and even "Mr Smith" are common on the customer registers of the large utilities. Lowly paid door-knockers will take any name they are offered, rather than none at all. It goes without saying – though it will be said here – that a door-knocker has absolutely no rights of entry and no right to have sight of any documentation from any dweller.

Students have also proven to be adept at identity fraud, obtaining goods in the name of others by using their *id's*. Occasionally they do it to each other, plundering rooms of personal information for use in credit applications; sometimes they do it to their parents, and it is not unknown for them to do it to the parents of other students at whose homes they have stayed. Hardest of all to prove or disprove, sometimes they do it in collusion with others to themselves; passing personal information to allow others to apply for credit in their name and to receive goods in their name at a time when they will have an alibi of being elsewhere, perhaps abroad.

> "But the risk of hubris is ever present..."

In a large multiple household of say six people at any one time, with some coming and some going, finding an individual perpetrator and proving their guilt may prove to be quite impossible. Students – as well as younger college age kids – will also be highly IT literate, adept at scanning, in the use of programmes such as *Photoshop* to copy and forge highly credible personal documentation including old utility bills, identity cards, bank statements, birth certificates. Technology, boredom, poverty, ingenuity, ambition and opportunism are incendiary components of potentially serious financial crime.

There is no limit to the fecundity of the creativity of young intelligent people: the *Facebook* generation. But the risk of hubris is ever present. Flushed with his own success, the retiring *jackal* may be tempted to wish to bask in his glory, seek the adulation of others, go after a payout of admiration as well as that of financial gain. The likeliest outcome is that of failed copycat attempts, growing awareness of predation by Creditors, and envy among peers. These are all preconditions for detection, pursuit and failure. Pride goes before a fall.

The Big Bad Wolf

*Worse than this would be the metamorphosis of the marginal jackal into a fully-grown **Big bad Wolf**, perpetrating criminal fraud on an industrial scale, say by the mass manufacture of false identity documentation accompanied by multiple application fraud hits on a financial services player. Big bad **Wolves** inflict real high visibility damage to the credit ecosystem and cannot be allowed to exist They invite their own destruction by their ferocious and ruthless greed, and the Lion of the law will go to extreme lengths to hunt them down and lock them up. The excuse of misguided youth and immaturity is not available to a vicious Big Bad Wolf, however tender in years.*

In sum: of any of the tricks and tactics described in this book, students are the most likely to have the gall, the intellect and the recklessness to do them and get away with it. Again, this is not an incitement to anyone to do anything, merely an acute observation. But aspiring *jackals* do not have to have academic pretensions; any household in a densely populated area of landlorded properties which contains an assortment of impecunious young people with time on their hands will grow its culture of non-payers. And of course, it goes without saying that most students and most young people are of course law-abiding and would never dream of payment avoidance. They are the growing next generation of Always-Pays who will take their part in the ecosystem of debt payment and debt avoidance of tomorrow.

15.0

Coming in from the Cold

WHAT'S IN THIS CHAPTER

There may well come a time when a Hold-out may wish to lead a less stressful existence, or perhaps their circumstances have changed. It is possible to become debt-rehabilitated and the options are summarised. For others the need to come in from the cold may take the form of depression or even suicide ideation. There is equally a need to recognise and to be able to avoid predators and vampires upon the weak. In dealing with Debt Charities, the Debtor needs to be clear about their boundaries. He may want to leave some of his historical liabilities out in the cold when he comes in...

Coming in from the Cold

"There is always hope"
Anonymous

Many of the debts which the Hold-out avoids and evades may never be linked back to him: he will have escaped scot-free. Just as it was a matter of individual conscience somewhere between taking credit at the outset and receipt of a demand for payment later on, when he took the conscious decision not to pay, he is at liberty in his conscience to forget such debts and let them lie with the sleeping dogs, for in truth even Creditors forget. Once a debt gets to a certain age and condition it gets written off the receivables ledger. It is no longer an asset with any real substance; it is formally struck off the Debtors list and is forgotten.

But what if enforcement is unavoidably pressing, if circumstances do not permit physical escape, if the sheer stress of always having to look over one's shoulder has begun to wear the Debtor down?

Remember Ronnie Biggs

Ronnie Biggs owed the Government rather a lot of money; beyond this he owed them the return of his person to serve a further 28 years of jail for his part in the "Great Train Robbery" of 1961. Moreover, in Rio de Janiero, where Biggs had ensconced himself with a new Brazilian wife and fathered a son who became his ticket to continuing undisturbed residence at liberty in Brazil, it was hot, not cold. But like the spies of John le Carré legend,

> Biggs was old and tired and wanted to come home, "walk into a Margate pub as an Englishman and buy a pint of beer". It is not recorded whether he ever enjoyed that privilege on his return, but Biggs did indeed come home to face his own personal music, which was a return to gaol before eventually being released on compassionate grounds. If an arch criminal can come in from the cold, eventually be released to live out his remaining years quietly, then of course the Hold-out Debtor can hope to be rehabilitated also.

Circumstances do change: perhaps a new relationship starts up or an old one dies, perhaps there is a decline in health such as that which prompted Ronnie Biggs to come home, and now it is opportune to close with the financial past also. In most cases the Debtor's credit status is shot; it is not a question of being able to gain new credit at this stage, more one of being able to make a new start without being continually harassed with notifications of the impending consequences of the past.

To be quite clear, at the point where the Debtor does decide to settle with his Creditors, he is not going to be permitted to simply start again and run up more credit as if the past had not happened.

"...rehabilitation of credit score does not take place overnight despite what a DCA might suggest."

The road to earned good financial reputation for those Hold-outs who are not young and able to show a continuous address history of living with their parents at a "good" address is hard-paved and long. They need to prove themselves again as being financially responsible. But there is hope to be gained from the very quarter that initially condemns the indebted to an existence without credit: the misery curve.

The Judaeo-Christian ethic that underlies the Social Capitalist system within which we live is, despite its extrinsic appeal to self-interest and rapacious greed, essentially optimistic and forgiving. The economist Joseph Schumpeter defined Capitalism as "creative destruction", in other words recognising that economic enterprises, including private consumers, will fail. But people are able to rise up again just as managers of so-called phoenix enterprises reappear in business shortly after declaring their previous corporate vehicle insolvent. Credit scoring

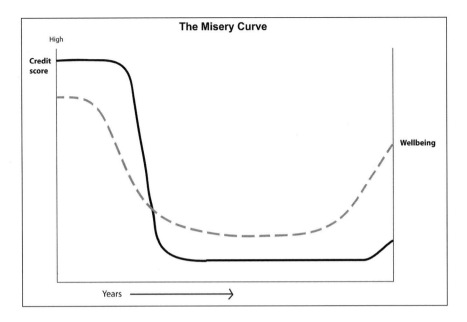

systems have at least the benefit of being impersonal; they do not hold grudges.

Credit reference agencies will track the descent of someone suffering debt problems down the "misery curve" over several years. Relationship breakdown, illness and unemployment may separately or together pull down a consumer's credit score, which will bump along the bottom until, for some of life's survivors and thrivers, they pull themselves together, find new relationships, train for new jobs and gradually rebuild their economic worth.

This will be reflected in their credit score as they acquire new bank accounts and manage to remain within the financial disciplines set by their bankers, and as they assiduously pay for the utilities they enjoy at their new abodes. In time they will successfully apply for credit again. Over a lifetime, 5 or 6 years is not long. People can and do become credit-rehabilitated. But to be clear, rehabilitation of credit score does not take place overnight despite what a DCA might suggest.

The Roads to Recovery

A very successful *jackal* may be completely unrecognised as such by dint of his agility and invisibility. He may have an alter ego as a member of the *sheep* or *cattle* class of payers. Others may have taken some knocks in the course of their journeys. How can they start again? Advice is best given by a competent, qualified and licensed adviser, and can be had for free from *Citizens Advice Bureaux, National Debtline or CCCS:* all debt charities providing excellent, objective, anonymous and professional advice.

If debts are pressing unbearably and running away is not the solution there are some clear routes to rehabilitation, all of which will be considered in terms of their suitability by the Debt counsellor.

Debts Less than £15,000

Debt Relief Order (DRO)

If savings are less than £300 and any car is worth less than £1000 then a *Debt Relief Order* can be obtained through a licensed Debt Counsellor, including the Debt Charities. The adviser will assist in the completion of a *"Common Financial Statement"* which he will attest under his power as a licensed adviser to be true. This document lists all the outstanding debts to be addressed under the *Debt Relief Order* and also sets out a schedule of income and expenditure.

There will need to be a surplus of available monthly cash of less than £50 after all necessary expenditures are taken care of for a *Debt Relief Order* to be allowed as an option. A *Debt Relief Order* will give relief from all debt chasing by affected Creditors, no repayments need to be made and the debt will be written off after one year. The cost of approximately £90 to the Debtor can be spread over the life of the *Debt Relief Order*.

Administration Order

If Debts are less than £5000 and the Debtor has had a CCJ awarded against him, a Debtor can apply to the Magistrates court for an *Administration Order,* making one monthly payment to the court which will distribute it proportionately among the Creditors.

Debts Greater than £15,000

Individual Voluntary Arrangement (IVA)

This a formal arrangement granted by a magistrate if 75% of Creditors by value agree to it, and can be suitable if the Debtor can demonstrate the means to make regular payments of instalments to pay back between roughly 30% and 70% of debts covered within the IVA (this is negotiated by the debt counsellor), normally over a period of less than 5 years.

It avoids the £500 cost of bankruptcy as well as the stigma of this route. Again it gives relief from Creditors included in the IVA, but does not stop others granting credit or pursuing for non-payment; bankruptcy is still possible if payments under the IVA are not kept up.

Bankruptcy

If debts are over £15000 and less than 75% of Creditors by value can be persuaded to take part in an IVA or informal repayment arrangement, this may be the only remaining option. It does cost around £500 to enter into bankruptcy; all assets come under the control of a Government-appointed Official Receiver who will receive any monies earned by the bankrupt and pay him out money to live on. But at least the bankrupt can be discharged after just one year and start again. Alternatively the Debtor can wait to allow a Creditor to pay the cost of bankrupting him. This is often the better option.

Debt management Plans
(also available for debts less than £15k if no DRO suitable)

Because these are not sanctioned by a court or Official Receiver Debt

Management Plans are defined as informal, ie they are made between the parties – Creditors and Debtor. Debt Management companies will for a fee attempt to negotiate discounted repayment plans on behalf of their Debtor clients. In other words, they will try to get Creditors to agree that instead of paying back £1 for every £1 owed, the Debtor pays back say 40p or 50p.

They do this for a fat fee, and continue to attract criticism from the Office of Fair Trading for posing as charities and front-loading their fees to the beginning of any negotiated repayment plan so that they get fully paid first. Over 100 Debt Management companies were warned that they would lose their licences in September 2010 by the OFT unless they cleaned up their acts. "*In some cases, it appears that business models may be set up to take the maximum amount of money from a consumer regardless of their circumstances,*" the OFT report said.

Avoiding Vampires at all costs

Some of the most vicious of the breed of Debt Management Company vampires will even push Debt Consolidation loans as the solution. These loans roll up existing debts into one very large debt which will invariably be secured by a charge on the Debtor's home, if he is an owner-occupier, thus converting unsecured loans into secured loans. For the Debtor this is one of the worst possible outcomes, unnecessarily put his home at risk. It would never be suggested by a Debt Charity acting in the best interests of the customer and not intent on earning itself commission payments. Almost every Debtor would in fact be better off if they increased their mortgage with their existing lender to pay out other Creditors rather than take out a consolidation loan which will be at a higher interest cost than a mortgage. Even this would be a last resort only after other remedies above (other than bankruptcy) had been attempted by a charity debt counsellor acting in the Debtor's best interest.

The **real** Debt charities – *CAB*, National Debtline and CCCS – **charge nothing** and are much more credible to both Creditors and the courts system as acting professionally and **for free** in the interests of the Debtor to miminise his debt repayments and also to maximise his income including any benefits to which he may be entitled, something which the debt management companies are not qualified to do. Debt Management Companies and Claims Management systems are arguably *parasitic vampires* preying on those *cattle* and other sundry herbivores too bovinely stupid to be inoculated in the womb with the intelligence to resist their blandishments in the red-top classified ads.

Being Careful with Debt Charities

It must not be forgotten that the big debt charities are ultimately funded by government, and that they play very much by the rules of the Establishment. Often comprised of ladies slightly older than "a certain age", the volunteers tend to be middle-class products of the morality of the Anglican church. There still adheres a certain Victorian attitude to their "progressive/conservative" outlook. In other words, they will only support a Debtor who demonstrates that he is willing to pay what he can and tells them what they believe to be the truth.

Debt charities can be useful allies to the Debtor coming in from the cold, for the *Common Financial Statement* which they sign off on effectively becomes a fact of documentary evidence as far as a magistrate is concerned. This means that if a *CFS* states particular cost elements in a Debtor's budget as being necessary, the magistrate will not question them further. A Debtor had better be able to be prepared to defend to the debt charity volunteer why they need to spend £x per week on buses, and £y on heating.

Kidney dialysis machines, young children and elderly parents may all require extra spending on utilities which will bulk up a household budget and thus reduce the amount that a Debtor will need to offer Creditors as instalment payments. Heavy smoking due to addiction is an acceptable expense, but gym membership is discretionary and not allowable. This may run contrary to apparent common sense, but it is at least useful to know what to expect.

Avoiding Desperation

Very sadly, people in serious debt arrears do regularly succumb to addiction, depression and worse. The *Child Support Agency* has had to account for a large number of suicides of desperate fathers who felt so hounded by the vicious threats of jail, loss of housing, loss of driving licence and thereby the means to earn a living that they killed themselves. In October 2009 Somerset journalist Ross Hemsworth alleged 61 suicides "caused by CSA harassment" and suggesting that the CSA should be charged with manslaughter. It might sound callous to speak of *lemmings* being hounded to their deaths by *dogs*; no doubt the *dogs* did not intend this, and the people concerned were not mindless rodents.

They were vulnerable human beings unable to cope with the isolation of relationship breakdown, lack of access to their children and the equivocation of a government bureaucracy which demanded their money but was deaf to their human needs. Other notable debt suicide cases in recent history included Derek Rawson who owed 16 credit card companies over £100,000 when he hanged himself in 2004 and Mark McDonald who owed £65,000 to multiple card and loan providers. Both had pledged their houses to try to restructure their debts and both had low incomes. Suicide can be a real and tragic outcome for those who lose their way.

"Those deeply in debt are stated by these studies as being as much in need of psychiatric counselling as debt advice."

There are around 5500 suicides in the UK each year. That equates to 18 per 100,000 males and 5 per 100,000 females. One person in 65 will attempt suicide at some time in their lives. Debt is a key factor in what is known as "suicide ideation", the development of ideas for killing oneself, and the companions of debt, including relationship break-up, bereavement, unemployment and heavy caring duties, are significant additional factors.

Studies have shown that Hire Purchase, housing related debt, child support, credit card and mail-order debt are primary causators of suicide ideation in people heavily in debt. Those deeply in debt are stated by these studies as being as much in need of psychiatric counselling as debt advice.

"Studies have shown that Hire Purchase, housing related debt, child support, credit card and mail-order debt are primary causators of suicide ideation in people heavily in debt. "

Happily for those who seek them out, the Debt Advice Charities are trained to recognise clients who appear to be under mental stress as much as financial issues; they can and do signpost people to agencies such as *The Samaritans* who can provide help.

In the wonderful feel-good movie *"As good as it gets"* Jack Nicholson as the misanthropic Melvin finds himself crying at his piano in mourning over the dog which he had been looking after for his sick neighbour and has had to give back. He catches himself crying and starts laughing : *"Over a dog! Over an ugly dog!"* That it should be so in terms of Debtors' attitude to the *dogs* of debt collection... Thankfully there are solutions to debt and life goes on even after bankruptcy. Keeping problems in perspective is everything. Better to be a live *jackal* than a lamented *lemming*.

Getting ready for a bumpy Landing: après moi le déluge!

On 14th May 1935, the much maligned "Wickedest Man in the World", Aleister Crowley, was finally declared bankrupt. He managed this from a starting point of an inheritance worth approximately £6M in today's money, but had been living on his wits ever since the early 1920's. What is notable about his bankruptcy was the number of Creditors: thirty eight unsecured and ten who were partly secured.

Crowley owed money to lawyers, tailors, wine merchants, a moneylender, solicitors, hotels, restaurants, opticians, masseurs, a dentist, a bootmaker, a shirtmaker and a hosier as well as to numerous friends and well-wishers. In total his bankruptcy amounted to £4695 8s 1d. Today this would equate to roughly £272,310, not a large sum in absolute terms even now, but prodigious for a man widely known to be larger than life and completely unreliable. The point about Crowley's bankruptcy is that he managed to stave it off for so long and could have so many Creditors.

> However "wicked" or depraved Crowley really was, he was undoubtedly highly resourceful and courageous – possessing the kind of bravery that led him to climb high crumbling chalk cliffs without ropes as a young man and becoming a highly acclaimed Himalayan climber. His artistry was in keeping his front going even when his situation appeared hopeless by maintaining relationships with his Creditors, making promise after futile promise. He is thus worth studying just as much for entertainment as for wisdom.

Even further into the realm of legend, Hagen, a villain-hero in the famous *Nibelungenlied* Middle High German epic poem, found himself betrayed and surrounded during a celebratory banquet in the court of his enemies the Burgundians. He immediately grabbed the young son of his treacherous host and cut off his head.

Realising that he must shortly pay for his own earlier treachery with his life, Hagen thus massively increased his liability in a final act of defiance. This was the courage and resolution of one who knows that he may be doomed, but he is not without resources and options. Robert Maxwell, the litiginous, thuggish pension swindler and larger than life publisher and bully was a real life example of such a man. Faced with ruin when his theft was exposed and his attempts to prevent disclosure had failed, he is thought to have simply stepped off his cruise yacht to certain death by drowning.

Happily, those contemplating bankruptcy do not need to resort to harming anyone physically to make their point. But there may be lessons in these histories for the hard-pressed Debtor regarding human behaviour in extreme circumstances. Some will lose heart and become suicidal while others fight to bitter end as we have seen, under the motto: "*Après moi le deluge*".

The Debt-Gamer

Games Theory is a branch of applied mathematics which seeks to apply logic to

"Happily, those contemplating bankruptcy do not need to resort to harming anyone" predicted human behaviour in set situations. A classic example is *"The Prisoner's Dilemma"* where two suspects are separated by the police and offered reduced sentences if one will give evidence against the other: what to do...?

Each prisoner is in a dilemma. If he does not confess but the other does, then he will receive a high jail sentence while his colleague gets a low one.

If he confesses, and the other does not he will get a lower sentence, but at the price of betraying his colleague. If they both confess, they may both get a lower sentence, but perhaps they may not have been convicted if neither had confessed; finally if neither confesses they might both escape conviction for lack of evidence, but if convicted, they will both get the highest available jail sentence.

Games Theory can certainly be applied in behaviours around debt. Thus: given that it is possible to obtain a Debt Relief Order if one has debts of £15,000, what point would there be of declaring bankruptcy, or allowing oneself to be made bankrupt for £16,000? The struggling Debtor may well think: if one is going to go down, why not go down with a bang... "bigtime"? Today this typically occurs by "robbing Peter to pay Paul".

In other words, a Debtor will borrow from a new lender in order to repay an old one. Credit cards are the obvious solution for the desperate, especially if they are nominally employed home-owners who are somehow keeping the payment roundabout going. It is of course fraudulent to deliberately apply for credit with the intent of not paying. But it is not fraudulent to take out one loan to help to pay for another, is this not indeed what so-called consolidation loans are all about? Just like helpful drug dealers, helpful money lenders will always be around to invite the unwary to ingest their drug of choice to the point of self-annihilation.

In Aleister Crowley's day, there was no data-sharing between credit bureaux and his credit was kept alive by his bluster and promises, and perhaps by showing documentation purporting new publishing opportunities. Today's "credit revolver" will make the minimum payments demanded by credit card companies each month and will keep seeking new cards or loans for more credit.

"Just like helpful drug dealers, helpful money lenders will always be around to invite the unwary to ingest their drug of choice to the point of self-annihilation"

Obviously debt grows eventually either to unsustainable levels, or to the point where new credit dries up. In terms of games theory, this might be the optimal time for the revolver to get off the roundabout, as its downward spiral thenceforth simply increases his debt liability without giving him any more credit assets (money) to play with. Depending on his appetite for extreme and suicidal risk, games theory might naturally forbid entirely that he should ever pledge his property to consolidate or re-structure his debts: that would mean he would actually be committed to either repaying them or end up homeless – the route to suicidal desperation: game over.

This is the sort of risk one takes in stepping off a cliff, wondering if by exception one will someone escape the certain forces of gravity. Instead the debt-gamer will ensure that once credit has been granted and while he is still keeping up payments, he either sells up and transfers overseas any proceeds from fixed assets such as houses or cashed in pensions which would otherwise be consumed in a bankruptcy, or else transfers assets to a trusted confidant.

He will do this knowing that it is fraudulent, but calculating that he can get away with it. Of course Creditors will later turn out to be disappointed, angry and potentially vengeful, eg willing to bankrupt the debt-gamer, or even to try to involve the *Serious Fraud Office* (SFO) in a prosecution. The gamer will have considerations in his mind such as:

- The likelihood that the SFO will try to prosecute if there is no "smoking gun" of asset transfer at the stage of debt delinquency (if asset transfer occurred earlier, who is to prove there was malice aforethought?)

- The willingness of Creditors to potentially throw good money after bad in a civil case

- The prize at stake, is it worth all the effort?

- Impact of the denouement on his future life, eg life after bankruptcy if it comes to this.

If bankruptcy does turn out to be inevitable for a gamer who has played his chips to the point of exhaustion, it need not mean the end of life, just the end of a chapter. Americans are optimists and they know this: they call it Chapter 11 in regard to commercial debt. The bankrupt can start afresh, inspired by the likes of Abraham Lincoln, Walt Disney and Kim Basinger – all of whom picked themselves up and made their way to distinction and success.

Lastly under this heading, it must be observed that games theory fully applies in the approach of the Creditor or DCA. The strategies that the Creditor or DCA applies are gambits. Indeed at any one time the Creditor or DCA will have a "Champion" gambit (a particular letter or call script in sequence with other specifically scheduled letters and calls) which he is always ready to test against a possibly better "Challenger" gambit in terms of better effectiveness in securing more cash from Debtors.

The Creditor or DCA tries to influence the Debtor in ways analogous to the Prisoner's Dilemma by painting a dire outcome, which will become more dire if the Debtor does not capitulate, not least by the addition of interest, fees and costs to the original debt; as a variant on this, the DCA will at a later stage offer to settle for a significant discount if the Debtor settles now. Thus the strategy starts as bullying and ends in pathos and derisory gambling.

People do business with people they like

Part of coming in from the cold for anyone in debt may mean making restitution – payment – to a lucky few Creditors. Who will they be? The dogs of the Debt Collection Agencies believe that he who barks soonest and loudest will be the one to get paid. But almost by definition the majority of the debts assigned to them are for discretionary payment items. Principals do not farm out secured debts for collection, because they do not need to, which is the very point of having security, eg a registered charge on a property via a mortgage. Of course the Debtor will be at pains to settle or make an arrangement to pay over a longer term with such priority Creditors in order to keep a roof over their heads, or in the case of certain government debt obligations, to maintain their liberty.

But the Debtor is at liberty to decide who they pay. Shall they surrender to the barking dogs, or shall they favour people who may have favoured them in the past: family and friends? The Debtor who is in a position to make settlements because they can at least afford to part pay is actually in quite a strong position. Creditors can either choose not to settle and hope that a legal enforcement process might leave some meat on a bone which is not quite picked clean; but if they don't settle with an offer which can afford to be well under 50% of what is owed, they risk that other Creditors will take up the offer, so that there will eventually be nothing left for them, and they will get nothing. It is a classic reversal of the so-called prisoner's dilemma.

16.0

Beware the Magic Bullet?

WHAT'S IN THIS CHAPTER

An emphasis on anticipating the moves of the opponent has been a constant theme of this book. Thus it is logical to examine current developments in the credit industry to anticipate how their approach will develop over the coming years. The theme is repetitive, it is two-fold and complementary. Driven by a focus on cost effectiveness Creditors will contract out more debt, while all sides of the industry continue to promote data sharing and ever more sophisticated customer segmentation and prediction models. This will all work to the extent that customers or Debtors cooperate with the industry as members of the Facebook generation by sharing all their data – or not… it is nonetheless great news for Jackals.

Beware the Magic Bullet

In the perpetual Darwinian struggle between Creditors and Debtors, Creditors and debt-collectors are forever seeking more effective ways of getting Debtors to pay. Highly aware that for every Debtor there are likely to be at least 5 unsecured Creditors chasing each pound in his pocket, Creditors find themselves in the ticklish situation that they are eternally in competition with each other, but in order to have effective intelligence on Debtors, they need to cooperate by sharing address data and payment data.

"...If all collectors fire the same"silver bullet" at the same time, then they will all be shooting at the same very few stray cattle and sheep who have escaped the net of initial collection efforts"

Nonetheless, each is continuously searching for the "magic bullet" which will solve their problem of getting hold of the Debtor as first in line, and securing any payment from him ahead of the onslaught of competing Creditor. Thus they are like *seagulls* each trying to scoop up a little fish who is foolish enough to offer himself by appearing on the surface. Only one is likely to succeed to get a meal from him, which *seagull* will be quickest?

How to avoid traps

For the Debtor the surest way to avoid being caught in a trap is to be aware of its construction, knowing where it is sited, what it is designed to catch and how it operates. Thus the potential target will know how to avoid the site of the trap, learn not to resemble desirable prey, and discover what steps to take not to become enmeshed. No matter how fiendishly clever the technology, the trap or the battle plan if it cannot be brought to bear because the enemy will not engage, it cannot

> *succeed. This is as true of American cyber-war in Afghanistan today as it was for Sun-Tzu 2,000 years ago. So in this section we look at some of the old/new approaches being assembled by the credit industry which is already sensitised to the fact of hard economic times, increasing numbers of Debtors who truly cannot afford to pay and the desperate need to be seen to be an efficient hunter by their paymaster client Creditors.*

It is said that when the student is ready, the teacher will appear. It has also been said that it is an ill wind that blows no one any good… The student is currently very ready in the form of Creditor principals, not least government, but also the credit collection industry: everyone is desperate to cut cost and do more for less. These are hard economic times: hence the ill wind. And just who will it do good for? Credit Reference Agency *Equifax* is ready to provide the answer with its own particular brand of snake oil, promising the means to *"more efficient collections, with more money collected and less money spent collecting it"* (quoted from a conference reported in a credit magazine).

Of course if all Creditors buy the same snake oil remedy – or we should say "silver bullet" and all fire it at the same time, then they will all be shooting at the same very few stray *cattle* and *sheep* who have escaped the net of initial collection efforts – TO THE COMPLETE NEGLECT OF HARD-TO-COLLECT DEBT. *Goats* and *jackals* will be completely ignored … The same generic approach metatastises into a whole brewing infection of similar approaches:

Data mining

The sources of attack and ensnaring which the Hold-out Debtor will be at pains to avoid start with the basic application of data mining. Closely related to collections scoring, data mining involves collating large volumes of data containing relevant Debtor attributes. It seeks to find patterns in apparently random occurrences of successful payment recovery, looking to determine specific attributes which can be sorted and counted. The customer Debtor ledger is filleted to provide lists of customers with specific attributes, for example to be likely to pay after a judgement has been obtained at County Court, or to be party to an application fraud, or likely to be at home to a doorstep collector.

The more data available about a specific Debtor the more susceptible they are to being categorised in a data mining exercise. If a *sheep* is correctly and accurately categorised as not being a *goat* or a *jackal,* then it will definitely be pursued. If an animal at large remains a grey shadow, it will be ignored.

Propensity to pay

> The more data available about a specific Debtor the more susceptible they are to being categorised in a data mining exercise

Using data mining and scoring, including so-called "blackbox" neural scoring" is a means to determining individual customers' individual propensity to pay, or the likelihood that they can be induced to pay. Data used for this purpose includes specific postcode (wealthy or poor), time at address, number of credit relationships, use of both white and black CAIS/Insight/Share data to demonstrate previous history of payment or non-payment. The value of this data to Debt Collection Agencies (DCA's) , who have not traditionally been party to it because their principals, who did the data-sharing on the basis of earlier customer consent to data share, were not confident of the right of data access as extending to their agents, the DCA's

The value that DCA's place upon this approach is betrayed in more than one sense by the following quote from one of their number: *"This has been particularly prevalent when determining whether to litigate following conclusion of any collection cycle"* (Mark Taylor, Incasso). *" In the current financial climate it is imperative that Creditors are using litigation as a last resort and trying to ensure that they engage with Debtors to agree repayment plans and "rehabilitation strategies".*

When this code is translated what he is actually saying *"right from the horse's mouth"* is:

"It is not economic to pursue litigation unless you are absolutely confident that the Debtor will then pay... today we just don't have the money to litigate so we rely on Debtors behaving like good little **sheep** *and paying up when we can inveigle them into talking to us".* So by inference, if the Debtor gives every sign he will not pay, and certainly does not talk to the DCA he has every chance of succeeding in not paying.

Affordability Scoring

Out of the same stable as data-mining and Propensity Scoring, Affordability scoring is yet another magic potion touted by Credit Reference Agencies (CRA's) Note that while propensity scoring seeks to discover a customer's likelihood of paying, Affordability scoring tries to assess whether they can afford to pay. At the margin of course, a Debtor might well be able to afford to pay, but have no propensity to do so, at which point the CRA would no doubt suggest litigation with all its attendant costs.

Affordabiility scoring is based on modelling the likely circumstances of a customer based on **postcode** (*"You are where you live"*), **age** (you will be either single or married , and you will have such and such a level of education and likelihood of either being on benefit, a blue collar or white collar job, or indeed retired), **sex** (breadwinner, housewife, dole jockey..) and **CAIS data** (you will either be a home owner if you are shown to be paying regular mortgage instalments, or paying rent or living with parents if not, again depending on your age and postcode...)

Of course these data elements reinforce each other in the imagination of the data modellers, for example in terms of predicting - or is it guessing, which would really be a snake-oil sale? - that a 31 year old woman is likely to be a professional part-time mother of two children with a gross salary of £45,000

> "Purveyors of Affordability scoring are at best selling modelled guesstimated "stratified" average values, building hypothesis upon hypothesis to the point of fairytale."

and either will or will not be able to afford to make regular payment of £1500 on her third credit card in addition to an existing two.

But before we start to worry how Orwellianly omniscient the Credit Reference Agencies are today - as they would have their Creditor customers believe – consider that they do not actually possess any *salary i*nformation. Although they would undoubtedly like to be party to an information flow about how much goes into and out of an individual's current account in terms of salary and spending, banks do not have the right today to give or to receive such highly intimate and private personal data; nor do employers have the right to share information on their employees incomes, save to certain Government agencies such as HMRC and the CSA. Yes, that last point was indeed predictable.

What is key, however, is that the purveyors of Affordability scoring are at best selling modelled guesstimated "stratified" average values, building hypothesis upon hypothesis to the point of fairytale. On occasions where they have been bold enough to predict that a given consumer would have a property, they have been proven embarrassingly wrong. Affordability scoring is at best a work of imagination drawn by a one-eyed modeller in the gloom, if not quite in the dark. It is the work of half wit and at best only vaguely indicative.

Further evidence of this is the advent of a competitor offering called "**accurate propensity modelling**": it gives the game away in its title by suggesting that propensity modelling, of which affordability scoring is one variant, is generally *inaccurate.* While the purveyors of this also-ran silver bullet claim that it predicts not just the likelihood of the Debtor paying, but how much they will pay, this claim somehow overlooks the sovereign decision-making power of the Debtor either not to engage with the collector at all, or to decide themselves how little they will pay.

And in a world where greed is always eventually stronger than fear, it is very likely that the 31 year old female imagined above will indeed get her next credit card.

Geographical recession impact segmentation

The equivalent of a dirty cobalt bomb to destroy whole populations, suggestions that complete areas of the country be "red-lined" as being likely to contain higher proportion of Public Sector workers likely to lose their jobs and become unable to pay are made quite seriously by credit industry insiders. While no credit reference agency will know which of two neighbours living near "The Ministry" mega-shed of civil servants in Newcastle are indeed public servants, refusing credit to both of them will certainly avoid much business being done. Does this have the ring of fair trading about it?

CIFAS use by Government

" Civil Libertarians as well as goats and jackals can take heart that their freedom of choice in sharing their personal data is thus not for sale by their government."

The Credit Industry Fraud Avoidance Scheme (now CIFAS) was developed by financial services companies as a data-sharing user group with data accessed as part of credit application processes via the Credit Reference Agencies. CIFAS members are made aware of any potential fraud at a specific address whenever they use a Credit Reference Agency to obtain a credit score on a new named applicant. The scheme has proved valuable in highlighting names linked to addresses where there have been previous incidences of fraud, thus enabling new frauds to be prevented.

Rather late in the day, the *Lion* of Government has woken up to the potential of CIFAS and is arrogating its right to plunder a kill made by lesser jungle beasts. Thus it plans to take data shared by others without sharing its own data with them. Civil Libertarians as well as *goats* and *jackals* can take heart that their freedom of choice in sharing their personal data is thus not for sale by their government. Those with evil intent had better watch out, however. *Cohabiting couples who either jointly or separately make credit applications and/or pay bills to financial services companies, utilities, telecoms companies or retailers from the same address will in future gain instant scrutiny and likely prosecution if they:*

- Attempt to claim a single person discount on their council tax

- Sub-let a council property to a third party who makes credit applications and pays bills from that address

- Attempt housing benefit fraud (single mother bringing up kids, lover living in undeclared)

- Attempt to obtain driving fraudulent driving licences or passports in someone else's name who is known to be living elsewhere than the application address.

Credit Reference Agency Bounty Hunters

> "Those with evil intent had better watch out, however"

The credit reference agencies are also competing in the feast to supply government with data inadvertently authorised and consented to by consumers when they applied for credit. While CIFAS is merely a conduit for data through the pipelines and engines of the Credit Reference Agencies, the CRA's themselves have the data matching and modelling power (which CIFAS does not possess) to create the lists and reports of suspected perpetrators of wrongdoing. One large CRA has voiced its ambition to become a "bounty hunter", presumably being paid for results in detecting and naming specific malefactors who it can show are enjoying benefits from Government to which they should not be entitled based on their lifestyles and proven spending patterns.

So are the wicked doomed to meet their collective come-uppances as a result of all this radar detection activity? Certainly, if they maintain old behaviours they will be detected, just as radar detects metal components in approaching aircraft. But just as the Mosquito fighter was designed and built largely of wood rather than metal in the Second World War so that German radar could not pick it up, and just as Stealth Fighters overfly enemy territory undetected in the Twenty First Century, so too the highly adaptable and un-stupid evil-doers can adapt.

They will simply take care not to have a credit history at the same address as someone complicit in one of the above-named crimes and thus otherwise vulnerable to detection. The live-in lover will have an address somewhere else, or will simply disappear entirely into the ether of the cash economy. People living under one roof who may not continue to enjoy certain benefits and tariff reductions if they declare the fact of this, will take care not to both apply for credit or have payment and billing histories at the same address.

In this way the bounty-hunter scenario may, in the cold light of day, play out differently to the vision being portrayed by both Government and the CRA's at the point where both get down to agreeing a formal contract. Bounty hunters get paid on results by bringing bodies in, dead or alive, and traditional debt collection also works on this contractual basis. The CRA's on the other hand are used to asking for money merely for providing information.

If the Government insists only on paying based on results delivered by the CRA, eg money recovered from some fraudulently claimed benefit, this will not rhyme with the CRA insistence on money up front. Will the two parties be able to agree when it gets down to negotiating the detail? But some Government minister will get promoted and CRA shares will continue to be a good investment as the money rolls in. The Hold-out will learn and successfully adapt his behaviour: the *jackal* will hide.

Speech analytics

When one considers that the only contact which Debt Collection Agencies every have with their customers (Debtors) it is unsurprising that they are intrigued by the ethereal medium of voice as an identifier and as a means of validation. There are at least two technologies be promoted which focus on voice as a source of truth and value.

Validation technology underlying speech analytics is said to have originated in Israel as a means of identifying potential terrorists at security checkpoints. Based on the much older lie-detector principles, speech analytics record voice patterns in a so-called "normal" and unstressed range, showing speech graphically on a computer screen. If a subject is under stress, ie lying, their voice is likely to betray this stress by playing outside the normal range of voice modulation. However, as with lie detection equipment, this test is not infallible. A very large UK utility experimented with the technology in the late 1990's and found that it was not reliable at that time so that the application was discontinued. It quite simply failed to detect some individuals who were proven by other means to be lying.

Speech Analytics can also mean sophisticated call recording and data retrieval, used for audit trail or customer record validation purposes. In other words, customers can be reminded of promises made and held to account on specific issues from earlier conversations. As such this is really a productivity and efficiency tool and not of real concern to the unwilling payer save that it may be used to remind him of what he said or promised previously.

Both of these applications require that calls are recorded. Any Debtor who finds it politic to engage with a Creditor or their Debt Collection Agency agents would do well to question and confirm the extent to which their voice record is to be analysed and what use any analysis is to be put to. Some might even decline to engage with the Creditor or his agent until notified in writing regarding this issue: it may be fertile grounds for a dispute based on personal liberties and the use of personal data.

Debtors who do not engage with their Creditors by phone will of course continue to be untroubled by whatever potential this technology has to offer in the future. *Jackals* will definitely hide. But they will assiduously be looking over the horizon as to the nature of any new silver bullets being forged, taking the opportunity to look in the shop windows of the Credit Reference Agencies and Debt Collection Agents by checking out their websites regularly. Forewarned is after all forearmed.

Magic Bullets or Duds?

A range of additional tactical approaches recently being applied by the credit industry may also provide useful intelligence to the Hold-out Debtor as to future trends in collections and enforcement approaches.

Use of charging orders for low value debts

Pushing against a trend by banks and finance houses to seek to place a charge on a Debtor's property, sometimes for debts as low as £600, which would enable the Creditor to seek from the courts to force a sale of the property via an Order for Sale, the Office of Fair Trading has set out guidelines requiring "proportionality" in terms of the value of any loan compared to the value of the Debtor's property. This gives the green light for Debtors to appeal to magistrates not to grant such orders on these grounds. It underpins the need for Debtors to assiduously read all mail and especially court documents and to seek early free debt advice from the debt charities.

Use of the High Court to enforce evictions.

To avoid the delays inherent in relying on the county court process which can be up to 16 weeks for bailiffs to obtain a warrant for eviction, landlords may in future attempt to provide at the county court stage for later enforcement via the High Court which would be a more rapid process. This will doubtless be more expensive for the landlord client, but could allow him to benefit overall by either renting or selling the property more quickly.

Possible Increase in Debt Sales to Specialist Debt Purchase Companies

The business of commercial sale of consumer debts to be collected by third party companies originated in the USA, and the practice is relatively recent in UK. After some initial market frenzy between debt sellers (banks, finance houses) and buyers, the enthusiasm of both sides cooled. Debt sold by a bank to a third party does not automatically become easier to collect because it has a new owner. In fact, a Debtor can usually take heart if his debt is acquired by one of these self-styled sophisticated collection organisations. Having bought a debt for pence in the pound, normally after it has been well and truly touted around a number of collection agencies without any sign of the Debtor being willing to pay, Debt Purchase companies are very unlikely to invest significant sums in enforcement.

> "A mooted trend for banks to unload low value instalment repayment plans devised by Debt Management companies and Debt Charities is good news for Hold-out Debtors"

A mooted trend for banks to unload low value instalment repayment plans devised by Debt Management companies and Debt Charities is good news for Hold-out Debtors. Such plans typically require low priority Creditors to pay just £1 per month over many years. The logic of the purchaser is that if a debt is "performing", ie the Debtor is actually paying, they are buying an income stream, probably paying only around 5p per £1 of debt bought.

> "What if the Debtor becomes aware that they are paying a Debt Purchaser and then simply stops paying?"

What if the Debtor becomes aware that they are paying a Debt Purchaser and then simply stops paying? It is very unlikely that a debt purchaser will be willing to invest any money in pursuing such a Debtor who subsequently refuses contact. The age-old dilemma for the (new) Creditor then begins: is the Debtor still at the address, have their circumstances changed so that they can no longer pay? In the Debtor refuses contact at this point by not answering mail or phone calls, he feeds the computerised decision engine of the Creditor with the clear message:

"This account will never pay, give up!"

The same scenario beckons with the advent of increased debt sales by water companies, led reportedly by Severn Trent. If a water company has sold its debt, then it has got past the decision as to whether to sue the customer, and decided that it is not worth it. So why then would a Debt Purchaser come to any different conclusion, specifically if the Debtor refuses contact? Is such a development not a clear signal to the Hold-out Debtor: *"You don't need to pay!"*? These latter "magic bullets" in the making do look like duds, only threatening to snag the odd stray escaped *sheep* who might take them seriously.

17.0

Money From America?

WHAT'S IN THIS CHAPTER

One way not to pay is to have others pay on your behalf. While many people instinctively look to family for support, this can lead to bitterness and long term relationship disruption. There is a large number of charities which will help people who can convince them that they are deserving cases, some of which are locally based in a specific town or region and others created to support people in specific industries.

Money from America

One way not to pay is to get other people to pay on your behalf. For Irish relatives who did not emigrate to the USA in the Nineteenth and Twentieth Centuries and who chose to stay to scratch a living from their native sod, the hope of "money from America" was often all they had to sustain them. Diasporas of emigrants across the world still do habitually remit money to relatives at home.

"...there is help to be had from unsuspected quarters"

Thus for the Can't Pay, the family is a primary source of initial help. However, debts among family members can cause the kind of bitterness that blights lives and ultimately splits families, particularly siblings as the "haves" resent having to support the "have nots" and the "have nots" resent the success of the "haves" and snipe at them for their meanness, even when they do provide. Thus debt counsellors often class debts to family and friends as priority debts, just as friends who lend books sometimes inscribe on the flyleaf: *"You cannot keep this book and my friendship"*.

But surprisingly there is help to be had from unsuspected quarters, albeit only for those thin little *sheep* and *cattle*, the Can't-pays who demonstrate compliance and rectitude. Gas, Electricity and Water companies all have arms-length funded charities, now usually operated by professional charity administration companies, which give financial assistance to customers who can demonstrate real hardship and are prepared to be means-tested by submitting to a debt counsellor helping them to complete a *Common Financial Statement* and making a submission for a charitable grant on their behalf.

Trades or guilds often have a charity which will pay grants to people who have worked in their particular industry, for example *BOCI* is a charity which will help people with a background in the Meat trade. In addition there are charities specifically targeting the elderly, ex-service personnel and families. *Soroptimist* and *Rotary Club* charities are to be found in every large town: grants can often be had from them, sometimes in the form of prizes for demonstrated achievement in overcoming hardship.

"...grants can often be had from them sometimes in the form of prizes for demonstrated achievement in overcoming hardship"

The supplicant may need to craft an application which stresses illness, addiction or single parenthood and give examples of how they are working to overcome these, but need a specific amount of money to assist them; and may have to attend one of their many dinners and fundraising events to win the prize of a grant on offer.

Sometimes there are specific annual prize grants to aim for. These can be for the purposes of furthering education, affording medical help or simply to assist with setting up a family home. In each case the supplicant must be prepared to cooperate in demonstrating their circumstances, including some form of means testing. There will be virtually no effective controls on how a grant is actually used once paid out.

Finally, there are hundreds of small local charities which will make ongoing support payments to people who can demonstrate hardship or help with purchase of necessary white goods or other household major purchases such as carpets. The local Citizens Advice Bureau can provide a list of potential donor charities to consumers who approach them seeking help with managing their debts. Some of these charities are listed below:

www.turn2us.co.uk   www.charisgrants.com   www.anglianwater.co.uk/awaf
www.britishgasenergytrust.org.uk   www.edfenergytrust.org.uk
www.uutf.org.uk

If you don't ask, you certainly won't get, so why not ask?

18.0

Sheep May (not) safely graze ...

WHAT'S IN THIS CHAPTER

Unfortunately many people in debt are taken advantage of by the unscrupulous and we have seen earlier how we have all been programmed to comply with those who tell us that they are in authority and we have erred... If only the meek and mild could find the initiative to challenge their pursuers they would find that they have plenty of ammunition and ways of resisting. We look at someone who could not reply and someone else who did...

Sheep May (not) safely graze …

Beware of the Jungle

Sadly, being willing to pay does not prevent people getting into debt, and on its own, it is not enough to get them out of it. Credulity, personal vulnerability and willingness to pay go hand in hand. It is perhaps cruel to call the gentle souls who have this combination of attributes **sheep**, but to the **dog** and **vulture** collectors of the Debt Collection Agencies they are the perfect prey. First they succumb to the blandishments of the marketing and advertising **hounds** who herd them willingly to the trough of easy credit, initial payment holidays followed by instalment or lump sum payments which carry horrendous rolled up interest penalties if payment dates are missed.

These hounds have volume targets to meet in terms of numbers of *sheep* gated and penned into apparent cheap or free credit deals. Would-be consumers are gulled into becoming willing Debtors who pay while they can but, because of their natures, are easily tempted to take more and more credit with additional providers. They have no forward planning or contingency strategy to deal with the many accidents that Life invents for them, and when some of them stumble the *vultures* are there to devour them.

Sophie's Story

Sophie is single, fortyish and has been unable to work since she witnessed a horrifically violent street attack which did not involve her directly. She suffers from post traumatic stress disorder and speaks in short staccato

> bursts between long silences so that anyone listening to her can tell that she is distracted and confused. With just £50 savings, she lives alone in a housing association flat and has no idea how to deal with 8 Creditors to whom a total of £9000 is owed. She does not smoke or drink but has virtually no money over from her Employment Support Allowance benefit and thinks she cannot afford to see a dentist.
>
> She is aware that she could apply for a Debt Relief Order, but she has been told by Debt Collection Agency vultures that if she keeps up her repayment plans, some of them at just £1 per month, her credit record will be refurbished and she can apply for more credit. Some of the vultures are asking her to increase her payments, while others are not being paid anything. It is in her nature to want to pay; and she dreams that she will one day be able to get more credit. So she struggles on with bad teeth and walks everywhere to save money. She has no idea that she has the option to pay absolutely nothing, that no one is going to sue her, because she has absolutely nothing to take. Sophie is a real person except that she is not called Sophie. Sheep may not safely graze...

Debt Propensity/addiction

Arguably people like Sophie become addicted to credit; they are sufficiently unsophisticated that they cannot see that the other side of the credit promise is the debt burden. So like an alcoholic wanting to protect his stash of liquor, even while they are deeply suffering the consequences of over-indebtedness, they still want to hold on to the promise of more credit.

"Just as more booze is the last thing that an alcoholic needs if he is to recover, the sheep addicted to the teat of credit cannot see that more credit is actually the last thing they need"

Just as more booze is the last thing that an alcoholic needs if he is to recover, the *sheep* addicted to the teat of credit cannot see that more credit is actually the last thing they need. It is what made them sick *sheep* in the first place, and it will do so again if they are given free access to it. If only they could pay the £2 to the Credit Bureaux to see their credit record, they would be under no illusion that the cocktail cabinet will be closed to them for the duration, with no time off for good behaviour.

Sheep savages vulture?!

While it might be the stuff of allegory or fairytale, it is not too hard to imagine a scenario where, with a little help and encouragement, a *sheep* might turn on a *vulture*. They are already on the hook of communication, and they probably have not got the resourcefulness to take the evasive action of a *jackal*. But if only they had wit, they would not be completely without defence. Let us imagine the following conversational gambits led by a *super-sheep* with newly invigorated with defensive instincts:

" I want you to know that I am recording this call in the event that I need to complain to the Office of Fair Trading about unfair collection activity on your part."

" I am on benefit and I am entitled to pay you just £1 per month, you cannot do anything about it, so why are you harassing me? I intend to report you for this".

"I am under medication from my doctor for stress and feeling very depressed and unwell; You are pushing me over the edge...I am asking you not to harass me when I have told you I can't afford to pay you anything. "

"Are you a debt collection agent or a debt purchase company? How much did you pay to purchase my debt? "

"How much would it cost you to take me to county court, how much to get an enforcement order, how much to pay a bailiff to come out and get nothing? How much money are you prepared to throw away trying to collect from me?"

"If you are threatening to sue me, please be clear and tell me exactly what you are going to do and when, otherwise you are breaking your industry code of practice and I can report you and even get the Office of Fair Trading to withdraw your licence to operate."

"If you do take me to court, be sure that I will get free advice from the Citizens Advice Bureau and I will ask for the hearing to be transferred to my own locality so that I can appear to defend the action."

"The fact that this debt has been passed to you means that the Principal did not think it worth taking me to county court, so promise me that you will if you dare!"

*"I don't want to hear what you **may** do or what you **might** do, tell me exactly what you will do and when, otherwise you are just hot air."*

"We both know you aren't going to try to sue me because you can't afford the cost on the one hand, and you know I can't pay you on the other."

"How much would it cost you if you really did send a collection agent to my door: £25 or £35... so when can I expect them so I can be sure to be in?"

"So you promise that my credit record will be restored if I was able to pay you, even though I have told you that I am recording this call?"

"Ok, so you agree my credit record won't be restored anytime soon and you can't afford to sue me, so I think we are all done here."

"Can you give me address details please for the Credit Services Association and the Office of Fair Trading so that I can report you to them?"

"If a *worm* can turn, so can a *sheep*..."

While it was the blustering failed Labour chancellor Denis Healey who mocked Sir Geoffrey Howe that being attacked by him was like "being savaged by a dead sheep", Howe had the more progressive impact on history. He it was who turned on arch-matriarch *elephant* Margaret Thatcher to demolish her leadership of the Conservative party and effectively her prime-ministership in the House of Commons.

If a *worm* can turn, so can a *sheep* as demonstrated by Sir Geoffrey. *Sheep snagging* by the devious *vultures* of the Debt Collection Agencies can be put an end to only by the *sheep* themselves by refusing to continue to cooperate with their bullies and abusers. Given the zoological constellation of character-types who populate the world of credit and debt to form an entire self-sustaining ecosystem of herbivores and carnivores however, this is not predicted to happen anytime soon.

Part Two:

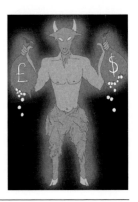

Tricks and Tactics

This second part of our exploration of the ways in which people successfully manage not to pay their Creditors builds upon the system knowledge we have gained in Part One. It looks at specific products and services and how payment for each one is today being evaded. **Once again, we take pains to state that this is not for the purposes of incitement to either pay or not pay, but simply to explore, understand and inform.** First of all we must take note of a couple of key enabling strategies which open the way to avoiding or evading payment for numerous products and services. Thereafter we will examine the peculiarities of individual goods and services as to how they are contracted for and billed, how enforcement is attempted and how consumers can use knowledge of these peculiarities to avoid payment.

19.0

Master Enabling Strategy # 1:

Illegal Use of Car Number Plates

Master Enabling Strategy # 1:

Illegal Use of Car Number Plates

Most people spend many hours of their lives encased in the metal enclosure of a motor vehicle, during which time the only way to identify them, including for the purpose of holding them to account for payment, is the number plate of the car they are driving.

An example of the law of unintended consequences

In Germany during the 1980's there was a system of traffic control cameras which contrived to take a photograph from the front showing of the occupants of a car exceeding the speed limit, and which was sent to the registered keeper's address together as photographic proof of the offence. Anecdotal evidence abounded whereby drivers were confronted by their understandably angry spouses brandishing pictures of themselves with some inconvenient third party of the opposite sex. Such cameras have not been introduced widely in the UK.

Whether they drive for pleasure or for business purposes, the activity is intensely expensive and is under the constant scrutiny and revenue milking of taxation, insurance, fines for speeding and parking infringements, and not least fuel consumption. Hence in addition to police cameras specifically linked to computers which capture number plate data and check that a given car is taxed and insured, similar private systems are used on petrol forecourts to determine that a car is not stolen; and on car parks to capture numbers of cars which may have parked without permission and thus be eligible for penalising by imposition of a fee.

> "Government and commerce thus rely not just very heavily, but quite completely on the currency and accuracy of number plate data to tie car-users into personal accountability..."

Government and commerce thus rely not just very heavily, but quite completely on the currency and accuracy of number plate data to tie car-users into personal accountability, liability to pay and proof of non-compliance in case of infringement. Heaven forfend that the system of reliable number plate identification as a means to personal validation should break down or indeed be susceptible to circumvention – yet it is! Even worse from the point of view of government and commerce, the system is so fraught with opportunity for manipulation, fraud and evasion that the classic organisational response to deadly weaknesses applies:

1) Don't talk about it

2) Don't admit to the facts of it happening

3) Use dire punishments to crush anyone caught exploiting the weakness

If a motorist receives a penalty notice for an offence they did not commit in a location where they have never been they are automatically liable to pay any fine by virtue of being registered as the keeper of the car to which the number plate

> "As with cloned credit cards, extreme proof is needed by a victim to demonstrate the facts of cloning..."

associated with the alleged violation belongs. Anyone who cannot provide a cast-iron alibi of their whereabouts including witnesses and documentary evidence when confronted with an allegation of past misdeeds which will have occurred perhaps 6 weeks ago simply will not be believed. As with cloned credit cards, extreme proof is needed by a victim to demonstrate the facts of cloning.

How hard is it even to remember, never mind prove, where you where at 3:00pm 6 weeks ago? And even if a motorist can forensically demonstrate that he was in Timbuctoo at the time of an offence it will be suggested that he gave use of his car to the driver and was thus liable as the keeper. There is annoyance at the very least for the victim if not outright hardship and unfairness. Of course for some people, this might suggest they will clone the number plate of someone they dislike...but in every case some unfortunate motorist is likely to suffer consequences if their number plate is copied for the purposes of payment evasion.

Stealing Plates

Surprisingly, over 40,000 sets of registration plates are stolen from cars in the UK each year. As a method of cloning this does have the disadvantage for the perpetrator that the victim discovers their victim status as soon as they look at their car again after the plates have gone. Thus victims are able to promptly contact the police and DVLA to make them aware both of the fact of this crime and their own innocence as victims of it. The number plate will immediately be published to police forces, petrol forecourts and no doubt sundry car parks and security company databases, thus rendering its life as a means to securing fraudulent credit very short indeed.

Buying Copy Plates

While UK websites which advertise replacement registration plates routinely require proof of keeper-status of the number plate being sought via DVLA car registration documentation, it is undoubtedly possible through careful research to buy number plates from abroad which have no such scruples or restrictions. One approach is to buy "show plates" which are ostensibly for use off-road and which can be bought legally for this purpose in UK. Moreover, just as "*everybody on the housing estate knows...*" a dodgy plumber or electrician who will be prepared to help to circumvent utility meters, so certain individual people who work in the thousands of garages which can supply number plates around the UK can no doubt also perhaps be bought.

Self-manufacture of Plates

Many of the frauds which can be perpetrated using false car registration plates are by definition "one-time", ie they cannot easily be repeated without detection once committed and the number thus compromised. This means that the plate used would not have to have any longevity or durability. In fact high gloss quality photo would will do very well... With access to a computer and scanner and an A3 printer, it would be easily possible for almost anyone to photograph and reproduce a high quality life size copy of a real number plate.

Which Plate do they use?

The thoughtful perpetrator will be aware that police technology will increasingly use the data-mining techniques used by the credit agencies, but instead of identifying "goods" as the exceptional creditworthy payer capable and willing to repay credit advanced, these techniques are used to identify "bads". Such "bads" are number plates in the wrong place at the wrong time on the wrong make of car, for example a number plate from a Ford Focus based in St Helens and normally commuting to Liverpool at 8:00am on a Monday morning being picked up on a Vauxhall Vectra in Plymouth at that time, perhaps repeatedly.

If national police computers ever do become clever enough – and of course while this has to be seriously doubted, dedicated and thoughtful criminals stay out of jail by taking no chances – they might even be able to spot both sets of plates being used at the same time in real time and direct a squad car to the "wrong" one by GPS Satellite Positioning technology.

The thoughtful criminal will thus select the car to clone by inspecting local supermarket car parks which will tend to have fewer cameras then paying car parks. They will certainly choose a car which exactly resembles their own, and they will even note the presence of car window stickers or distinctive items on the victim's car (which is what the police will ask the victim to describe in order to distinguish his own car from the cloned one). By observation they may easily detect the sex and even the appearance of the true owner of the number plate they intend to clone.

Really wicked and confident criminals might even go back to the original car park (knowing that people tend to do supermarket shopping at regular times) in order to adjust the appearance of their own vehicle to take account of changes in appearance adopted by the victim in an attempt to distinguish their car, having become aware of it being cloned. Thus, during the lifetime of the use of a particular cloning coup, they will be driving the "right" car and in the right area, making it very difficult for them to be identified as *"the bad guy"*. It has been estimated that between 10,000 and 25,000 cloned plates are in use across the UK and as many as one car in every 250 which enters the inner-London congestion zone does so using cloned plates in order to avoid the £8 congestion charge fee. However the breadth of the forecasts above is an indication that no one really knows the true size of the cloned car population: it could be much larger.

Foreign Plates

Using a foreign plate immediately makes the statement: " I *am from another jurisdiction and pay my tax and insurance there*", especially if displayed on a newish quality car. Perversely, if the vehicle looks dirty as if having travelled a long way recently, this only adds to its shine. However, this statement may not be quite so credible on a visibly old right hand drive vehicle. Foreign cars may be driven for a year on their home country plates and insurance arrangements, so a new car with such registration plates can be presumed to be a temporary visitor. If the vehicle is old and incongruous enough to display UK window stickers or others signs of being comfortable in its UK surroundings, it may well attract attention and questions as to how long it has been in the jurisdiction.

According to the European Union Press Office non-resident drivers (ie using foreign plates) represent around 5% of the road traffic in the EU, whereas the share in the EU of non-resident drivers committing speeding offences is 15% of all speeding offences. A foreign registered car is also three times more likely to commit offences than a resident driver. There are distant moves afoot to promote data sharing on foreign plates, but this appears to be remote for the foreseeable future. Drivers who commit traffic and parking offences using foreign plates and who are not captured *in flagrante* seem highly likely not to have to pay unless they specifically volunteer themselves.

What are false plates used to evade payment for?

Because number plates are a quasi-identifier of personal identity in the mindset of computer programmers, car users immediately qualify as credit-worthy payers, members of the vast herds of sheep and cattle who can be directed by traffic lights even when the streets are empty to stop and start and turn left and right when bid – just by a coloured light! The system of traffic management relies on people behaving in predictable ways, and having apparently been selected into the population of car-keepers, by a kind of reverse logic possessors of registration plate identity look like safe bets for payment systems also.

Car Tax

Penalties for non-payment of car tax range from £80 for non-renewal to £1000 if the case is taken to court. If a number plate has been cloned and its owner is unaware because the cloner has not committed any traffic offences or incurred parking fines which would result in lettering to the victim's address there is effectively no individual "victim" who is made to suffer loss. So long as the original plate holder continues to tax the original car, there would appear to be no limit on the length of time for which car tax could be evaded unless a sharp eyed traffic warden were to spot that the tax disc looked photocopied or forged.

Car Insurance

The same logic applies to car insurance. A number plate forger who otherwise drove within the law and was lucky enough not to be involved in an accident whether of his making or as a passive victim in his own right, might be able to continue to drive undetected or unmolested for a very long time.

Traffic Violations and Parking Fines

Anyone using a cloned registration plate who commits a traffic offence or incurs a fine for parking in the wrong place will incur documentation being sent to the real plate holder and thus alert them to the fact of cloning, thus completely compromising the use of the false plate. They will likely escape the cost of the violation if it is only captured on camera and indeed could continue to commit a whole series of such infringements for a number of weeks.

But if their red-light jumping or speeding attracts the attention of a real life constable of the law the complete cloning fraud will very likely be immediately unravelled. Arrest and a stiffish sentence even for a first offence will be inevitable given the premeditated calculation of the crime and the danger to the entire system of regulating and funding traffic management it presents if widely copied.

"Drive-off" Theft of Petrol

Approximately £14,000,000 is reportedly stolen from petrol stations in the UK each year by motorists quite literally *driving off* without paying. If the average cost of filling up a car with petrol is £70 that equates to 20,000 occurrences of drive-off theft annually. How is this done?

Motorway service stations often have prepayment systems as mandatory for the purchase of fuel, as may those in known high-crime locations such as Liverpool and much of the urban north of England and similarly unpleasant parts of inner London. Where such precautions are in place drive-offs are effectively prevented. But supermarket forecourts during daytime in leafy Surrey or sterling Stirling still widely give credit from the point of the petrol pump during the expected march into the busy payment kiosk, which is now indeed a shop for browsing in in its own right. The motto of the supermarket has always been to stack produce high and make it visibly tempting and available on the basis that: *"If you can't steal it, you can't sell it".*

Perhaps they overreach themselves in this regard on the petrol forecourt with an excessive reliance on cameras and number plate recognition. Someone wearing a baseball cap and sunglasses during the appropriate weather and who is driving a clean newish car will have no trouble gaining a few minutes credit. If they have cloned several number plates and are driving a very common make and colour of car, eg metallic or black, they are quite likely to be able to make an easy criminal escape around the next corner to switch their stick-on photo-paper plates.

"...it is not thought that there is any near-term solution to the cloning of number plates"

Once again the cloning is compromised immediately upon the committing of the crime, but for a commonly appearing car type, the population of clone-prone and thus disposable plates must be fairly inexhaustible... up to a point. If black BMW's in any one location are known to be driving off without paying for their petrol, then petrol kiosk attendants will eventually be instructed to require prepayment for any such vehicle seen lurking at a petrol pump, and the criminals will move on somewhere else.

Number plate crime prevention Trials

While trials involving number plate recognition have taken place in the Birmingham area involving the use of computer chips embedded in the registration plate, it is not thought that there is any near-term solution to the cloning of number plates. The national *Automatic Number Plate Recognition* (ANPR) system which automatically recognises number plates captured using CCTV is reported to be unavailable for real time analysis, simply because of the vastness of data needing to be processed at any one time. There is no imminent solution to the vast lurking problem of number plate cloning; it remains wide open and easily available even to the first time amateur criminal.

20.0

Master Enabling Strategy # 2:

Move abroad

Master Enabling Strategy # 2: Move abroad

In contrast to forging number plates, it is completely legal to move abroad. Any Debtor may do it at any time, and when he does so he does not just remove himself physically from close pursuit by his Creditors: he escapes into another jurisdiction where any further debt chasing must start again from scratch. Worse than this from the perspective of the Creditor, any attempt at debt enforcement abroad has to contend in many cases with a new language, a new legal system and in the absence of the large armoury of credit bureau data sharing tools which are so widely available in UK.

The thoughtful Debtor may consider that, like the apocryphal Japanese tourist escaping the jungle tiger, he effectively does not have to outrun the system, just to put other more easily catchable Debtors between him and his pursuit. In other words, if we recall life from the perspective of the debt collection organisation, they have thousands of cases to pursue, tightly limited budgets and plenty of easier cases to collect close at hand.

> "...by demonstrating their fleetness of foot in moving away successfully to a place of refuge, the Debtor signals that having moved once in this way, they can do it again"

How hard are they really going to try to pursue a Debtor who has moved abroad? Not least, by demonstrating their fleetness of foot in moving away successfully to a place of refuge, the Debtor signals that having moved once in this way, they can do it again. So if a Creditor were indeed to be so bold as to pursue them in one foreign country at significant cost, they could simply move on...

The step of moving abroad is generally effective in defusing pursuit against all

Creditors, no matter what their propaganda might state. This specifically includes the **Child Support Agency**, whose remit only runs in UK and even **HMRC** and the **Student Loans Company**. All government debt agencies rely on sheer terror of their enforcement powers to offset the fact of their bureaucratic bumbling sloth and inefficiency. From the other side of the bars of the cage of his UK domicile the *Lion of the Law* looks a lot less fearsome. He can roar as much as he wants, and yes he can invest money in pursuing debt abroad and will doubtless do so if there is significant criminality involved.

Yet everyone knew that Asil Nadir, the former Polly Peck entrepreneur, was living in North Cyprus from 1993 to 2010 while actively "being pursued" by the Serious Fraud Office on 70 counts of alleged false accounting and theft. When he eventually returned to face his demons, just like Ronnie Biggs in Brazil before him, he did so under his own volition for his own reasons and at a time of his own choosing. Most Debtors who move abroad have no such notoriety or criminal charges pending against them, and no doubt they sleep soundly most nights.

Within the European Union there is provision for debt collection abroad using a *European Payment Order* which must be presented to a local European court. At this stage, even if the Debtor is temporarily surprised and cornered by having to deal with this, they can still apply tactics to delay and obfuscate proceedings, including request for transfer of the hearing to a different court, or raising a dispute, for example, stating that the billing was incorrect. How easy is it to produce alleged copies of letters claimed to have been sent disputing a debt, which have allegedly never been answered?

"No wonder so few graduates abroad make payment to the Student Loans Company."

Quite simply, by continually withdrawing up the mountain on to higher, more rocky and inaccessible ground (the *Sun Tzu* defence against a more powerful opponent), the *jackal* has every prospect of exhausting the resources of the Creditor who has decided to continue funding expensive *hyenas* to keep chasing him.

Not least, even while proceedings are in gestation, he can move country again...

If he moves outside the EU and avoids commonwealth countries whose law will resemble that of UK and be more comfortable and familiar for his pursuers to deal with, again he makes pursuit more expensive and formidable. No wonder so few graduates abroad make payment to the *Student Loans Company*.

In terms of making himself less findable, the Debtor can also resort to changing name; if female by getting married. He can take a "job" rather than a career by working in a casual occupation perhaps in tourism or services, working in the black economy by being paid cash for casual work, thus not even being on the radar of the new host country tax and legal system.

He can rent rather than buy, thus keeping himself off local land registry databases. If he manage to avoid contact with Creditors for more than 6 years, including avoiding to acknowledge or correspond with them , then UK debt will automatically become statute-barred after this period. This will not apply to HMRC debt or to legal fines, but the CSA will not devote any resources to pursuing maintenance on any child who has turned 19 years of age.

21. 0

Master Enabling Strategy #3:

Live in a mobile home

Master Enabling Strategy #3: Live in a mobile home

This is the ultimate step to mobility: having no fixed address, while still possessing a certain degree of comfort and shelter from the elements. It is of course a fairly extreme step in the sense that it creates other problems: need to continuously find somewhere to park overnight, issues of personal security and risk of loss of possessions if they are all in the mobile home.

Against this it obviates the need to pay rent or council tax, and anyone in a mobile job (see earlier sections on lifestyle) would find it easy not to pay income tax. An accommodation address for necessary postal communication could be provided by a postbox shop or an understanding friend; so much the better if they have a "good" postcode for credit application purposes.

> **"This is the ultimate step to mobility: having no fixed address…"**

Not least it makes "flitting" at home or abroad a matter of extreme simplicity. And what if the mobile home has foreign plates because it was imported from abroad? See below on the advantages that these can confer.

22.0

Alphabetical Listing of Payment Avoidance Methods

by Product or Service

Alphabetical Listing of Payment Avoidance Methods by Product or Service

Banks

If a bank holds good security against any loan or mortgage then it really does have the whip hand. In other words if in a distress sale situation, where perhaps the price of the asset might be depressed due to general economic conditions, the bank can still force a sale and be confident of recovering its current loan value and costs of enforcement out of the balance, then the Debtor is truly on the hook. At the point where there is negative equity the Debtor can physically walk away, leaving the keys to a property, albeit the debt will attempt to follow him unless he makes himself bankrupt or absconds.

However, in the case of an unsecured loan the bank is exposed to the willingness of the Debtor to continue to pay, and if his salary or other income is regularly being paid into this bank, then the bank can continue to add costs and fees to an overdue loan and increase the amounts being sucked out of the Debtor's current account. He can of course change banks to stop this happening. At this point the bank is just like any other Creditor and the evasion and escape techniques described in earlier chapters are fully available to the Debtor.

Bailiffs

Enforcement agencies have learned to call those they coerce "customers" and the work they do a "service", both of which are logically correct if one adds the epithet "involuntary". To summarise what has been discussed already, bailiffs who are not enforcing on behalf of government agencies may never use force to enter or break their way into a property. Bailiffs acting on behalf of HMRC or in order to levy against magistrates' fines may break down doors to enter. But to enforce all other types of debt they may only enter "peaceably and with the permission of the occupier".

If the occupier keeps doors and windows (including upstairs windows which the bailiff may legally use a ladder to enter through) firmly closed, does not open or allow the bailiff to enter "to discuss matters", the bailiff will be forced to withdraw. They are paid to turn up, and paid more if they can levy goods, but there will be a limit to the money which a Creditor will be willing to pay to have a bailiff keep going back to fail again. The bailiff has no powers to call upon the police to help him enter.

A car belonging to the Debtor which is parked close to his home can be clamped or towed away, so the cunning Debtor will contrive not to allow this possibility to arise by keeping any vehicle at some distance from his home and under physical cover if possible.

Car Tax

Master Strategy number one above discusses how criminals illegally evade car tax by using incorrect number plates. Car tax cannot be legally avoided by anyone wishing to drive a car on UK roads, other than foreign cars which have been legally imported and may be driven for up to a year in UK on the assumption that car tax has been paid in the country of origin .

Council Tax

Councils are entitled to charge council tax on all private dwellings within their catchment area, based on the assumption that there will be two adults living in each property. While there is no increase in the bill if three or more people share the same home, a 25% discount is available to sole occupants.

There is therefore massive fraud by people who ostensibly live alone, but in fact allow a lover or a lodger to live with them. This is detected by councils based on intelligence from neighbours – so one way the discount fraudster can encourage discovery is to allow regular noisy sex with the live-in lover to disturb the peace through the party wall. Councils also acquire data-sharing files from credit reference agencies which include data such as:

- Who is on the voter's roll

- Who is recorded on the post office address file

- Who is applying for credit and paying bills at this address

Thus any council tax discount fraudster will be very concerned that anyone living undeclared at their address does not receive any mail addressed to them there, but uses some other accommodation or postbox address for their mail instead. Added to this, some three people in every thousand to whom council tax is billed succeed in evading payment each year to the extent that the council eventually has to write the debt off its books. Councils pride themselves in their diligence and persistence in tracing and enforcing against Debtors so this 0.3% successful evader population is evidence that a small *cadre* of *jackals* survives in the urban desert.

Landlords also find ways to evade council tax by declaring properties exempt due to temporary void status or being under refurbishment, but can generally only get away with such exemption for 6 months at a time. On the other hand, once a tenant has moved in the landlord has every incentive to declare them to the council so that they as occupiers and no longer he as landlord become liable to pay the tax.

Anyone who does not pay council tax at all will eventually be prosecuted by the council and liable to bailiff action to levy goods once a *liability order* has been obtained from a magistrate. As an arm of government they have draconian powers of enforcement including *deduction of earnings* directly via an employer (if they can find out who that is), and even a short term of a few weeks in prison, although this may become less likely with the ever increasing pressure on prison space through a combination of growing criminality and budget cuts reducing prison beds. Enforcement is likely to take at least 6 months and perhaps longer for the creative delayer. Ultimately Master Strategy Number 2, discussed above, of leaving the country is highly likely to succeed in allowing the Debtor to evade payment for arrears indefinitely. No figures are available for extradition orders to bring back arch-council tax evaders to face the consequences of their misdeeds. This could be because the number is zero.

Child Support

Has any Government Agency attracted more vitriol and derision than the CSA? It is lumbered with creaking IT systems, and routinely reports debt as being "compliant" if a Debtor makes just one monthly payment a year and pays nothing for the other eleven months. Yet dozens of its reluctant clients (non-resident parents or *NRP's*) have committed suicide as a result of its oppressive collection methods which can include withdrawal of driving licence and passport; *deduction of earnings* at source without needing to go to court again once a liability order has been granted; *charging orders* and *orders for sale* to make non-resident parents homeless; and indeed jail.

The CSA is also widely vulnerable to fraud but, perhaps because of inter-departmental resource wrangles, appears now to be much less interested in pursuing this. The joke on the taxpayer is that for so-called "parents with care" (the recipients of money collected on behalf of the children of Non Resident Parents or *NRP's*) on benefit as so many are, there is a direct incentive to claim that they are not being paid by the NRP, while secretly accepting cash in hand from them and continuing to fraudulently accept benefits, thus getting paid twice. This is easy if they allege that they fear violence from him, as we will see below in a moment. So how then do Debtors or NRP's, avoid paying the CSA?

Threatening Violence

If an NRP threatens to harm any of the beneficiaries of debt to be collected from him by the CSA it is widely known that the CSA will cease activity against him in order to avoid endangering his ex-partner and her family. NB, threatening to do violence to oneself does not count, so if an NRP kills himself this is not a statistic on which the CSA measures its success.

Moving Abroad

Because the government agencies are now plugged into Credit Reference Agency data sharing programmes the CSA will be aware of any attempts by non-paying Debtors to sell a house as a means to avoid payment and it will accelerate moves to obtain an injunction against the NRP to stop them selling their house; and indeed to take a charge on the house so that the CSA gets paid first on any sale. However, if the NRP is compliant and makes initial payments, and then subsequently decides to sell their house, no such action can take place. If, while remaining compliant by making payments, the NRP then sells his assets and places them abroad, again there is no case for action to stop them. If subsequently the NRP, having sold their assets and placed the proceeds abroad, stops paying, that is too bad from the perspective of the CSA. The NRP will have succeeded in evading payment. Is this rocket science, a state secret or actually quite obvious?

Holding property and Bank Accounts jointly

The CSA has obtained new powers to require banks to disclose money in bank accounts held by NRP's, including the ability to receive regular data extracts from banks to monitor banking transactions. Thus they will be empowered to observe when money comes into a bank account and to use a *garnishee*-type power to have it withdrawn and paid to them. *They cannot do this for joint bank accounts*. They will equally struggle to obtain *charging orders* and *orders for sale* on houses being lived in by the NRP and their new partner. Thus any NRP who decides that for their own reasons they cannot leave the UK may find themselves incentivised to place their assets either jointly, or even entirely with a third party such as a new partner.

Ignoring Debt Collection Agencies completely

Such is the evident impotency of the CSA's computing and accounting systems that they appear to completely lose overview of any debt farmed out to a Debt Collection Agency (DCA) for collection. NRP's attending debt counselling sessions repeatedly report that while a debt is with the DCA for collection all CSA in-house internal collection activity seems to have ceased. CSA staff tell the NRP that they cannot deal with the case because it has been farmed out; and the DCA cannot tell the NRP how much current liability for ongoing maintenance he is incurring.

This is a chaotic situation, which only benefits the NRP! So the NRP has effectively been given more time, even though their current liability for ongoing child maintenance will continue to accrue and is not visible to or collectable by the DCA, or indeed anyone so long as the account remains with the DCA. The good news from the perspective of the reluctant NRP is that, having trialled debt farm-out to DCA's, the CSA is likely to do much more of this activity in the future due to reductions in internal womanpower through government cuts (From the perspective of public policy and use of public money, of course, this situation is a catastrophe.)

In any case, the overwhelming majority of NRP's reportedly succeed in continuing to defy DCA's who have been commissioned by the CSA by not paying. They have recognised that the DCA will never spend their own money on legal enforcement and that debt being sent for collection to a third party DCA has been given up on for traditional collection in-house as uncollectable: they have effectively been given a payment holiday by the incompetence of the CSA.

Being Self-Employed

It is very easy for the CSA to obtain a *Deduction of Earnings Order* (*DEO*) for those who are employed, particularly if the NRP has a "career" rather than a job. ...eer means that one is hooked into remaining with a particular empl... Visibility to recruitment consultants means very clear visibility as a high profile milk cow to the CSA, whereas anyone in a mere job with no particular attachment to it, and in an occupation where there is high turnover and they can quickly move on, is much better placed to keep moving to avoid and stay ahead of the *DEO*. People working in a freelance capacity through an employment agency also have significant commercial clout with the agency: if it is quick to implement the *DEO* they can simply move on to another agency.

Not least an employer is coerced by threat of fines for non-compliance to cooperate with the CSA in imposing the *DEO,* while anyone self-employed has a self-interest in being non-compliant if they are minded not to pay. Famous footballers routinely fail to cooperate with the CSA, relying on the fact that what the CSA really cares about is to be able to show numbers of "compliant" NRP's in order to hit targets with its political masters rather than maximise income for the parent with care.

Thus instead of paying between 15% for one child and 25% for three children or more of their weekly income of hundreds of thousands of pounds, they wait for the "Default Maintenance Demand" which is just slightly above the UK average weekly wage – a pittance not just for footballers but for most of the self-employed who will earn significantly more than this.

By paying the Default Maintenance set by the CSA the self-employed NRP can in perpetuity avoid having to pay based on their real income without further challenge and without any risk to their bank accounts or houses. This may be a cop-out for the parent with care, but it makes for good statistics to report to government on how successful the CSA is.

Credit Cards

To apply for a credit card with the deliberate intent of not paying the balance is of course criminally fraudulent. It is a fact, however, that the majority of distressed *sheep* who trot into the offices of the credit charities present with a number of credit card debts in addition to struggling with utility debt. It remains very possible for consumers to acquire numerous credit cards despite the protestations of "the credit industry" that they now use shared data about credit cards to avoid lending to customers who appear to have too many to the point where they be becoming "over-indebted".

In a *Ponzi*-like manner, credit from new cards is used to fund minimum repayments to existing Creditors until credit is exhausted. Whether this is premeditated fraud,or as a result of *lemming*-like reaction to finding oneself on the drug of free credit is moot, probably un-provable in the individual case, and certainly not worth pursuing in the eyes of the credit card company in terms of attempting to seek prosecute someone who genuinely can no longer afford to pay.

Anyone so minded may decide to take the advice of lawyer Stanley G Hilton as described in his book: *To Pay or Not to Pay* and hire a lawyer to sue the credit card company for inveigling them into debt. This might cost quite a lot of money in legal fees for each Creditor thus to be challenged and occasionally it might even work, or it might not... Thus the *jackal* would observe from afar and wonder: when a *goat* seeks out a *hyena* to defend him from a pack of *dogs* in a process presided over by a *lion,* who will ultimately get eaten?

Debt Collection Agencies

Tactics to defeat debt collection agencies, who like bailiffs are an involuntary "service" to the overdue Debtor, have been described in depth in earlier chapters. In a word the Debtor can evade paying by pretending to ignore them, not taking any calls or making any responses whatever.

Electricity

Billing and payment arrangements are very similar for electricity and gas. Both largely rely on a new customer making themselves known to the supply company; they rely on the customer to tell them when they arrived, ie when billing should start, and not least on the customer to report the starting meter read. The classic payment avoidance tactics that apply to both products are therefore discussed under **Gas** below.

Theft of Electricity

If anything, electricity is even more open to non-payment and theft (known as "illegal abstraction of electricity") as it can be slightly less dangerous to work with than gas. For example, it is quite easy to bypass an electricity supply and disguise the fact of this by burying or plastering over wiring – although highly dangerous. By contrast, anyone trying to bypass a gas meter illegally has the problem of cutting into the supply pipe and engineering a t-junction solution which will not be immediately obvious to the next meter reader, if playing with leaking live gas has not already wiped out most of the evidence by killing the would-be perpetrator in the attempt through a devastating gas explosion.

Thus physical intervention to avoid billing and thereby payment is easier to carry out than for gas. It is very common for late-night takeaway outlets not to pay their electricity bills and indeed to be cut off. This apparent Armageddon is not, however, the easy solution for the electricity supplier that it appears. Most such commercial outlets then simply bypass the supply and are immediately in business again. Utilities do not routinely invest in checking that *disconnected* means *staying disconnected* by regularly inspecting for continued use, particularly as this might involve someone being prepared to work after 0900pm when many of these outlets first open...

The problem gets worse for the supplier because, having been without a supply for 28 days – at least nominally so whether or not the connection has been bypassed – the commercial takeaway customer is legally entitled to seek another supplier who cannot outright refuse to supply, but may demand a hefty prepayment to do so. For the by-passer this problem doesn't necessarily arise so long as he can keep the current flowing undetected. If things get really hot in terms of follow-up, the takeaway can simply change its name and nominal proprietor and start again as a so-called *Phoenix*... Easy, really. One wonders if these people ever pay taxes either?

Domestic customers can also illegally but easily bypass meters by interrupting the supply ahead of the meter and reconnecting behind it. Wires are much easier to re-route, to bury in plaster and to reconnect to a distribution fuse box out of sight of the area of the meter. Given proposed developments for remote electronic meter reading, meter readers are supposed to be a dying breed. Already, many are being made redundant and those that remain are aware that their jobs are under threat.

> "Meter reading is a low-skill but stressful activity, involving shy door-knocking and rapid scurrying in and out of domestic properties"

Meter reading is a low-skill but stressful activity, involving shy door-knocking and rapid scurrying in and out of domestic properties. People who do meter reading for a living tend to be introverted loners who hate personal contact; they just want to get in and out, terrified of physical confrontation or worse.

Long since contracted out by utilities to third party data reading contractors, meter reading is the Cinderella occupation of utility supply, which itself is not exactly a scintillating theatre of excitement. So how much reliance can be placed on these very low-paid and much abused apparatchiks to sniff out and investigate possible malfeasance by householders?

What Barry does – illegally and not recommended

Barry is a real person who pays very little for his electricity because he steals most of it. He has drilled a very small hole in the side of the Bakelite meter-housing at an angle which is not obvious even if a torch is casually shone upon the meter. Through the hole he pokes a cocktail stick to jam the little cog-wheel of the meter so that it no longer goes round and thus the meter stops recording.

When the meter reader comes round, Barry always goes and stands helpfully beside him to direct him to read it. This makes the shy meter reader even more eager to take a read and go, so Barry has been successfully stealing electricity for many years. He gets away with it because he is careful and thoughtful. He smears the hole with shoe polish to disguise it when not in use. When he wants to do a washing in his washing machine, in goes the cocktail stick; but he is also sure to let the meter run undisturbed several days a week.

He also keeps careful records of how much electricity he is allowing to run through the meter so that the supply does not fluctuate significantly. He knows that his supply company will compare his usage with that of his neighbours, but he also knows that within certain limits, utilities have to recognise that there are high and low users. Not least, Barry always pays his low electricity bills on time, so he appears to be a model customer. He has worked out that if he pays something rather than trying to get away with nothing at all, he can get away with long-term theft.

The Stupidity of Cannabis Farmers

While it is illegal to import cannabis seeds into the UK, under certain conditions the police will not be too strict with an individual smoking it for his own use; but woe betide he should try to grow it himself and sell it. This may or may not appear to be a logical approach by the *Lion of the Law*, but ours is not to reason why... The fact is that growing and selling cannabis, as well as being highly illegal, is an easy way to get rich quickly for the unscrupulous.

But unlike Barry, so many of them are dyed-in-the-wool stupid. Being criminals they are morally indignant at the idea of paying for their utilities; so they use lots to heat houses and flats to keep their tender plants warm and thereby signal very clearly that they are not just incredibly high-end consumers, but indeed so consumptive of energy that the only possible explanation can be that they must be growing cannabis.

Even if they weren't drawing attention to themselves by running up huge bills which continue unpaid and thus give themselves highest priority for disconnection to halt the loss of revenue, just by using so much publicly supplied and highly visible energy, whether electricity or gas, they are signalling: " *I am a criminal growing cannabis, come discover and arrest me on the easy*

> "There is a moral here for the immoral and it is that Gordon Gecko was wrong: greed is not good"

basis of a warrant of disconnection". There is a moral here for the immoral and it is that Gordon Gecko was wrong: greed is not good. Excessive greed is stupid. But more than this, stealing is itself of course wrong and always to be condemned, no matter how "clever" the act of abstraction.

Dumb and Dumber? Using Forged Meter Tokens

In drinking establishments of low repute it is apparently not uncommon to be offered cut-price electronic token meters for use in electricity or gas prepayment meters with the promise that these will give access to half-price fuel. While the initial promise may be true, ie that the tokens actually do work, the utility will of course discover that electricity or gas is being consumed without payment when the meter is reconciled. The first way that this can happen is during a "must-read" meter reading which must happen every two years. While this might seem a generous degree of leeway, doom in the form of discovery lurks much earlier and ironically by the hand of the perpetrator himself.

Every time that a token meter is re-charged at a *Paypoint* outlet it uploads a current meter reading to the **Electronic Token Meter** (ETM) system of the utility. So whenever the credit on the forged ETM card runs out and the electricity or gas user reverts to using their own card, the meter read uploaded to the Electricity or Gas supplier's energy accounting system will reveal a sudden jump forward in the meter read.

As the supplier regularly reconciles the amount of energy recorded by the meter with the value of energy sold to that meter, it will become apparent within a month or so of reversion to using the correct ETM card that energy has been used and not paid for. This will generate an automatic notice from the utility warning the consumer that that the utility suspects illegal use of an unauthorised ETM card; that they intend to make an early inspection to validate the meter, and that prosecution may follow if there is indeed proven to have been theft; and not least that the consumer will now have to pay a second time for the energy used by paying up to the utility supplier for the gap in recorded payments to it.

But what if the forged ETM card can be re-charged or exchanged for yet another one from the dodgy character in the pub, so that the correct card is never used again? There will be no early signal to the utility that payments are missing for energy consumed and no early threat of dire consequences. The utility will run a regular report on non-consuming ETM's and identify this one as such a non-consuming meter. So long as the consumer does not use their correct ETM card there will be no certainty as to whether the property is now occupied or empty. Perhaps the consumer has no cash and has "self-disconnected"? Perhaps there is no one there any longer, which would explain the apparent non-purchase? In this case, by avoiding contact with the utility the consumer may well succeed in avoiding detection until the next run of "must read" meter readings. Even these visits can be deferred for some time by the appearance of non-occupation.

> "But what if the forged ETM card can be re-charged or exchanged for yet another one from the dodgy character in the pub, so that the correct card is never used again? "

For utilities they are a costly chore and there is a recognition in terms of the targets that they set themselves under the previously referred-to "law of large numbers", that they will never succeed in reading all the meters they set out to. Hence targets for meter reading are generally in the 95% range. The *jackal and hide* tactic of waiting out and exhausting the opponent can yield dividends here too for the fraudulent thief of energy.

Jackals do not stay overly long at a given property; for them a time horizon of two years is perfectly adequate. They can even take comfort in the fact that utilities are more complacent in their approach to needing to know who their customer is for properties with prepayment meters: if the customer has to pay, why bother knowing who he is? The other side of this coin is that if he does not pay and they still don't know who he is, they are completely undone when he moves on. He is virtually untraceable.

Fines

According to the *Public Accounts Committee* of *the House of Commons,* just 30% of fines which remain unpaid after 6 months are considered recoverable. The amount of unpaid fines and penalties increases year on year and in excess of £1 billion, older than 6 months, is believed to be uncollectable.

"From the point of view of a payment refusee, however, non-payment might appear a very attractive option, specifically if the refusee is not encumbered with assets to impound or houses to have sold from under him"

This appears to be extremely serious for a government which can no longer afford the £41,000 per annum which is costs to put a fine non-payer in jail; indeed to do so would only make the Government's finances worse.

From a citizenship perspective therefore, non-payment of fines is a real threat to social cohesion if it cannot be backed up with prison. From the point of view of a payment refusee, however, non-payment might appear a very attractive option, specifically if the refusee is not encumbered with assets to impound or houses to have sold from under him. With a high degree of irony therefore, it is the sort of person who is perhaps most likely to incur civil and criminal penalties short of a prison sentence who is most fitted in terms of attributes to be able to resist paying those fines!

Gas

Most of the following applies to electricity as well as gas. In earlier chapters we have often referred to Sun Tzu with his emphasis on confusing the opponent. All that this ancient master has to say is relevant in spades with regard to utilities.

The Example of Lawrence of Arabia

The other example we might look to here is the more recent guerrilla, Lawrence of Arabia. Analogous to Lawrence's opponents in the First World War – the Turks on the Arabian peninsula – utilities shift large volumes of customer on "railway track" processes. Laurence used camels. His technique was to blow up the railway tracks of the Turkish Army, curtailing their freedom of movement of large volumes of troops and ordnance. The Debtor jackal too finds ways of "blowing up the tracks" of the stultified processes which large utilities have engineered to railroad Debtors down particular paths and thus adding delay after delay before he finally decamps to another oasis.

The average annual UK domestic gas bill is said to be around £900 and rising, while across the UK 5,500,000 people are estimated to live in fuel poverty, ie needing to spend over 10% of their net incomes on heating and powering their homes. The industry (including electricity companies, for all of them supply both electricity and gas) has now developed literally thousands of different tariffs to bamboozle the consumer and has been actively criticised for its opaque pricing and failure to align charges promptly to movements in the gas wholesale price. Price movements over the medium term have been in one direction: upwards. Little wonder then that there is wide resentment of utility profits as well as extensive levels of debt owed by hard-pressed consumers for a good which is necessary for life.

Around 30,000 people die each year in their own homes of hypothermia, largely because they are too frightened to switch on their heating. Pity poor Phil Bentley then, Managing Director of *British Gas*, who earned a mere £1,249,000 reported salary and bonuses in 2009/2010. It may or may not be "wrong" not to pay your gas bill; but can it be right for someone licensed to dominate an oligopoly for a basic human need to earn quite so much?

So what are we to make of the fact that the domestic gas industry is unable to prevent at least one gas consumer on average in every hundred from successfully evading payment for their full year's gas supply? Of those people who move out of a property without paying their final bill after 6 weeks, only 40% are ever persuaded to pay up and the other 60% is eventually written off. Even for those cases where the gas industry discovers a new address, only 1 customer in 20 of those holding out and not paying have traditionally been pursued through the county courts. And even when they are sued, only around 25% of these pay up. Yet again this is a story of *cattle, sheep, goats and jackals* each behaving to type and each paying or not paying as a matter of their nature and training. It is very possible for a domestic consumer not to pay for domestic gas without ever breaking the law.

> "It is very possible for a domestic consumer not to pay for domestic gas without ever breaking the law."

We have already discussed some of the tactics used to defeat gas and electricity bill collection in the section **Dealing with a Determined Collector** and the Sub-section **Defence in Depth.** Without re-visiting this in its entirety it sets out basic tactics which can include:

- Pretending that no one is in the property

- Delaying the debt path

- (illegally) Falsifying readings to minimise bills

We will now list some of the specific practices which hold-outs use to minimise or successfully evade gas debt in particular altogether. We start by emphasising that everyone has a right to a domestic gas supply, that no supplier is entitled to refuse one although they may make onerous conditions such as the prepayment of a deposit of (in practical terms) two thirds of the annual *Supply Charge*, and that *British Gas* remains the "Supplier of last resort", which will always be looked to by the Regulator *Ofgem* to supply a struggling domestic customer.

The consumer has numerous champions including *Ofgem* and watchdog quango *Consumer Focus,* and the gas companies are very concerned not to be shown to be acting against their own published codes of practice in regard to debt collection and enforcement, which could be used against them by *Ofgem* to limit their licence to continue to trade and at the very least cause them acute embarrassment, loss of face and potential customer switching to other brands.

The Bains Case Cock-up

In July 2002 British Gas disconnected the gas supply of an elderly retired couple named Bains due to non-payment of their winter 2001 gas bill. The couple did not phone to seek re-connection and sadly died of hypothermia the following winter, even though it turned out that they were not without means to pay. In the rush for cover that followed a predictable storm of criticism in the worthy British Press, British Gas stated that they had not informed social services of the plight of the Bains due to the restrictions of the Data Protection Act.

The Information Commissioner reacted to this hot potato being tossed onto his lap by accusing British Gas of completely misunderstanding the purpose of the Data Protection Act, and responding that they should have interpreted it to mean that where someone was in mortal danger, personal data could indeed be shared with social services to save them. This of course assumes that the error-prone utility would have had any idea that the Bains were elderly, vulnerable and suffering, which itself is doubtful.

After the Bains tragedy the utility industry hurriedly formed an agreement among themselves that in future no domestic gas supply would ever be left physically unconnected to a gas supply: instead where they forcibly entered a domestic property to extract a credit meter, they would in future connect an electronic token meter (ETM) as had long been the practice of the electricity industry. This self-serving step – ETM's can be programmed by the utility to take at least 40 pence in every pound to pay for debt (and sometimes much more), leaving just 60 pence for heating – does not prevent the fuel poor from continuing to freeze because they don't have any money to buy pre-payment tokens, but it does mean that if you have money, you need never be cold, even if debt evasion fails. So the utilities have done their duty, but old people still freeze to death in their homes each year.

Writing to utility to announce move-in (optional to waiting for their contact):

This is a bold attacking strategy, which if over-egged may attract early unwelcome attention:

- Declining to offer to pay by direct debit, insisting on quarterly cash.

- Declining to supply full name and explicitly refuse consent to data sharing. Insisting on company writing to acknowledge data share refusal and to explain how they will assure this.

- Adding a goodly figure to the actual meter read (to later insist if probed that whoever moved out must have given a dodgy final read). Hence if the true meter read is 4000, by giving a start read as 6000 the new user can consume 2000 units before reaching the actual meter read of today as free gas.

- Declining to supply phone or email contact details.

Finding a sucker-supplier

From a high of around 18 gas suppliers at the turn of the century, competitive consolidation reduced the number of utilities providing domestic gas to just 6 some years later, but new entrants continue to emerge. Some of these insist on direct debit as a pre-condition of supply in the belief that this assures they will get paid. Some are founded by eco-idealists who want to deliver "green" energy to a grateful world; many these new companies try to cut corners or have optimistic assumptions about how easy it is to get paid. They tend to be sales-led and focus on growth of new customers without much consideration of controls. A jackal will find it much easier to play a new supplier than a traditional one. Not least the new supplier will tend to out-source much of their back office and collection activity, which makes for longer chains of communication, less ability to command and control; and having a widely dispersed customer base makes it hard to economically justify field visits and enforcement for one lone

> *jackal out in the boondocks. NB, green energy is mixed up with all the other energy sources when it comes down the pipe or out of the socket, so any über-sheep dumb enough to pay over the odds for such a tariff arguably deserves to pay for the jackal too – he would no doubt argue.*

Amending the first bill by phoning in a new meter read to the utility voice answering system.

A first bill may be sent early based on an estimate to test the willingness of the consumer to pay, specifically in cases where the utility believes there may be a problem. Debt chasing will also be programmed to be rapid and rigorous for a first bill, so why not draw its sting? If a bill is received for £100 and a new lower meter read is immediately phoned through to lower it to £10, some weeks grace will be had while the account is re-billed at the lower figure. If this £10 is paid as cash through an anonymous middleman such as *Paypoint* in cash this will benefit the hold-out in a number of ways:

1. They establish some initial credibility as a payer at very little cost; this positive payment history will then programme further correspondence and debt chasing to regard them as lower risk, starting later in a more dilatory way and escalating more slowly, buying more time again.

2. They maintain their anonymity and possibly their true identity if paying under an alias, thus making themselves harder to trace later.

3. They withhold their banking details which provide not just a personal identifier but a possible means of enforcing payment after a judgement via a *garnishee order*; or indeed a possible means to finding their employer.

If a new lower reading is sent in at any time to most utility billing systems they will re-bill to the new read. This re-starts the entire cycle through the debt path.

More intelligent utility systems may be set to question amended reads if the amount outstanding has progressed to the first visit stage; but even if the utility refuses to accept the new read, this then becomes a useful bone of contention and "justification" if ever in dialogue with them as a reason not to pay.

Name changes

In a court of law the utility must sue a specific named customer, there is no point in suing "*The Occupier*", although they may be obliged to seek a *warrant for disconnection* of supply for this "Occupier" if he will not give his name and does not pay. Occupiers are discussed in depth earlier in this book. Furthermore the entire threat of loss of credit status for non-payment is dependent upon the utility being able to accurately name their customer with no doubt as to validity.

It is a serious misdeed in the eyes of the Data Commissioner to confuse John Henry Smith with John Harry Smith, potentially disclosing data about the wrong individual or damaging the wrong individual's credit status. Thus the utility will be at very great pains to validate the name of their customer; and once they have that customer on the bill they have a potential cash yielding asset which they will not lightly release from the account.

One classic way not to pay a utility is to remove oneself from the account as a named customer. Obviously if this customer is the only name on the account the utility will only be willing to do this if the account is paid up fully and thus closed either because the customer has changed supplier or has moved out. This is of no use to the *jackal* whatever! He therefore needs to exchange his name with that of someone else.

Basically the utility will agree to names being added without much ado, because they think they are getting more *cattle* to milk if others on the account do not pay. What the individual account holder can do is to subtly change their name, more than once, rather like in word games, so that by a series of subtly small "typographical corrections" Jack Johnson becomes Zac Jensen.

It is easier if there is more than one name on the account. More can be added with less focus on validation and control while the account is still in credit and then others more easily subtracted. All of this is likely to be easier still with new "sucker suppliers".

Talking to Sales and Customer Service and avoiding Debt Management

As with any romance the faithless lover can get away with more when the tryst is new and the other party dewy with expectation and trust. Customer service staff are highly focussed on customer retention and get roughly 10 days training in customer satisfaction techniques for every one day on collections. They want to please and if a customer whose account is new and still not due for payment calls them, they really want to help.

Furthermore utilities routinely use students, temporary contractors and in-betweeners at weekends and in the evenings. These jobbers have absolutely no commitment or career skin in the game with their employer and precious little training. They have to take phone calls at unsocial hours supervised by losers who have been bullied into taking the late shift: no one wants to be there. They are prime meat to be asked to do something slightly gullible. Hence if a *jackal* wants to amend a name, he will never call debt management and never in normal office hours. It will be done via sales or customer service late in the evening or Saturday afternoon.

Resisting the Gas Debt Enforcement Path

Ways of affecting not to live in a property have already been discussed. In order to obtain a *warrant of disconnection* in mainland Great Britain utilities need to demonstrate that they have made a "first visit" and left a notice of intention to disconnect. The utility representative who carries this visit out is increasingly an outsourced debt collector who may also work part-time as a bailiff.

Without a warrant of disconnection, which he may try to feign or bluff possession of at the point of first visit, the utility field representative has no right of entry. The Utility Debt Representative may even present a **"dummy warrant"** at the first visit stage. This is a lookalike copy of the warrant which can only be issued by a court at a date AFTER the first visit has been made without any offer of payment by the customer. Such tactics by a utility would be contrary to their published code of openness and fair dealing, but may nonetheless be attempted by a hired hand contractor whose only concern is payment on success.

Otherwise the Utility Representative on first visit will be at pains to obtain meter reads and inspections, to validate who is living at the address, all of which will increase the incentive commission he is paid by the utility. These people are largely paid on results and they have boxes to tick to add more commission.

One strategy for the holdout at this stage is to provide this individual with the "proofs of residence and identity" that he seeks, again as discussed earlier, either as the Holdout in their true guise who has "just moved in", or under a new forged alias with forged lease agreement showing a recent start date; or alternatively putting forward some new named occupier (why not an East European whose previous whereabouts cannot be validated?) as the new customer.

The Utility Representative's objectives are simply to be able to prove that they have visited the site and to get as much data as they can without getting beaten up – and they are all terrified of that outcome. They will certainly get paid more incentive reward if they come away with a payment, but this is so rare at this stage that they do not expect it. The new customer will not let any documents out of their hands for photocopying, but they can be absolutely certain that the Utility Representative has no expertise whatever in validating a passport or work pass, or in spotting a forged lease. He will be only too happy to tick boxes on his worksheet to show that he has seen these documents so that he gets paid a little extra for providing the information.

Location, location, location

A holdout who lives in a remote rural location will have a longer respite than someone living among a crowd of chimneypots. A locked farm gate, a dog running loose, a long driveway to a front door, the absence of a letterbox: all are disincentives to the hired lookout utility representative. Frequently these people will pretend to have made a visit when they in fact have not done so, even when the location is close at hand, just in order to make a commission. They are in no hurry to have a guard dog chase them down a farm lane.

Door Locks

As a medieval siege would inevitably progress to battering down the gate of a castle keep, so the front door becomes the object of attention at the stage of enforcement of a warrant of disconnection. Such warrants are enforced on daily "runs" by a team of three including the utility representative, a hired locksmith and a National Grid Engineer.

On a good day from the point of view of the utility this team might be able to carry out 8 disconnections and reconnections. Let us not forget what we learned about the Pareto 80:20 rule earlier. The utility is under severe budget discipline to make the best use of its resources. They will always prioritise the 8 easy disconnections which give them 20% of effort and time over the 2 difficult cases which will take up 80% of available time in a day. It will cost possibly £1500 per day to employ this team. They do not want to be spending a whole day to resolve a £500 debt.

Most door locks are commonly available and thus easy for locksmiths to open as they recognise the type and have the tools. However, there are unusual types of locks which are very difficult to break, to the extent that most locksmiths on a disconnection run would have to walk away. Such door lock systems have features such as key control, such that keys cannot be copied, saw-resistant bolts, anti-drill features, bolt assembly protectors, steel door-frames.

Meter test request

A customer may refuse to pay a gas bill on the basis that they cannot possibly have consumed the amount stated: the meter must be wrong! Perhaps they say that they have been away most of the time. They can demand that the meter be tested prior to pay anything for their gas. Again this will buy time, particularly if the customer makes himself unavailable or keeps putting off the appointment with the specialist meter test engineer who will call.

Meter Manipulation

Customers have in the past succeeded in manipulating meters by various means, including tilting them, cutting off their electricity supply, using strong magnets. Today's meters have been engineered to resist such tampering, but this will not stop determined evil-doers from trying, even though some Electronic Token Meters and modern "smart meters" have anti-tampering detective controls.

Special Needs

A customer who is wheel-chair bound or who is shown to have severe learning difficulties may be incapable of physically accessing an electronic meter, or be unable to get to a purchase point to buy credit and hence unsuitable as a customer for an electronic token meter. If they can demonstrate hardship to one of the charities such as *Citziens Advice Bureau* or specifically to *Consumerwatch* this will again buy time before the utility attempts to install an ETM. Similar extraordinary consideration must be given to the elderly and to people with young children; by themselves these factors may not prevent a disconnection (and ETM reconnection) for non-payment, but they can add weight to a story of hardship in the context of utility misdeeds or errors causing mis-billing and inappropriate and heavy-handed enforcement attempts, buying more precious time.

Deceased

This ploy is a variant on the "just moved in, previous occupier gone" gambit. In this case the named account holder is reported to the utility to have gone to where he will not be returning from. Depending upon the level of previous contact and payment history, such a statement may or may not be believed by the utility. If it is directed by mail to a specific unit such as "Billing Department, Deceased Section" it will likely be conveyored onto a slow under-manned and incompetent deceased process which will elicit a sympathetic response and a request for final reads if sent by an "executor" at a different address. Again this will buy time, particularly if the executor lives in a different town and can justify their inability to provide prompt reads. If they then provide an obviously incongruous read, say 6 odd digits for a 5 digit meter which bear no resemblance to the actual read, then they can point out the misunderstanding later with another read… buying more time.

If, however, someone at the same address announces the death of a co-habitant account-holder the utility will simply invite that person to assume responsibility for any outstanding bill as someone who has been a beneficiary of the supply under the Gas Act. (The same applies for electricity). Such a move confers no advantage on the would-be hold-out.

Customer Relations

Customer Relations Departments are a branch of Sales. Their role in life is to protect the utility brand from unpleasant and brand-damaging publicity. They often report directly to the Chief Executive so as to have short lines of communication to be able to minimise potential damage quickly. Like Legal Departments, Customer Relations Departments work on the "Downside only" rule. If they do their jobs thoroughly by providing cautious advice, they labour unnoticed but well-rewarded, but if their advice leads to controversy and brand damage their careers are destroyed: so why take risks? Hence they will always act conservatively and assume the possibility of the worst outcome for their careers if they get their advice wrong.

Therefore, any customer with a pungent claim that they are being wronged will get a very ready ear. Any complaint to them will be ineffective if on the day of disconnection, with the utility disconnection team at the door; by then it is too late. They are at their most open to over-riding the enforcement process (which is always within their power) at the point just before the final disconnection with its potential for confrontation, mayhem and bad publicity on a doorstep.

Change of Supplier

If a gas consumer is in debt and attempts to change supplier, the existing supplier has 28 days to object to the customer leaving on grounds of the debt after they have been advised of the change by *National Grid* which administers the national gas accounting system. Unbelievably perhaps, but even the very largest gas suppliers have been shown to be incompetent in working through the checking process of would-be leavers and then following through with an objection, which would prevent the transfer going through. In the case of one of the very biggest of all, its ability to successfully prevent customers leaving in time to meet the 28 day window was traditionally around only 60% and sometimes as low as 40%. How could this be?

The answer is that behind the scenes utilities are always having to cope with backlogs of work of various kinds, created by the so-called law of large numbers, whereby minor process flaws emerge and small numbers of customer accounts that are incorrect in some way grow unnoticed over time and then start to create disproportionately more work to fix, creating staff shortages. The utilities are ever having to cut corners with their processes and the boring billing department (boring but vital to the company's revenue!) is always a prime place to look for bodies to stop doing *task a* for a while in order to do *task b*. Then staff are asked to do *task a* and *task b* together, which is too much so they make a hash of both.

The moral for the canny Debtor is that if under pressure from impending disconnection, but with at least one month's grace (in order for any transfer to take effect) it is always worth their while to try to sign up with another supplier as yet another escape avenue. If the odds of winning are 40%, then multiple attempts over a series of weeks may mean that one attempt will succeed.

If a Debtor is able to send a gas company a new supply contract showing that they have moved supplier, this again will buy time. If they use their right to turn up at the magistrates court to contest an application for a *warrant of disconnection* (which should have been cancelled if the contract is more than 28 days old) then the magistrate will throw out the warrant.

Obtaining court referral and re-scheduling delay

The utility needs to have a court magistrate sign any *warrant of disconnection* which will give them the legal power to enter a Debtor's property, if necessary under police supervision, in order to disconnect the meter and reconnect with a prepayment meter. Most warrants in England are processed by utilities at *Northampton Bulk Issuing Centre* which deals with them in bulk on the basis that very few are challenged by the gas consumer.

However, the customer always must be notified under the *Human Rights Act* 28 days before the court hearing to give him the opportunity to attend court in order to defend the action, or equally importantly to use his right to have the case heard in his local court. This notification will give him the address of whichever court is proposed by the utility to which he can write to obtain a referral to the court nearest to his home.

At this point he can choose to either attend court, perhaps clutching copies of "unanswered correspondence" (which they may not really have been sent) to object to the issue of the warrant. The utility court representative will be taken unawares and the case will inevitably have to be halted for investigation and re-presentation by the utility, probably for at least a month. Alternatively, the defendant Debtor can notify the court of his intention to defend and then send the court a last-minute sick note signed by his doctor. This again will surely lead to re-scheduling and delay.

The Phantom Occupier

Utilities write off hundreds of millions of pounds as uncollectable Occupier debt every year. Very frequently a consumer moves in and out of a property without ever making contact so that the utility has no idea who to bill. But they are also vulnerable to the "phantom occupier" who never was. If we imagine a gas meter reading 5000 when *customer a* moves out and giving the same reading when *customer b* moves in a month later.

What if *customer a* reports that he had only used the meter up to 4000? *Customer b* gives a start reading of 5000, so who has used the missing 1000 units? Is *Customer a* lying to minimise his final read to reduce his final bill? Is *Customer b* lying to maximise his start read to gain 1000 units of consumption before his account starts to bill? Or was there another occupier in that month, perhaps the landlord decorating the property and needing to heat to dry it out?

It is the unfortunate disposition of the utility, just like someone being born ugly, that they can do nothing about this vulnerability. Customers who are in love with their credit rating can keep it pristine while taking a few units of gas or electricity or gas back from the behemoth utility supplier, provided they have a credit meter. And of course in the above scenario, there is nothing to stop *customer b* from declaring their start read as 6000.

Neither *customer a* or *customer b* knows that the other has understated their consumption by 1000 units, but the result for the utility is a phantom occupier account for 2000 units. Even if both customers declare different readings on the same day, moving in and out hours apart, the utility still has no way of knowing who provided the false reading. Do they want to encourage the new customer to move to a new supplier by being heavy handed at the outset?

The Pièce de Résistance:

Changing Supplier and Changing tenancy together to evade debt

This leads us neatly to the final king's move in the chess game of utility debt evasion. A utility can, as we know, object for debt if a customer in debt attempts to change supplier. They cannot prevent *customer b* from choosing a new supplier if they declare to a new supplier that they have just moved in and are therefore not *customer a.* A utility nominates itself as a supplier to a consumer address by contract with the consumer.

A new consumer is free to choose a new supplier at their supply point (address) and by definition they have no liability for any debt of a previous customer. The new customer need not even necessarily have to prove to the new supplier who they are, although it is more certain that they will be accepted and therefore succeed if they can clearly show themselves to be someone who has no association with the address on a credit record. Students, live-in lovers, conniving sub-letters, undisclosed multiple occupiers of whatever hue: all can take advantage of this fact.

Time and Timing

Again and again the benefit of time gained has been stressed as an outcome of various debt evasion methods, but to what end? In the end we are all dead, and time is all we have between us and that certainty. Success in life is largely about creating time, opportunity and freedom to act, or in the case of the

Holdout Debtor, to avoid being acted upon. Saving time for the debt evader, Hold-out or *jackal* is like saving money. In the words of the old Scottish proverb: *"Many's a mickle makes a muckle"*.

In other words elements of time all add up. In the case of utility consumption, added time means not just added time of debt evasion, but added time during which more of the utility service is enjoyed. It also means opportunity for the *jackal* to plan his next move and engineer his next coup. Time is combined with successive strategems akin to a Russian retreat strategy, such as successfully used to wear down the armies of Napoleon in 1812 and Hitler in 1943, simply withdrawing further and further into a desertified wintry landscape which offers no succour to the pursuer.

But timing is also of the essence for the evader of energy utility debt. Once an account has progressed past the *first visit* stage, utility systems and procedures are tuned to be alert and to suspect any customer contact as being potentially fraudulent and evasive in intent. Certainly, once a warrant has been issued, if the three man team of utility debt representative, *National Grid* Engineer (the organisation used to be called *Transco*) and locksmith arrive at the door, these three Horsemen of the Apocalypse will only be deterred from forcible entry to force-fit a prepayment meter by documentary evidence on the doorstep that there is a new customer living there in place of the one they had sought to enforce against.

What about Smart Metering?

It is currently envisaged that a Great Britain mainland system of smart metering will be rolled out for all domestic gas and electricity meters between approximately 2013 and 2015 while certain large UK suppliers propose to roll out their own smart meter solutions prior to this with the hope of integrating their solutions into the approved GB plan. What does this mean for anyone trying not to pay their gas or electricity bills?

Smart meters will be able to be remotely converted from credit meter to prepayment and indeed back again by the supplying utility. They will supply accurate meter readings at all times, enabling timely and accurate billing. Such system features might appear at first pass to change the game completely for consumers and Debtors. They give control to the utility to prevent the Debtor from continuing to use the gas or electricity supply without having to pay for it. It is highly likely that utilities will prioritise properties with previous histories of non-payment in trying to introduce these meters, so the cards appear to be stacked against the struggling Debtor or would be hold-out non-payer. Not least, it is the consumer who will pay for these meters to the tune of an estimated £9 per customer per year.

The Government believes that consumers will benefit overall by having access to more information about their energy consumption, motivating them to reduce consumption and to switch supply to cheaper competitors. (But if the largest suppliers thought this was a threat, why are they piloting their own smart meter solutions?)

The truth is that any consumer savings are highly speculative, ie they may not happen, but the Government will be helped in being seen to work towards its international carbon emission targets and the utilities will save massive amounts of money on staff. There will no doubt be a boom in utility shares when the stock market focuses on the emerging story. Again, Government and commerce call the shots for their own benefit and the consumer is the *lamb* to be led to the slaughter.

"...the history of large computer projects in the UK is not auspicious for either the government or the utilities"

But there remain large areas of uncertainty. Firstly it will be a long time before all properties can have these meters installed, so there will continue to be scope for Debtors avoiding payment at least until this happens. Secondly, the rules of engagement have yet to be set out including consumer protections which may also give cover for the Won't pay. There are major human rights and data protection concerns surrounding smart meters: the radio emissions they use to transmit date to central data receiving stations may be hazardous to human health, particularly if meters are fixed to a wall next to a bedroom only a few feet away from a sleeper's head.

Significant amounts of personal data, including lifestyle data – what appliances a consumer uses when, when they get up and go to bed, when they leave their home and return – can be inferred from smart metering data; it remains to be seen whether consumer consent will be required to allow utilities to transmit and use this data. This might well give a consumer the right to refuse the meter on grounds of human data protection and human rights. It is also highly likely that with a large roll-out programme, utilities will place their efforts on properties where customers are not resisting in the first instance, allowing time for hold-outs to continue to keep existing "dumb" credit meters.

But … It is not clear whether so-called inter-operability of meters between suppliers will actually work. In other words, if a consumer wants to change from one supplier to another, we are not yet informed how the changeover, including all the metering read data, will work. There are weaknesses being planned into the system which will eventually be exploited by enterprising Won't pays. Call centre staff at utilities will be reduced by 20%, teams of meter readers and enforcement staff will be made redundant. Thus work capacity and skill capability will be reduced, making it harder for utilities to deal with the exception who is the determined debt Hold-out. It is likely that smaller suppliers will struggle with the cost and complexity of implementing and managing new metering technology early, these may well be weak in terms of controls and enforcement.

So what can the hold-out Debtor do if faced with a supplier who seeks to install either their own smart meter solution or a new smart meter as part of GB-wide plan approved by the Government?

1. They can initially ignore all communications and refuse access to meter installation

2. They can appear at any court hearing to enforce meter installation to plead for non-installation on the grounds of potential safety concerns with radio

wave emissions, refusal of consent to data sharing under the *Data Protection Act* on grounds of privacy.

3. They can immediately seek another supplier, considering especially a small one , at the same time changing tenancy so that there is a new customer to whom the existing supplier cannot object for change of supplier on grounds of existing unpaid debt.

4. If all else fails they may decide to move to another property, ideally remotely sited and with poor access, which may be a lower priority for later smart meter installation.

In summary, while smart meters do at first pass appear to impact upon the opportunity for a customer not to pay, there will be a number of years before they become universal and there will be means to avoid them during this time. Consumer protection rules have yet to be fully established and these will undoubtedly provide some comfort to the Hold-out Debtor. There are also significant commercial, technical and security concerns to be dealt with by the utilities before this strategy can be said to have succeeded on their part.

Not least, because metering data reading and meter switch on and switch off will be electronically controlled, the system will be an irresistible challenge to armies of hackers who will almost inevitably learn how to hack into meters to change meter reads in order to manipulate and minimise bills; and also to fool utilities into thinking that meters are switched off when there are really on. Not to forget: utilities will stop their two-yearly programme of meter inspections to detect for irregularities and illegal energy abstraction as a cost-saving "benefit" of the smart meter project. This will mean that intelligent (criminal!) meter-manipulation and meter-bypassing activities will be much less susceptible to inspection and detection.

Summary on Gas and Electricity Payment Avoidance

This lengthy exposition has demonstrated that both gas and electricity processes are intrinsically vulnerable to manipulation and evasion by a determined Hold-out who can find ways not to pay without becoming vulnerable to criminal prosecution. For the determined criminal these processes will always be susceptible to undermining without early detection even with the advent of smart metering in years to come..

Parking ticket Fines

Because there are effective means to collect parking ticket fines it is not illegal to refuse to pay them per se. But if a bailiff has clamped your car and threatens to impound it or even have it scrapped, as he is entitled to do if he has a *warrant of execution* as a result of a court judgement for non-payment of a parking ticket fine, then the temptation to pay will be irresistible for any motorist with the means to pay.

However, as *the Scotsman* newspaper reported in an article in June 2010, of 55,000 parking fines remaining uncollected in Edinburgh at that time, many over 4 years old, a significant number could not be collected because the vehicles were not registered with the DVLA. Westminster council, reportedly the largest parking authority in the UK wrote off £55M in unpaid tickets in 2009.

There almost one in five of all tickets issued remained unpaid with diplomatic number plates accounting for a large proportion of offenders and other "untraceable" foreign number plates another significant contributor to the total. But the Westminster problem with foreign and diplomatic plates is unsurprising in contrast to the problem in Edinburgh. It would appear that widespread number plate cloning is alive and well.

If UK-plated vehicles which defied parking ticket fines were plated with genuine numbers, it seems likely that in the near-term future remote camera systems will soon detect cars driving without being taxed, enabling the police to stop them and bring their drivers to book, not just for non-payment of parking fines, but for driving without tax or insurance. The same applies to those using stolen number plates. Drivers using cloned UK plates, on the other hand, appear likely to succeed in getting away with their evil deeds indefinitely for reasons discussed earlier, providing that they adhere to road traffic regulations and are not stopped inadvertently for other criminological reasons which might otherwise lead to their detection and apprehension.

Payday loans

Payday loans companies have flourished like locusts after a plague in the wake of the recession of the early 21st Century. They have been encouraged by the tightening of unsecured lending by traditional banks, the commercial failure of a large doorstep lender, *Cattles,* and the massive growth in immigration of low-skilled and thus low-paid labour to the UK. An APR of in excess of 1500% is not untypical of this sector, in other words complete and utter usury and exploitation of the poor and gullible. Customers are usually allowed to borrow up to £500 for a month (although the median loan is closer to just £100) and pay an administration charge as well as an eye-watering interest rate.

The cynical promise is made to the customer that they will not be credit searched. This is true, but only for the reason that these customers will not be on the credit reference agency radar; they have often just arrived in the UK and live in the cash economy so they have no credit record either good or bad, which is why they are not creditworthy to traditional lenders, and there is therefore no point in credit searching them. So the "benefit" of not being credit-searched is a mere inevitable recognition of the futility of doing so from the lender's perspective: it confers no advantage on the hapless borrower.

To qualify for a loan the prospective borrower generally needs to show their last two payslips, a utility bill, a bank statement and bank card and a photo id. They are often interviewed to validate that they are a real person.

Who are the payday loan companies? It turns out they are the same crew

"The big secret is that payday loan companies, just like DCA's, are 'all mouth and no trousers'"

which populates the debt collection agencies and debt outsourcing companies under a different brand. Many are financed by private capital and hedge funds as potential get-rich-quick vehicles. They are would-be banks run on the cheap, but without the in-depth information and data mining resources of banks.

The big secret is that payday loan companies, just like DCA's, are "*all mouth and no trousers*". The 1500% interest fee they charge covers the fact that they are completely naked underneath their bluster and have no effective means to deal with the non-payer, who is after all mobile, asset poor and uncreditworthy. The business model of the payday loan company relies entirely on recruiting sheep

"Any payday loan Debtor can make the choice of simply not paying and is almost certain to get away with it"

as customers and hoping that they will meekly pay. Goats are not pursued. Payday loan companies have no effective means to chase and enforce debt other than lettering, phoning and blustering. They do not routinely share data with other credit providers as they generally do not have the IT resource, commonality of customer base and membership of datasharing groups such as CAIS.

Any payday loan Debtor can make the choice of simply not paying and is almost certain to get away with it. Yes, unpaid debt will be sold, but only to another outsourcer of the same ilk who uses the same surface scratching methodology to try to intimidate the faint-hearted into paying. There is virtually no chance that any debt to a payday loan company will ever be followed up into county court. The business model is based on bluff.

Thus we can cry into our tea-cups over *Help Loan*, one such payday loan company, which was reported by *BBC Moneybox* as charging an APR of 1877% for a £50 loan over 14 days. This obscenely greedy operator was subjected to a fraud which attacked its paper thin controls by making multiple credit applications using cloned customer identities. It had to stop operating after issuing more than 9000 loans to fake customers. As a collections back-up it used *Intrum Justitia,* a typical UK debt collection agency which employed the typical debt collection agency approach as described elsewhere in this book.

Petrol

It is theft not to offer to pay for petrol having drawn it through a pump into a motor vehicle fuel tank on a garage forecourt. By number plate cloning as discussed above, and in an economic climate of increasing poverty among the disadvantaged classes accompanied by ever-increasing fuel prices, it is inevitable that undetected and unrecovered *drive-offs* will also keep growing. Garages will need to look out for individuals wearing baseball caps and sunglasses as minimal disguises. Perhaps these will have to be removed in future before a motorist is served petrol, just as motor cyclists are required to remove their headgear when entering a bank.

Rent

People who are not fortunate enough to own their home outright or live as the guest of a parent or indulgent friend typically spend between 25% and 40% of their net incomes on rent. In London the figure could easily exhaust all a young person's or unskilled worker's wages, so that sharing is almost obligatory. The landlord class has always been associated with the worst excesses of capitalism, appearing to live on the fruits of the work of others, resented and hated for taking money so that tenants can enjoy a basic human need. But such is the way of the world. There will always be landlords and those unable or unwilling to pay them, but needing access to a roof over their heads just the same.

Squatting

The classic way to enjoy rent-free accommodation is to enter and occupy it without permission. Squatting has long been associated with political radicalism on the one hand - people who insist that capitalism is immoral and that all property should be freely available - and with a bohemian life style led by artistic types on the margins of society not least associated with *the drug scene*; and betimes a mixture of both these *demi-mondes*. Nonetheless squatting is recognised as a fact in law and society. There may be over 20,000 active squatters residing in UK properties, having entered them without the owner's permission, at any one time. Once in possession they may acquire certain legal rights and it requires a landlord to obtain a *court possession order* in order to have a bailiff evict them, if necessary with the assistance of police. There are clear legal rules which squatters need to follow before occupying any property such as not using violence or causing damage to locks and windows on entry. Some squats in UK have been able to subsist for many years and this is undoubtedly a way not to pay rent. A specialist advisory service exists in London under www.squatter.org.uk and they produce *The Squatter's Handbook,* giving a detailed guide as to legalities and methods, which extends beyond the scope of this book.

Overcrowding and subletting

For the majority to whom the idea of squatting is synonymous with squalor the idea of recognising a landlord's right to charge rent is not quite so abhorrent. Tenants very commonly sub-let parts of rented property in contravention of the common *shorthold tenancy* agreement, sometimes with a nod and a wink from the landlord, and sometimes in complete secrecy. Certainly, in the case of housing associations and council-owned properties such evasion of basic contract terms is deemed as fraud and can lead to eviction and prosecution if detected. But once again, they are pathways to at least reducing payments for an impecunious tenant, if not altogether trying to evade payment, as is the case with squatting.

Withholding of final month's Rent

Landlords are largely powerless to prevent a tenant from withholding the final month's rental payment for a *shorthold tenancy* to their repeated frustration and despair. Rents are normally due in advance on the first day of each month and a landlord will be aware of non-payment within days of an expected bank transfer. But the process to have a tenant evicted takes longer than the remaining term of the lease and the penalty of eviction is one that the tenant has already prepared themselves to stomach by either giving or accepting notice to leave at the end of the current tenancy in any case.

While landlords could in theory ask for more than the standard one month's deposit, this might severely limit the pool of financially capable tenants and lead to void periods, which would cause a similar financial loss as the inability to claw back a deposit based on claims of damage caused by the tenant.

In addition, the landlord can of course withhold the deposit to make up for the lost final month's rent, this means there is nothing to cover any damage; while he can refuse to supply a reference for a new tenancy, this still does not generate him any cash. References are easily forged and new landlords often very keen to accept any reference at face value just to have the property rented at times of flat demand.

Restaurant meals

Aleister Crowley (whom we have met earlier), would-be magician and mysticist, writer, traveller, mountaineer adventurer, libertine, bigamist, drug addict, alcoholic, bisexual orgiast and bankrupt who has since been voted the 73rd greatest Briton of all time and during his lifetime was also known as *"the wickedest man ever"*, started life as the heir to a family fortune of around £8M in today's money and the beneficiary of undergraduate study at Oxford. By October 1937 at the age of 62 the money had long since gone and he was living on his wits.

Long a habitué of the Café Royal on Piccadilly Circus in London, he organised a sumptuous meal, hiring a private salon for the evening for his many friends.

Before coffee was served, and having dined on the best wines the house could offer, Crowley downed his brandy and excused himself - as the other guests assumed - in order to visit the restaurant's restrooms. In short order, he retrieved his coat from the cloakroom, boarded a taxi and disappeared down Regent Street, leaving the bill for around £12000 in today's money unpaid. How was he able to do this? In fact the deed was simplicity itself: he was known to the restaurant and had only recently dined there on his birthday at a similar meal which was paid for by cheque by his latest lady companion.

What the restaurant management could not know and what he did not disclose, was that he did not intend to pay and never intended to return. Crowley committed *"long day fraud"* by building credibility as a patron, who was never entirely reliable about timely payment, but was at least long known to the management. They must certainly have been aware that their notorious patron was an undischarged bankrupt since February 1935. But such was his charm and force of personality that he continued to command credit with the restaurant, up to that one last time.

It was a one-time coup, and in committing it he was at least true to his reputation, so that the friends who were left to explain their surprise to the head waiter might be unsurprised at the behaviour of a man whose motto famously was: *"Do what thou wilt shall be all of the Law!"* One does not suppose that Crowley suffered many pangs of guilt on this basis, although the hotel management must have bitterly regretted not having better considered the risk they were taking in allowing him to run up a very large restaurant bill. One might have less sympathy with them therefore than if this fraud had been perpetrated on a small owner-operated restaurant.

Restaurants tend to keep a close eye on large parties as the time to pay the bill approaches if the patron and customer is not known to them. Perhaps then the story of the Oxford medical students' graduation dinner is apocryphal as it describes how they succeeded in not paying for their large group celebration marking the successful crowning and end of their university careers. The group piled into a large and busy local restaurant, having already clearly had a lot to drink, indeed some of them were obviously already drunk enough to need to be supported by their friends. But as the group was cheerful and friendly and it was after all graduation time, the Head Waiter allowed them to take their seats in a separate section of the restaurant. None of the staff noticed the one diner who did not move or drink his drink or eat his meal all evening – all his drink was drunk and the meal consumed. Calling for the bill, the students began donning their coats and making for the door, pointing to their silent companion who appeared to be slumped in his chair. " Just leave the bill with Charlie, he won't mind paying!" they laughed, as they rushed out of the building.

When the waiter touched the last silent member of the group slumped over the shoulder, he discovered at last that he was talking to a corpse, which had been filched from the mortuary of the local teaching hospital. The reader must make his or her own mind up as to whether this story is true, or is it an urban myth?

More realistically, it is easy for couples to manufacture a "row" towards the end of a meal, particularly if they are sitting near the door or indeed outside at a table in the street. The lady will suddenly start to shout at the man, get up and hurry away to make a dramatic exit. The man will look alarmed, call after her and pursue her still call to her to stop... and off they go. If she is wearing heels, he can probably run faster than her so it is useful that she makes her exit first. The restaurant staff, if they notice what is going on, will always have a moment or two of hesitation while they try to work out what is happening. If the couple have stolen a coat from another cloakroom somewhere, perhaps this may be left draped over a chair to suggest that there will be a return? Not likely.

The Payment Evader who got complacent

It is also amusing to recount a further recent and real life account of persistent and ultimately unsuccessful payment avoidance (amounting to theft), not least from the curious perspective of the detective story. Janis Nords, described as "a penniless Latvian" by The Times, managed to avoid payment of £5,500 at a number of prestigious London restaurants by leaving hurriedly with his girlfriend without paying. Rather gallantly, when caught he exonerated his lady as an accomplice but, perhaps much worse, labelled her as being entirely stupid by suggesting that she was unaware of what he was doing as he hurried her away from each restaurant. Having got away with it six times, he might have been considered to have become an expert on the practice of "eat and run", but it seems he committed some fatal errors – just like in the familiar detective story:

- *He repeatedly committed the same offence in similar restaurants in the same area: it might be expected that word would get round and that staff might therefore be alert to potential attempts at running away without paying*

- *There are hints of hubris in his use of the moniker of Lupin, reputedly the name of a famous fictional 19th Century French thief. Hubris is always associated with personal misjudgement, disconnection from reality and a predictable comeuppance in classical tragedy, while although true to form in these regards, this story appears to be entirely farce.*

- *He asked for his jacket at the cloakroom of one restaurant to be able to go out to smoke: suspicious!*

- *He became nervous finally at the fatal restaurant by continually walking in and out for a smoke, no doubt to reconnoitre his means of escape.*

- *Perhaps due to his smoking habit, he was unable to outrun the waiters chasing him. A determined runner might have trained for the event of having to outpace the hired help.*

For style, brio and overall achievement level in terms of cash value, Aleister Crowley back in 1937 trumped Mr Nords by a considerable margin.

But to be very clear: any and all of the above scenarios amount to fraud (taking credit with intent not to pay) and theft. Restaurants could prevent this occurring by taking the example of inner city pubs who are less dewy-eyed about the quality of their customers than more expensive restaurants and habitually swipe a credit card as the meal is ordered.

Sex

Arguably, on those hopefully majority occasions when no money changes hands, sex is always paid for, but that might be the subject of a different book. Commercial sex is illegal in UK, so that any contract between the parties which involves payment of money for sex cannot be legally binding. The client is under no legal obligation to complete his (or her) part of any bargain after receipt of the agreed service or indeed after early receipt of the cash consideration element of the deal.

Prepayment may well be the solution for contractors who believe that they are likely to be thus affected. Protectors may not, however, be overly concerned that they need to resort to a court of law to extract whatever fee may be due: hence *caveat emptor* must be the watchword for any such dubious transaction whether it is decided to offer payment or not. After all, one may contract more than one bargained for...

Student Loans

The Student Loan Company (SLC) continues to be widely regarded as aloof and incompetent.

What has the Student Loans Company got to be secretive about?

A mark of its lack of confidence in its own abilities was the SLC's appeal against the Information Commissioner in 2009 to avoid having to disclose its collection methods for fear that this would make it easier for Graduate Debtors to avoid payment. This affair revealed 22 months of foot dragging by the Information Commissioner before acting to prompt the SLC to comply with the law on disclosure, reportedly a mendacious denial by the SLC as to the existence of a manual describing the aforementioned collection methods and then a sheepish admission and disclosure by the SLC when under

---

pressure by the Information Tribunal under a formal hearing at Law. What dreadful secrets were so fearful of disclosure?

Like many utilities the SLC uses an internal "debt collection agency" (called Smith Lawson and Company) to pursue non-payers. This is a trick to give the impression that the Debtor is under pressure from a real debt collection agency, designed to make them fearful and thus to pay. Having to resort to such tactics is a tacit admission of inability to secure payment by normal means and a sign of weakness in the Creditor. Intelligent Debtors would be encouraged at this desperate use of subterfuge, not intimidated.

The SLC sold £2bn of student debt in 1998/99 to Debt Collection Agencies and was doubtless keen to maximise the price it would receive for further tranches of debt sold to the private sector. By definition, as we have discussed earlier, any debt referred to a DCA or sold to a debt outsourcer has been given up on; the outsourcer will spend minimum money on trying to collect the easy money and let the tough stuff go.

As it turned out the tribunal did allow the SLC to keep secret its most sensitive collection methods, but by inference and with knowledge of other Government and private sector collection methods, these methods can only involve those already discussed in this book, in other words use of a debt path, escalating contact attempts and tougher verbiage, use of data mining techniques and sources such as CAIS and HMRC datasets to identify Debtors with a propensity to pay.

As we have already seen, there is no silver bullet, just hard grind to find the *sheep* among the *goats* who will pay if subjected to enough pressure. And equally, there are steps which determined Hold-outs can take to avoid these measures.

The simplest way for a graduate Debtor to effectively avoid repayment of student loans is to move abroad. President of the National Union of Students Aaron Porter was quoted on *BBC QuestionTime* as stating that *only 3% of student debt owed by graduates who had moved abroad was being paid.* No wonder then that the Student Loan Company threatens extreme penalties including usurious rates of interest to triple their standard rate against non-payers abroad. The mark of an effective collection agency is one which says what it will do and then does it. Threatening extreme measures at people living abroad is a resort to psychological terrorism and the impotence of the outraged and caged would-be *lion* with nail-varnish on its claws where they should be sharp.

> "Debts to the Student Loan Company are as ineradicable as a Sicilian Blood Feud, they are never forgotten"

One miserly weapon remains to the SLC: its debts are as ineradicable as a Sicilian blood feud, they are never forgotten. The normal 6 year statute of limitation on debts will not apply, nor can a Debtor escape student debt by bankruptcy. But by going away and staying away even mafia hitmen can be avoided, never mind the SLC.

Tax

It is illegal not to pay income tax for any private individual domiciled in the UK. As inevitable as death and taxes, however, is the persistence of people to try to evade payment for taxation. They will continue to do so by working in the cash economy and retaining anonymity; when under pressure people will also continue to migrate abroad from where they can fairly easily fend off collection attempts by keeping mobile and maintaining a low profile, again as discussed already.

Toilets

Many people are quite happy to pay the distress fee when caught short in a station to pay 50pence in order to relieve themselves. To the lifestyle non-payment *artiste* such a tariff represents both an affront and a challenge to their self-imposed regimen: *"Nil pende"* ("Pay nothing"). Hence rather than be contented with a sense of outrage that the toilets at Embankment in London have been converted to pay-toilets, the enterprising non-payer will make a mental note of free facilities on his regular routes, such as how to find his way into the Grosvenor Hotel in Victoria Station and how to look like he is on his way to a meeting therein, rather than use the pay toilets on the concourse.

Water

Anyone unlucky enough to have to live in Australia who compounds this infelicity by neglecting to pay their water bill is subject to the installation of a compulsory dripping water meter, which will just about fill a kettle in a day, ie enough to preserve life, but not allow a decent bath. Happy the denizens of England then who need never pay a water bill, safe in the knowledge that the *Lion of the Law* does not allow water to be cut off to domestic properties. Thus where energy utilities write off around 1% of sales, for the water companies the figure is closer to 5%. Word has got around that not only do water companies not cut non-payers off, they are also very unlikely to seek a county court judgement to enforce a debt for non-payment of water. At least one of the very largest has had a long standing policy of NEVER suing, while others will make statutory examples of individuals. But as we have already seen, getting a county court judgement does not by any means assure a Creditor of getting paid.

A straw in the wind of recent thinking by the water companies therefore was the news that *Severn Trent Water* was owed £159M by its customers and that it was looking to sell debt to the Debt Purchase, but at time of writing had been unsuccessful in finding buyers willing to pay the price it has been asking. The debate will have been around the low pence in the pound, hence the principal Creditor water company has more or less given up on anything close to full payment.

It is seeking to close its books on older debt and to save whatever face it may, for just pennies. A seller of utility debt will typically have filleted its ledgers of customers who own their own homes and might be cudgelled into submission by threat of a charging order; what will be sold will be sold on is lower grade debt owed by people who pay rent. No wonder that debt buyers will only be prepared to pay single pennies in the pound; they may not make even this back. For the hold-out Debtor, however, this mooted activity is an indicator that non-payment of water debt really can pay for them.

23.0

Does's and Doesn'ts

WHAT'S IN THIS CHAPTER

While this book does not recommend any specific action to any individual, the lists of what successful Debt Hold-outs do and do not do are indicative to the keys to success or failure in any attempt to avoid debt over time.

Does's and Doesn'ts

As this book does not make any specific recommendations to anyone, this chapter is not entitled "Do's and Don'ts". There is no imperative to be observed. Instead we address what the successful Debt Holdout or *jackal* does and does not do as part of their life pattern of successful debt evasion.

We have seen that there are two basic alternative and mutually exclusive strategies for the would-be debt avoider: one is to maintain a low profile at all times, constantly reinventing oneself and physically moving. This involves continuously finding new supplies of low-value credit, exhausting them and moving on – the "hunter gatherer" or *"jackal and hide"* lifestyle. The opposite is the high profile sedentary strategy: "Mighty fortress/empty shell."

In this case the Debtor builds up credibility and apparent reliability in a number of lines of credit over a long period to become trusted by a number of Creditors and often enjoy increasing credit lines, multiple credit cards being used alternatively and then paid off – followed by a series of high credit coups and disappearance: the so-called "long day fraud". When pursued at his erstwhile "mighty fortress" with its high credit visibility, perhaps having had at one time significant equity in a property, it is found to be empty, abandoned, an "empty shell", perhaps sold quietly shortly in advance of other coups.

The castle-dweller who has assets to lose will observe many of the does's and doesn'ts below, but having an eye to the fact that his exit strategy is longer and more complex and with much more to lose if he makes mistakes, on account of his asset base and his current good credit standing.

The "Does's" are behaviours that are consistent with successful payment avoidance, and the determined "hunter gatherer", *jackal* or Hold-out will take care to follow all of them: as with any detective story, just one major error can provide a vital clue to his pursuers and lead to his undoing. By contrast the "Doesn'ts" represent classical behaviours which will very likely lead to the Hold-out being positively identified, located and held to account.

Does:

Maintains anonymity towards neighbours.

Obeys civic and criminal laws carefully; he does not wish to betray his identity and whereabouts foolishly and needlessly.

Pays cash at supermarkets.

Keeps abreast of developments in the credit and collections industry (checking out their websites to see what they claim they can do for their clients) including new uses of technology, consumer legislation and stories in the press.

Talks to people in pubs, clubs and launderettes about what is going on in the area in terms of active debt enforcement, new ideas for payment avoidance.

Sells property via private sale, or at least avoids estate agents which routinely share data on properties for sale with credit bureaux. Otherwise Creditors may rush to seek injunctions on sale or to seek judgements for debt which will enable them to place a debt mortgage charge on the property, ensuring that they must be paid out on the sale of the property before any other proceeds can be paid to the seller (who is in this case the Debtor).

Reads his mail immediately he gets it.

Keeps good records of each individual debt owed including a schedule and forecast which estimates when each collections process is likely to become critical in terms of need to respond.

Plans ahead as to what he is going to do and when.

Ensures that he has reason to trust any partner or lover to whom he entrusts equity in a major asset. Maintains and nurtures this trust by exemplary love and consideration towards them at all times, knowing that if he falls out with them, he is lost, or at least his hidden ownership of the asset is lost!

Stays on good terms with his parents and maintain an excellent credit history at his parents' address by paying for services which he considers essential from that address. (nb, this is not the same as paying priority Creditors as recommended by traditional debt advisors, since in fact many of these priority Creditors can be avoided).

Is sure to establish on his medical record at an early stage that he has mental health issues such as *bipolar disorder*. Office of Fair Trading guidelines protect such people who may be subject to uncontrollable bouts of overspending. Lenders who are aware that a customer has such problems may find that excessive debts may be cancelled or set aside by a judge.

Marries a foreigner if marriage is for him. Thus he will have connections abroad to help him flit and start over. There will also be distinct tax advantages in the event that he needs to account to the tax authorities in his chosen domicile.

Does Not

Ignore mail or throw it away unread or delay opening it.

Panic.

Register to vote.

Join a supermarket card loyalty scheme.

Respond to shopper lifestyle surveys.

Use credit cards unless as a source of revolving and escalating credit prior to defaulting and at an address which he is happy to have disclosed and shared with other lenders.

Let bailiffs find his car.

Drink excessively or use drugs: to succeed he knows he needs to be in complete control of his faculties and judgement. This point is a major Achilles heel for many otherwise accomplished dwellers in the *demi-monde* of debt. It is the undoing of countless thousands of would-be j*ackals*.

Drink and drive: if and when he is caught his name will be spotlighted in the public domain and he will be criminalised, the last things he wants. Nor does he boast or tell people about his assets or income, knowing that it creates envy and jealousy and invites betrayal.

Own property in his sole name in UK. Better still, he does not have his name on any title deeds to any significant asset.

Promote himself on *Facebook* or other social networking sites.

Assume that friends, neighbours, ex-business partners and former lovers will withhold information about him to collectors trying to trace him. They are a prime and often very willing source, motivated by resentment, envy and thoughts of revenge.

Cheat, insult or humiliate his lovers and friends; they will have their revenge. His wife is number one on the list of people he does not want to disappoint.

Ever let things get personal. If he does, his emotions will cloud his judgement, he will be drawn in to conflict and is likely to make serious strategic errors. He is aware that a debt collector may actively seek to goad him to promote anger or guilt or resentment, and if they think they are succeeding they will only be encouraged to maintain their personal crusade to "defeat" him by collecting what he owes.

Use his address as a non-payer as the address from which he makes credit applications or continues to pay credit accounts which he considers vital.

Waste money by paying a professional debt management company to negotiate repayment with his Creditors or invest in "credit repair" including attempted CCJ removal. He knows that *Citizens Advice Bureau* or *National Debtline* have highly trained advisors who will do what can be done for free.

Allow himself to feel any sense of shame or guilt that he has an unpaid debt: it is just business for the DCA and so it is for the Hold-out Debtor.

Believe Debt Collection Agents' claims that adherence to a payment plan will protect or restore his creditworthiness: by the time a debt has been passed to a DCA his credit record is already destroyed and will remain so until many months or even years after he demonstrates regular income and regular payment of all commitments in full.

Pay Debt Collection Agencies or Debt Purchase companies one cent for unsecured debt such as credit cards, knowing that if anyone was going to sue or attempt to enforce through the courts, it would have been the Principal Creditor; DCA's are all bluster and no follow-through.

Regard solicitors any differently to DCA's. Again they mostly bluff, charging their client perhaps £25 to produce a letter to frighten sheep back into their pens. He will await production of a summons before taking a threat from a solicitor seriously.

24.0

Quo Vadis? (Where Next?)

Quo Vadis? (Where Next?)

So having read thus far, where to next? The reader by now has a good understanding of how credit management and debt management work, the blundering incompetence of large commercial organisations, and some specific ideas of what others have done to avoid and evade payment, using means that are both legal and illegal. What is he to make of all this information?

What is the worst that can happen?

According to the *House of Commons Library* note SN/HA/5525 being sent to prison for debt is a very rare occurrence. Apart from fraud, a prison sentence can happen only for specific types of debt. These include non-payment of:

- fines from the Magistrates' Court;

- council tax or business rates;

- maintenance for a husband, wife or children.

Even for these types of debt which are all "Government Debt" at the point of collection, imprisonment for non-payment is very rare; a prison sentence is regarded by the court as 'a last resort'. In an earlier chapter we underlined the free assets everyone is born with to at least some degree, including health, beauty and intelligence to some extent, and a good reputation. To this we should have added at least three "cats' lives" in the form of chances that the *Lion of the Law* gives to people found guilty of first or second offences, particularly if they are minor.

Because the jails are full, but also because the Legal system has a *Gladstonian* optimism about the corrigibility of human nature, magistrates tend to keep their harshest sentences for the unrepentant recidivist old lag types or *wolves* who appear entirely likely to do whatever brought them before the court again and again. A would be *jackal* who finds himself in court is unmasked as a *goat* who was not as clever as he thought. Perhaps he is not cut out for a life in the wild yonder, and should agree now to become a *sheep*? By consenting to live in a pen, he might yet avoid the penitentiary. This is the hope of the Law in its initial moralising mildness, but it is ultimately the decision of the one convicted.

The Fork in the Road

In medieval courtly poetry a major theme was that of a wandering hero trying to find his way in the world. In a Europe where there were virtually no roads an audience will have been familiar with the difficulty of making one's way across rough country. The hero would walk along a track which would eventually fork, so that he had to choose which of two paths to follow: left or right? For the sake no doubt of a good story the hero would inevitably choose the left hand path, which was fraught with difficulty and danger; indeed the Italian for *left* is *sinistro* – hence the *sinister* path was to the left, while that of *rectitude* and safety led to the right. In French the word for left is of course *gauche* which plays back into English meaning variously: *clumsy, tactless, green, ignorant, bumbling.* The reference back to the left handed path is evident: He who chooses the deviant, subversive left-handed path had better take care that he is none of these things, or he will come to grief as does ever the medieval courtly pilgrim-hero. It is a path fraught with risk of error and consequence.

So, now that we have the knowledge of how the credit industry, collections and debt enforcement work, plus insights into the tricks and techniques which are the bane of Creditors and collectors across the land: what will we do with this compendium? There can be no question that many of the stunts which are pulled by the animals of the allegorical zoology which we have portrayed to illustrate behaviours have succeeded for a time. For some people there may be a time and a place where they feel compelled by circumstances to resort to them; for others they will remain a curiosity.

It is, however, very unlikely that anyone can succeed in living very long the life of a *jackal* without it perhaps costing more in sheer hard work than it might save in payment withheld. And loss of effort and energy are the least of the risks that the behaviour of the jackal entail. There is a very short step between refusing to pay and constructing situations in advance where one clearly has never intended to pay, and lo, the *jackal* has become a *big bad wolf*, a criminal. The more often one crosses a line, the less significant the line appears to become, but the more likely in terms of increasing odds of detection or gratuitous mistakes fed by over-confidence and *hubris* that one will eventually be held to account for crossing It.

Life ultimately becomes a gambling casino, and habitual gamblers have a tendency of eventually losing. We draw towards our conclusion therefore with another vision, provided by the poet Henry Wadsworth Longfellow from *The Village Blacksmith:*

> "...when we make just one active suggestion in this book it is: "Keep it in your pants, and we do mean your credit card!"

"His brow is wet with honest sweat,
He earns whate'er he can,
And looks the whole world in the face,
For he owes not any man."

Nice work if you can get it. What do you do if you can't? It is said that when we take a lover, we do so for a reason, for a season or for life. Life is unquestionably a whole lot easier if one can indeed look the whole world in the face, has no need to run or hide and can find more constructive and creative things to do with one's time than to constantly have to invent new devices simply in order to live from hand to mouth. The world does not love the *jackal* and there may quickly come a time when he would rather not run and hide. In a word therefore, when we make just one active suggestion in this book it is: "Keep it in your pants, and we mean your credit card!"

Epilogue

Thus we take our leave of some noteworthy characters playing the parts variously of the *jackal*, the *lemming*, the *goat* and the *wolf* among others. As we say goodbye to Captain Blood, to Oscar Wilde, to Aleister Crowley and his nemesis Horatio Bottomley, we can remark that these older players were somehow much more accomplished, colourful characters than the modern escape artists. Step forward Jonathan Aitken to take a bow, alongside the hobby canoeist John Darwin and the hapless shed camper Steve Morris, not forgetting that other forgetful diner Janis Nords. These people are the stuff that newspapers are printed to portray and the pages of our morning journals would be dull without them. Quite a few of these men (no women!) went to jail as part of their career path, yet if their deeds brought them suffering in part, any one is only notorious because of the errors of judgment they made, which led to apprehension, exposure and reporting. By definition we know nothing of the unreported successes which only a Caspar Weinberger could postulate: the unknown unknowns...

If roguery was a frequent trait among them, must we not concede them also a certain outlandish romantic charm, for they certainly have provided us with some entertainment. Perhaps they have lived the fantasies that we dared only dream of. To a man they took independent action, against the prevailing legal and moral current and all good counsel that the *Citizens Advice Bureau* might ever dare deliver. (In closing we must not forget that even the debt charities are a tool of government, funded in great part by government grants and playing a tune at all times which their piper calls.)

If nothing else we can admire and occasionally even delight in the artistry of their inventions, their examples of sheer brass nerve and occasional personal courage, even if we do not commend one single step to anyone to imitate. *Jackals* and *goats* and *wolves* are part of the great ecosystem of credit giving and debt payment and avoidance. And so we return to the paradox of our beginnings with the quotation from Simone Weil: debts must be paid, and yet debts must not be paid. It is the way of the world: "Sock it to 'em!"

Bibliography

A Magick Life – a biography of Aleister Crowley by Martin Booth

Oscar Wilde by Richard Ellmann

The Prince by Niccolo Machiavelli

The Art of War by Sun Tzu

The Man who stole the Crown Jewels by David C Hanrahan

The Synagogue of Satan by Andrew Carrington Hitchcock

Dealing with your Debts Money Advice Trust 2010-2011

The Way to Wealth by Benjamin Franklin

Deal with Debt in 90 Minutes by Graham Wilmott

Back to the Black by Graham Lawler

Getting out of Debt and Staying out by Tony Palmer

To pay or not to Pay by Stanley G Hilton

Debt Advice Handbook 8th Edition by the Child Poverty Action Group

Comp City by Max Rubin

The Road Less Travelled by M. Scott Peck

Man's Search for Meaning by Viktor Frankl

Seven Habits of Highly Effective People by Stephen Covey

INDEX